Trouble Man

The Life and Death of
MARVIN GAYE

THE ECCO PRESS

An Imprint of HarperCollins*Publishers*

Trouble Man

Steve Turner

FIRST ECCO PRESS EDITION PUBLISHED 2000

Designed by Cassandra J. Pappas

Library of Congress Cataloging-in-Publication Data
Turner, Steve
Trouble man : the life and death of Marvin Gaye /
Steve Turner.—1st ed.
p.cm.
Originally published: London : M. Joseph, 1998
includes index.
ISBN 0-06-019821-4
1. Marvin Gaye. 2. Singers—United States—Biography. I. Title
ML420G305 T87 M2000
782.421644'092—dc21

[B]   00-039361

00 01 02 03 04 ❖/QF 10 9 8 7 6 5 4 3 2 1

Contents

Contents

Introduction

Why Marvin Gaye? This is the question I've been asked most often since beginning research on this book in the autumn of 1994.

The first part of my answer is that as a biographer I'm drawn to artists who are bothered by spiritual issues. There was something tantalizing to me about a singer who seemed to scale the heights and plumb the depths, sometimes in the space of one album. He could express righteous indignation and rampant licentiousness with equal conviction. That was the initial puzzle. Then there was the way in which he died and the slow decline that preceded it. It had all the ingredients of a great mystery—drugs, sex, religion, violence, celebrity, art—and I was in the mood to tell a story rather than simply present a chronology of artistic endeavours.

Although this is a book about a musician I wanted it to be more than a music book. I wanted to provide the necessary background to his great recordings but to avoid getting mired in the sort of minutiae that only the most dedicated of fans or fellow writers would be interested to know. I will have succeeded if the long-term Marvin Gaye admirer discovers a lot of hitherto unknown information, and the casual browser, who only knows of maybe one Marvin Gaye album and half a dozen singles, is entertained by this story of a wounded anti-hero and his times.

The chapter titles, and to an extent the structure of the book, were suggested by *The Writer's Journey*, Christopher Vogler's study of the principles of myth. The book title is, of course, borrowed from the movie for which Marvin scored the soundtrack in 1972, and seems to encapsulate the inner and outer turmoil that accompanied him all of his life.

My research began with a letter to Marvin's brother Frankie. His prompt return phone call resulted in me flying to Los Angeles for a meeting. For a short time it looked as though we might collaborate on this book, but later he changed his mind. I carried on, and made several more visits to America, including one to Lexington to visit the church in which Marvin's father was raised, and another to Washington DC, where his childhood friend, the late Buddy Comedy, took me to all the important sites from his early years.

I have had extensive help from many people and organizations, all of whom are listed in the acknowledgments. Some people have been particularly unstinting in sharing their time and memories with me, and for this I offer special thanks to Jan Gaye, Marvin's second wife, Eugenie Vis, his girlfriend during his Belgian exile, producer Harvey Fuqua, personal assistant Kitty Sears, valet Odell George, bodyguards Andre and Gerald White, Motown archivist Georgia Ward, ex-Marquee Reese Palmer, driver Joe Schaffner, writing partner Elgie Stover, European promoter and friend Freddy Cousaert, brother-in-law Mark Gaillard, producer Ed Townsend and church leader Shelton West.

In Lexington, Kentucky, Ann Todd carried out research for me into Marvin's paternal family tree, and the House of God Church made me particularly welcome when I visited and attended a Saturday service. In Detroit I was shown around the Motown Historical Museum by Christopher Alexander, and around Detroit by Michelle Fusco and Renee Monforton of the Metropolitan Detroit Convention & Visitors' Bureau. When I needed to extend my visit to Los Angeles, Sharon Wright of Virgin Airlines' press office in England sorted out my ticketing problems at the last minute.

During my research I was often asked if I was going to be writing a 'positive' or a 'negative' book about Marvin. My answer was always that I hadn't come to the project with the intention of either glorifying him or damning him. I hoped that whatever proportion of good and bad there was in Marvin's life would be in my final portrait. I didn't want to avoid the bad because it was too ugly and upsetting, or neglect the good because it was too mundane.

When I first spoke to Anna Gordy Gaye, Marvin's first wife, her advice to me was 'Write what you find.' That, in a nutshell, has been my motto.

Steve Turner, London, February 1998

Trouble Man

Prologue

New York City, May 1983

Marvin Gaye should have been on top of the world. He had just broken Barry Manilow's record by selling out five nights at the prestigious Radio City Music Hall on his first tour of America since returning from a two-and-a-half-year exile in Europe, he had a luxury suite at the Waldorf-Astoria on Park Avenue and there was a feature on him in the *New York Times* headlined 'Marvin Gaye Is Back and Looking Up'.

But something had gone drastically wrong with Marvin Gaye's life. At the age of forty-four he was a physical and mental wreck. Twenty pounds over his ideal weight as a lithe young Motown star, he was sweating his way through his shows every night. The membranes inside his nose were so badly damaged from heavy cocaine use that he couldn't sleep in an air-conditioned room without installing a vaporizer. More disturbingly, his mind was playing tricks on him. Wherever he went he heard voices threatening his life. One night he thought they were coming from the television set so he broke it open and tore out the wiring. Another night he was so convinced that the Devil himself was in his room that he phoned his bodyguard, Gerald White, a 457-pound ex-football player, who burst into the suite with a submachine-gun to find Marvin sitting up in bed with his head swathed in a towel and the number 666 stuck to his forehead on pieces of scrawled notepaper.

Gerald had grown accustomed to this level of paranoia. Ever since the tour had begun the month before, he had listened to Marvin's stories about how he was being stalked—how someone was planning to shoot him, stab him or put poison in his food. Now he had to be supplied with presidential-style protection to get him from hotel to venue and venue to airport. He never felt safe. Gerald and his brother, Andre, who headed up the security operation, always stayed in adjacent suites to assure Marvin of maximum safety. Even then they received constant phone calls asking them to check doors and windows or to look under beds and in wardrobes.

Then Marvin became fixated with the idea that his family might be threatened or that his home might be broken into. He told Andre and Gerald of the time that someone came to his house in Topanga Canyon when he was away and slashed the throats of his two Great Danes. He now had a bodyguard, Tex Griffin, a former heavyweight boxer from Pine Bluff, Arkansas, to look after his California home. He'd already asked Gerald to supply Tex with a .45 automatic. Now Marvin wanted a weapon for his father, who lived with his mother in a $300,000-dollar home on Gramercy Place in the Crenshaw district of Los Angeles. He was concerned that someone might try to attack them or take them hostage while he was away on this four-month tour. Gerald tried to dissuade him. He assured him that there was no serious threat to his or anyone else's life. Paranoia, confusion and auditory hallucinations were a common side-effect of a heavy cocaine habit. Besides, he had the best protection that money could buy. But Marvin wouldn't give up. He wanted a gun, and he wanted it now.

'All of my guns were registered to me and I wasn't going to give him one of mine,' says Gerald. 'Like I said, I knew he didn't need one. But he just insisted and insisted, and a friend of mine who was in the room at the time said that he could help me.'

That night an unregistered .38 Smith and Wesson was delivered to Gerald's suite at the Waldorf-Astoria and Tex Griffin was duly summoned. 'I gave the gun to Tex and showed him how to pack it in his luggage to avoid detection,' says Gerald. 'He then took it back to Los

Angeles and gave it to Marvin's father. Marvin was happy at last that his father had protection.'

Mr Gay had never owned a gun before. It didn't seem right for a preacher to have a gun, even for a preacher who hadn't preached for twenty years. Still, if it made his son happy he'd hold on to it. He put it under his pillow and hoped that he'd never have to use it.

Los Angeles, California, March 1984

Five months after the tour had finished, Marvin was in no better shape. The drug abuse, with cocaine and angel dust, had continued, he'd given up on his physical appearance and his career was virtually on hold. There was occasional talk of another tour, another album or work with contemporaries like Bobby Womack and Barry White, but nothing ever materialized. There were even advanced plans to set him up in Las Vegas like Wayne Newton. That way he could be near his mother, avoid the rigours of the road and yet still perform sell-out shows.

But Marvin had lost the motivation. The only thing he appeared to desire was oblivion. He couldn't write. All his important relationships with women had broken down, and he owed millions of dollars in tax. Making everything worse was the fact that he was back living with his parents, and his relationship with his father, which had never been good, was turning uglier by the day. Mr Gay had never shown his son any approval or affection. He had apparently resented him right from infancy, but he particularly resented him now that he was an international star whose income financed the family. Part of him delighted in the reflected glory, and he certainly enjoyed the trappings of celebrity that came his way, but his overriding feeling was of contempt. He hated what he considered to be the Devil's music and he hated his son's bad habits—the sex with loose white women, the indolence, the constant sniffing in his bedroom.

Yet it had been the father's disapproval that had made Marvin what he was. It was the desperate search for love, praise and reassurance that had propelled him into show-business, because it was only when he sang that he felt that wave of warmth and adoration he so needed. But after all the years of acclaim he had been left with nothing but a feeling of emptiness. Cocaine had been one of the few things he'd discovered that made the pain go away, but it had diminishing returns. He no longer took cocaine to get high but to avoid the agony of withdrawal.

His father was a flawed individual. Marvin knew that. He didn't sing the Devil's music, but he no longer went to church either. He didn't pay hookers, but he wore women's clothing and carried two French poodles around the home. He didn't take drugs, but for the past ten years he'd been a serious drinker. In some ways father and son were alike—proud but lazy men who liked talking about God and the Christian way, but who were too weak-willed to be dedicated disciples.

Marvin had recently asked his bodyguard Andre White to manage his affairs and Andre kept in regular contact to sort out unfinished business and motivate him to work again, but all that Marvin could talk about was his personal pain and his suicidal inclinations. He was worried about the intensity of the arguments he was having with his father and his father's habit of threatening him by saying, 'I brought you into this world, and if you lay a hand on me I'll take you out.'

Marvin asked Andre, to whom he referred as Dre, to record their meetings and phone calls. 'He liked me to tape our conversations so that we could listen back and pick up where we left off,' says Andre. 'Also, he would sometimes say things and then later claim that he had never said them and so we started recording everything as a kind of protection.' Their final taped conversation, which Andre would play back many times in the coming years, lasted for three hours. In the middle of it came this telling exchange.

Andre: Marvin, I hope you know your dad is not kidding when he says, 'I brought you here and I'll take you out of here'?
Marvin: Right. He does say that. Right.
Andre: Marvin. (*Pause*) Marvin, what's wrong?
Marvin: He means it too.
Andre: Man, you've come too far to start any shit with your daddy. Come on, man.
Marvin: Dre, why do you have to make so much sense all of the time? (*Laughter*)
Andre: It's the truth, and you know it.

Marvin: You know, the other night he did something that he has never done.

Andre: What?

Marvin: I was asleep and I felt someone rubbing my back. At first, I thought it was Mother because I told her I was having back-aches, but I detected the rub was too strong and I turned and looked and my daddy said, 'That will make it feel better.' Then he turned and walked away. He has never done anything like that.

Andre: Man, your daddy loves you! Why can't you see that?

Marvin: Dre, I know, but—

Andre: But nothing! You want to die and you're too chicken to kill yourself. But if you keep fucking with your daddy—he's told you what he'll do.

Marvin: I guess you're right.

Says Andre: 'Marvin paused when I said that and it was like a light-bulb lit up. He wanted to die, but he couldn't do it himself. He got his daddy to do it.'

Long Beach, California, May 1994

For the ten years since the death of his son, Mr Gay had lived in Californian retirement homes. His health remained good but his memory had shown marked deterioration. He could remember his fellow residents and the staff that tended to his needs, but not his wife Alberta or the family they had raised in Washington DC. Now he couldn't remember his own childhood in Lexington, Kentucky, or the preaching tours he had taken part in with Simon Peter Rawlings, who later became a bishop in the House of God. He couldn't even remember his own career as a preacher.

Lady Rawlings, wife of the late Bishop Rawlings, decided that the time was right to visit her old friend. She got together with some other members of the House of God—Shelton West, who had known Mr Gay since he was a boy, Bishop West's wife and Bishop Embury—and they drove down to the Long Beach retirement home.

Mr Gay came downstairs from his room and sat with his visitors in a communal area. He was dressed casually in a sweater, shirt and pants. He had lost a lot of hair since they had seen him before, but looked good for a man of seventy-nine, who had been reputedly in bad health a decade ago, and who had endured a major brain operation for the removal of a tumour. The main difference was in his demeanour. There was a vacant look in his eyes. The spark of recognition that once would have been there when surrounded by his Christian friends was gone. 'He didn't remember any of our names,' says Lady Rawlings. 'I tried to get him to remember things in Lexington. He only remembered a couple of things. He remembered a park that used to stand opposite his house when he was a boy and he remembered his oldest brother. He suddenly said, "It seems like I had a brother and he had something wrong with his head." That was his brother George.'

They spoke to him of mutual friends, hoping that something would fire his mind, but nothing worked. He pointed to an old lady, a fellow-resident, and told everyone that this was his new girlfriend. He sat at a piano and played them some songs. He gazed out of the window. He never once mentioned his son, Marvin Gaye, or the events of Sunday, 1 April 1984. It was as if they had never happened or had happened to someone else with the same name. There was no guilt, no remorse, no hint of personal tragedy. There was just nothing.

`It was strange,' says Shelton West. 'He could talk about things that were happening in the present, but he had no recollection of the past. It was as though his brain had conveniently blocked out all those events, as though they were too horrible to comprehend.'

1

The Ordinary World

He that troubleth his own house shall inherit the wind.

Proverbs 11:29

Marvin Gaye's father was born on 1 October 1914 in Jessamine County, Kentucky, the third child of twenty-three-year-old farm labourer George Gay and his wife, Mamie. They registered the boy simply as 'Infant Gay' but a few weeks later named him Marvin and gave him the middle name Pentz after the German-born doctor who had delivered him. Five years later, the family moved into a house on Adams Street, Lexington, close to George's father, Strawder.

Strawder had been the first in the family to adopt the surname Gay, the first to be born outside slavery and the first to preach. No one was certain where he'd picked up the surname but he'd started using it as a teenager. (His great-grandson, Marvin Pentz Gaye II, added the E when 'gay' came into popular usage as a term for homosexual.) The origin of his Christian name was equally mysterious, being spelt on various documents as Strother, Strouther, Strauther, Strauder, Strawther, Strader and Straughter as well as Strawder. Census returns from his adult years describe him as either a labourer or a painter. His obituary mentioned that he was also a Baptist preacher.

Born in 1869, six years after Abraham Lincoln's Emancipation Act, Strawder was the son of an unmarried mulatto woman from Montgomery County, Kentucky, named Margaret Anderson. She was a thirty-one-year-old cook, working in the house of a white couple, Matt and Sarah Anderson, and had presumably been one of their slaves. She had taken this family's name and Strawder was registered as Strawder Anderson shortly after his birth. Matt Anderson appears to have been a Christian with compassionate feelings towards his former slaves. In his will he set aside one acre of property to establish 'a colored Christian church' in Montgomery County.

If Margaret knew who Strawder's father was, she never documented the information. He must have been black because Strawder was registered as 'black' despite his mother being a 'mulatto' with two other mulatto children. We know nothing about his early years, but records in the Kentucky State Archives reveal that some time during the 1880s he dropped the name Anderson and became Strawder Gay. His son James passed on the story that the name came from a Frenchman who farmed in Nicholasville, Jessamine County. Having no children, this kindly farmer willed his property to Strawder while on his deathbed. The only problem with the story is that there is no record of Strawder owning a farm or of a Mr Gay farming in Nicholasville at that time.

What we can know is that the Strawder Anderson of the 1880 US census was Strawder Gay ten years later when he married Rebecca Garrett (also 'black') of Mount Sterling, Montgomery County. When he died at the age of sixty-one, he was sufficiently respected in the community to warrant a mention in the 'Colored Notes' column of the *Lexington Herald*. 'Rev. Strauder Gay died after a lingering illness,' read the entry on 22 September 1930. 'Wife, Rebecca; three daughters, Margaret Taylor, Mary Belle Taylor and Elizabeth Wells; three sons, George, Bert and James Gay.'

George Gay, Strawder's eldest son, married Mamie Watkins from Indiana and appears to have made her pregnant almost every year of her fertile life. The first child was born in 1911 and the last in 1933 when she must have been almost fifty. Thirteen of these children survived—nine boys and four girls—the third of which was Marvin Pentz Gay, the father of Marvin Gaye.

By the time the youngest children arrived the older ones had left home, but there was a more or less constant brood of seven or eight, which meant that the girls had to share the parents' bed while the boys slept in the living room, some of them on the floor. They were so poor that they often had to scrounge for food in the garbage cans of the better-off, cutting the rot out of apples and potatoes and baking the remains over a fire. Their poverty was made harsher by George Gay's behaviour. Although he worked when he could, he was a terrible alcoholic prone to outbursts of violence. If his wife didn't obey him he would knock her around. The children never actually saw him drinking but he always stank of a combination of whiskey and beer.

'We were all frightened of him,' remembers Howard Gay, who was born in 1924. 'When you're five or six years old you don't know what to do when your mother is being beaten and there's hollerin' and cryin' going on. When I got old enough God gave me the will to tell him to leave my mother alone and get out. I thought I was going to have to kill him myself, but he just gave up.'

George walked out of the family home and headed for Cincinnati. No one in the family ever saw him again. The next time they heard from him he was seriously ill but by the time they reached his bedside he was dead. This left Mamie in sole charge of her large family.

'She was a very beautiful mother but when you were in her home you had to do what she told you to do,' says Howard. 'She trained us to hold our heads up. We had to stand straight, sit straight and walk with our backs straight. If she caught us sitting with our heads bent over anything she would tell us that we should only bow our heads to pray. It may have made us appear stuck up, but that's the way we were.'

Her most significant contribution to the life of Marvin Pentz Gay was religion. When he was in his mid-teens, Mamie, who until then hadn't enrolled her family in a church, was converted to a new Holiness denomination, which had recently established itself on Lexington's Newtown Pike. No one knows why this busy mother was attracted to the House of God (or, to give it its full name, the House of God, the Holy Church of the Living God, the Pillar and Ground of the Truth, the House of Prayer for All People). It could have been the joyous celebration that offered relief from the tedium of mothering and housekeeping. It could have been the emphasis on personal holiness, which promised moral guidance for her young children. Certainly, the House of God would have been very different from the Methodist and Baptist churches she had known. It was here that her boys first sang in public.

'Our mother taught us all how to sing when we were very young,' says Howard. 'She used to sing spirituals to us and then when we were teenagers we had quartets at church and we used to set the place on fire. Both Marvin and our brother Clarke played the piano.'

Founded in 1918 by R.A.R. Johnson (Rufus Abraham Reid Johnson) of North Carolina, the House of God denomination was 'Hebrew Pentecostal', a black Holiness church, which adhered to aspects of Judaism. Like any other Holiness church it practised speaking in tongues, healing and 'tarrying', but it also kept the Passover, observed Saturday as its day of worship and avoided the 'unclean' foods (such as pork and seafood) prohibited in the Old Testament book of Leviticus. The women wore white veils, the styles differing according to their seniority. The pulpit bore the Star of David. The Ten Commandments were dutifully recited by the congregation at the commencement of each service.

The gospel preached at the House of God was uncompromisingly Christian. An individual was 'saved' through faith in Christ, whose death had been a punishment administered by God for human sin. But whereas almost all other Christian denominations believed that Old Testament ceremonial laws had been abolished by the advent of Christ, the House of God considered that they were still binding.

Being black in the South during the 1920s in itself brought hardship, but to be a black who refused to work on Saturdays, eat non-kosher meat or celebrate Christmas was to invite persecution. Yet this didn't seem to bother the young Marvin Pentz Gay, who was moved by the preaching of N. L. Henry, the pastor at the Lexington House of God, and who later described his early experiences of church as a time when he was 'enraptured by God'. So enraptured was he that he decided to become a preacher himself. The denomination required no special training for its ministers because it believed that the gift was received through an 'anointing' of the Holy Spirit. He left Booker T. Washington School in 1927 and went to work at the Hillenmeyer Nurseries on Sandersville Road, but within four years, at the age of seventeen, he began travelling as an evangelist with Sister Fain, a respected older member of the Lexington church. 'They set out for Florida in an old borrowed car,' James Gay later told the *Lexington Herald*. 'They made the tour begging gas, tires, parts and anything else along the way.'

His closest friend in the Lexington congregation was Simon Peter Rawlings, a solid, cheerful boy who was a year younger and who believed that God had appeared to him in a dream, calling his name and asking him to 'go speak to the lost sheep'. In 1934 Marvin and Rawlings banded together and travelled to Mayesville, South Carolina, to pastor the House of God church there. When their work was completed they went up to Washington DC.

It was while in Washington DC that Marvin encountered Alberta Cooper, a young black girl from Red Oak near Rocky Mount, North Carolina. Shy and poorly educated, she had been raised as a Baptist and had left school to work as a sharecropper. The young Gay struck her as a polite man, and she was impressed with his self-assurance. Even though he was physically slighter than his friend Rawlings, he seemed to exude more power.

In many ways Alberta was the ideal wife for a preacher in a male-dominated church. Her shyness meant that she was happy to hide behind a strongly opinionated man, and yet she had a strong personal faith. However, there was a problem. Alberta was pregnant. The reason she was in Washington was to avoid the scandal of being an unwed mother in Red Oak. She was living with her sister Pearl until the child was born. Untypically for an up-and-coming evangelist, Marvin didn't seem perturbed by the situation. The couple dated during her pregnancy and then married in a storefront church three months after the birth of her child, a son whom she had named Micah Cooper.

However, when the newly-weds moved into a housing project at 1617 First Street, close to the Anacostia river, Marvin changed. He didn't want to raise the boy as his son and accused Alberta of being a fallen woman. It was as if he felt that the existence of the illegitimate child gave him a moral advantage. Once, he made her spend the night in the main railroad station as a reminder of her sin. Micah was handed over to Pearl and her husband George to be raised.

Alberta had already survived hardship and brutality. Her heavy-drinking father, Sam Cooper, had died in prison when she was a child. No one now knows exactly for what crime he had been imprisoned but it involved violence. He may have killed two white boys for insulting his daughters, or he may have gone berserk one day after drinking some poisoned alcohol. Both stories have survived. Whatever happened, the result was that his wife Lucy was left a widow and his children—John Astor, Alberta, Zeola, Toley and Pearl—all had to leave school after completing sixth grade to work in the cotton-fields. They couldn't have survived as a family without the income.

'My daddy was a real mean man,' admits John Astor Cooper, the only one still alive today. 'He tried to shoot my mother with a shotgun but he didn't quite hit her in the head. He would come home after being out all night, take all the dishes out of the cabinet and break them up. He lost his mind and when that happened they sent him to Goldsboro and that's where he died.'

This background left Alberta educationally disadvantaged but it endowed her with compassion. After two years of marriage, she produced a daughter, Jean, and then, on 2 April 1939, a longed-for son, who was named after his father, Marvin Pentz Gay II. Two other children were to follow—Frankie in 1942 and Zeola (better known as Sweetsie) in 1945.

Later Alberta confessed that her husband had never wanted Marvin and that the animosity that characterized the father–son relationship was there at the beginning. Perhaps as a reaction to this she grew exceptionally close to her son, and their mutual admiration was obvious to everyone.

Marvin Senior's energy went into church work, even though it paid only a pittance. Other than a short period working for the post office and as a driver in the construction industry, he never had a full-time occupation, blaming a slipped disc for his inactivity. By 1942 the twenty-seven-year-old was known in the denomination as Elder M. P. Gay and had become General Secretary of the House of God for an annual salary of fifty dollars, even though the church he had established in Washington DC was really no more than an extended family gathering, which met either in local storefronts or at home.

'The church at that time had very few members,' says Polly

Solomon, whose father was also an elder in the Washington DC church. 'It was mostly our family and theirs. There were some aunts on the Gay side and Mrs Gay's mother. But we did everything just the same way that it would be done in a big church. We had a praise service with music, testimony and preaching. It was very active and everybody played a part.'

Marvin sang in the church from the age of two and enjoyed the atmosphere of the services, which started in the early morning with a Sabbath School and went on until the evening, with the grown-ups breaking down, speaking in tongues, uttering prophecies and performing miraculous healings.

'Our church was a very spiritual church and we were a very chosen people,' Marvin said in later years, as he spoke fondly of the people who had come to his home to worship. 'The body [of believers] was small but the spirit was intense, and very evident to anyone who passed by or came in. It immediately encompassed them.'

South West Washington DC, where the young Gays grew up, was a black ghetto, disadvantaged but not torn apart by street violence or gang warfare as later ghettos in the city would be. There was little crime, no drugs and virtually full employment. Bounded on one side by the Anacostia river, on another by the railroad tracks and on a third by the Fort McNair Military Academy, it was a self-reliant community where no one bothered to lock their doors and where parental discipline was firm.

Although Marvin grew up within easy reach of the White House and the Washington Monument his childhood play areas could have been in rural Kentucky. There were trees to climb, fish to catch and a community centre for social activities. Baseball and football were played on vacant lots, and Marvin learned piano at home. When he was thirteen he was hit in the left eye by a stone that his brother Frankie had launched from a slingshot and had to be hospitalized for three weeks.

His closest childhood friend was Buddy Comedy, a cheerful, adventurous boy whose mother became a second mother to Marvin. The two boys were so inseparable that they became known in the neighbourhood as 'Comedy and Gay', as if they were a show-business act with invented names.

'Everyone in the neighbourhood took up the responsibility for raising all the children,' said Comedy. 'Anyone who acted up would be disciplined on the spot by the first adult on the scene. Then they would tell your parents so that when you got home you'd get another spanking and have to stay at home on the porch and miss baseball.'

Although strict discipline was common, Marvin's father was exceptional for the inflexibility of his rules and the savagery of his punishments. The laws that governed the House of God also governed the House of Gay. There was no make-up or nylons for the girls, no sport between dusk on Friday and dusk on Saturday and no questioning of his authority. Movies and television were banned and a curfew enforced. If rules were broken the children were immediately grounded or beaten. His beatings could be vicious: Mr Gay used a leather belt, which he would administer on bare skin, producing red welts, for serious wrongdoing, such as provocation or disobedience, but also for such failings as wetting the bed, something all four Gay children frequently did because of the climate of fear.

In later life Marvin believed that his father delighted in giving these beatings and used delaying rituals to prolong his pleasure. He was a weak man who loved to punish others for their failings, a stubborn man who liked to see others bend to his will, a lazy man who couldn't stand to see anyone wasting time.

'I can remember my mother talking about Mr Gay as a fellow adult,' said Comedy. 'She would say that he was a very strange man. He wouldn't let his children be children. Most of our parents were aware of the implications of segregation. They weren't bitter about it but they tried to prepare us to deal with it. But Mr Gay didn't have any time for that. He thought that everyone should be religious just like he was.'

'We were a strange family,' admits Marvin's brother, Frankie. 'We were strange in the sense that we went to church on a Saturday and we didn't eat pork. There wasn't any cussing in our house. There wasn't any fighting. We were very much sheltered from the neighbourhood and I know that they looked on us as being very strange.'

In the House of God, the keeping of the law was paramount. Obedience didn't get you into heaven, but the desire to obey told you something about the state of your soul. Hadn't Jesus said, 'If you love me, you will keep my commandments'? The double bind was that even though you weren't saved by your good works you had to do good works to show that you were saved. Failure to live up to the standards opened the floodgates of doubt and fear.

This life was made even harder by the application of Old Testament standards, often accompanied by Old Testament justice. Under Levitical law the father reigned supreme in the family. 'If anyone curses his father or mother, he must be put to death,' read Leviticus 20:9. 'He has cursed his father or his mother, and his blood will be on his own head.'

The children were made to read and learn the Bible while their father imposed his interpretations. He would test them on what they'd learned and he let them know that if they broke his rules they were breaking God's rules. Remarkably, given later developments, Marvin was always grateful for this introduction to the Bible and gave his father credit for introducing him to Jesus. Yet his relationship with his father was ambiguous from an early age: he loved him, yet feared him; he despised his behaviour, yet respected his teaching; he wanted to please him, yet wanted to confront and challenge him. Above all, he wanted to win his love and support.

'The only thing Marvin wanted from his father was approval,' said Comedy. 'He was really happy when he was with his mom because she loved him unreservedly, flat-out. There was no doubt about it. It was a two-way thing. He was at his happiest when he was with his mom and able to do things for his mom.'

Because Mr Gay didn't earn enough to keep the family, Alberta had to work as a cleaner in nearby Maryland or Virginia. But despite her bread-winning role he treated her with disdain, frequently abusing her verbally and intimidating her physically.

'He would never let me do anything and he'd never play with me when I came over to visit,' remembers his step-son Micah Cooper. 'Once he pushed my mother down the stairs and I remember my uncles coming round to talk to him about that.'

Sylvia Inman, a niece of Alberta, who would visit the family in Washington, remembers her aunt having a low sense of self-esteem because of the constant cruelty. 'He made her feel like she was nothing,' she says. 'It was as if he was saying, "You had a child out of wedlock and I took you in. You better be grateful." I don't know whether he ever actually used physical abuse, but he certainly abused her mentally.'

Almost everyone who visited the home during this period remembers Mr Gay lording it over his family. The children had to address him as 'Father' rather than 'Daddy', and he didn't play with them. He spent much of his time locked away in his bedroom experimenting with women's clothes and make-up.

'He was really odd,' says Barbara Solomon, a cousin of Marvin, who once lived with the family. 'He would stay in his room while my aunt waited on him. She took meals in to him on a tray. Once in a while he would come out of his room all dressed up with his hair freshly waved. Everyone in the family was afraid of him.'

From the age of five Marvin would accompany his father to the annual House of God conventions in Lexington, where he would be given the opportunity to perform gospel songs. His father would play the piano while Marvin sang classic numbers such as 'Precious Lord', 'Journey To The Sky' or 'Through The Years I Keep On Toiling'. The women adored him and young Marvin became a platform attraction.

'Elder Gay could sing but he was quite mediocre,' says William P. Johnson, a contemporary of Marvin, who attended the conventions. 'Marvin, on the other hand, had a great talent from an early age. There would always be requests for him to sing at the adult services.'

It was during these large events that Marvin came to see his voice as a gift from God that could sway people's emotions. At the same time he sensed that his father felt threatened by the applause and the embraces from the women. It detracted from his glory. 'I think that one of the reasons people asked him to preach,' says Micah Cooper, 'is because they wanted to hear young Marvin sing.'

Music plays a vital part in House of God worship. Sabbath services, which last for at least three hours, always start with half an hour or more of singing, and the whole afternoon is punctuated by gospel music. Emotions can be gently raised with music but they can also be gently brought down in the same way. The important thing is not to get caught up in a merely fleshly response. In a typical service there will be choral performances, solos and duets, testimonies and impassioned exhortations by the preacher. The music is lively but not generational. A twenty-year-old singer might be backed by a seventy-year-old guitarist. An old man banging a tambourine might shout out words that sound like an echo from the plantations. No instruments are forbidden as 'the Devil's instruments'.

'What Marvin learned from the church was how to put his very being into a song,' says Larry Johnson, an elder from the Lexington church. 'He was not someone standing there singing a song in the way he had been taught but someone who was expressing what was in him. Pentecostals put everything that is in them into the song.'

The same year that Marvin attended his first House of God convention he and Buddy Comedy started school at William Syphax Elementary School on Half Street, a short walk from the Gay family home on First Street. 'He was playing piano right from the early days because his father would teach him,' said Buddy Comedy. 'The school would have special programmes for Easter and Christmas and Marvin would be chosen to appear in these because of his playing. They would write a part especially for him.'

From Syphax the boys graduated to William Randall Junior High, where Marvin was particularly encouraged by the music teacher, a bachelor called Levington Smith, who ran classes after school and at weekends for talented pupils. Marvin played keyboards and sang in the boys' choir. 'Levington Smith took a great interest in all the boys in our school and especially those who showed talent,' remembered Comedy. 'Our families would scuffle up the money to send the children to him for lessons on the violin, the piano or whatever. If you didn't have the money but you had the talent, he would teach you anyway. Marvin was one of his protégés. He gave Marvin a lot of instruction.'

At this time Marvin was unaware of black music outside gospel music. He'd never heard jazz, was ignorant of developments in R&B and never listened to a radio unless it was on at a friend's house. The first recorded music he could remember liking was the smooth-throated vocals of Italian-American singers such as Frank Sinatra, Tony Bennett and Perry Como. The only black singer he knew and loved was Nat 'King' Cole. At Randall he began entering talent competitions and in 1952 impressed staff and pupils with a rendition of 'Cry', the single by the white singer Johnny Ray, which had been a hit both in Britain and America and had launched Ray as one of the first heart-throbs of the 1950s. One of Ray's tricks was to break down weeping on stage and he carried a sob in his voice that would elicit screams from his young female audience.

'Marvin won the show based on that song,' said Buddy Comedy. 'He was so good he really had the audience going. Everybody was hollerin' and screamin' for this guy. Everyone from the janitor to the principal was moved by him and I benefited from the attention because I was his friend!'

Alberta was pleased, and encouraged her son, but Mr Gay was disappointed. This was 'boogie-woogie music', he said, and not appropriate for a member of the House of God. From his point of view Marvin's gift should be used exclusively to glorify God, not to celebrate carnal desires. There could be no compromise. Either you were in the world and caught up in its passions, or you were set apart for God and determined only to serve Him. The irony was that even as Mr Gay denounced his son for his secular ambitions and his stirring up of lust, he was beginning to experience his own battles with the world, the flesh and the Devil.

Although the House of God was a small denomination, it provided an arena in which Mr Gay wanted to succeed. He was already a member of the senior executive—the twelve-man Board of Apostles—but had his eye on the top job, that of Chief Apostle. However, in 1947 a split took place, and he saw his chance of success within the breakaway denomination, the Church of the Living God. He made his move, and was rewarded by being made a bishop in the new church. However, when he came to plant a church in Washington DC, it didn't take off. He was left with a grand title but no congregation, and it riled him that he had made the wrong choice.

Humiliated, he returned to the House of God two years later, only to find that his old pal from Lexington, Simon Rawlings, had been elected Chief Apostle. That in itself was a blow to his pride but what made it worse was the new ruling which declared that thirty-four-year-old Rawlings should hold the position for life. An argument erupted that would shape the direction of Mr Gay's life. 'He felt that there should be an election for Chief Apostle every four years but no one else agreed,' says Shelton West, current chairman of the church's Ministers

Council. 'You would have to accept that this was primarily because there was hope within him of being the head man himself.'

Having been overruled, Mr Gay seemed to lose his enthusiasm for organized religion. He carried on pastoring for a few more years but the motivation was lacking. Whatever had originally spurred him on to evangelism and teaching, whether it was the power of the Holy Spirit or simply the human desire for power and glory, had ebbed away. They still called him Bishop Gay but by the mid-fifties it was a title with no meaning.

'He just isolated himself after that,' says West. 'He never really dis-associated himself from the House of God but he didn't continue to attend. Things went on without him. He was a very proud man. He was laden with pride. He ceased to grow spiritually.'

Marvin would refer to it as the period when his father 'lost his heal-ing power'. When people would ask him about the religion of his father he would instead refer them to Bishop Simon Rawlings. 'He would tell them to talk to my husband,' says Lady Rawlings, 'because he knew that his daddy had left his power behind.'

His ambition thwarted, Mr Gay became lax about his own piety although he continued to expect high standards from his children. His clothes became increasingly feminine. He would wear colourful silk blouses and straight-hair wigs, and even his wife's nylon stockings. People in the neighbourhood questioned his sexuality. Was he homo-sexual, bisexual or merely eccentric? Alberta claimed that at least one of the unmarried brothers was gay, and Howard Gay would later serve a prison sentence for 'indecent and immoral practices' with a boy. But she also knew that his major weakness was women.

'He loved beautiful women,' remembers his niece Gloria Herring. 'He loved large breasts and large buttocks. My aunt had to accept that he had girlfriends. They were always referred to as "sisters" or "com-panions" and came from the church, but actually they were sleeping with him and I think he used his position in the church to get women. Because he was a minister I think a lot of the women felt it was an hon-our. They thought they were serving God by doing it and I think he felt the same way too.'

Barbara Solomon remembers times when he requested that Alberta bring food through to him in his bedroom while he was entertaining his women friends. He even attempted to grope Barbara when she was only fifteen. 'I told my aunt about the advance but she said he was just teasing,' she says. 'She told me not to take it seriously.'

His moral decline began to shock the adult members of the wider family, who had been led to believe that he was a 'man of God'. 'He was very sexually explicit,' says Sylvia Inman. 'He used to take pictures of his wife and other women in sexual poses. I didn't say anything about it myself as a child but I can remember the older people talking about these things.'

He even tried to tempt the wife of his elder in Washington to be unfaithful, something she never mentioned to her late husband and only told her daughter much later in life. 'He was telling her that she was young and attractive,' says Polly Solomon. 'I don't know whether he was trying to get her to do something with him or with another man. She refused but that didn't deter him. He came back a second time, presumably because he thought that she would eventually weaken.'

In 1954, South West Washington D.C. was subject to an urban renewal programme. Residents were moved to new housing in North West D.C. with the promise of being returned when the renewal was completed. That was the plan although, over forty years later, the site of the block where the Gays lived on 1st Street is still desolate and overgrown and the community centre has been replaced by a scrap-metal plant. The new Gay home was a two-storey red-brick house at 12 60th Street, just off East Capitol. A dirt track where families gathered to talk or play in the evenings ran behind the houses.

It was when he arrived here that Marvin graduated to Cardozo High School while Buddy Comedy went on to the more academic Dunbar High. Cardozo graduates were expected to become police officers or office clerks. Ninety per cent of Dunbar's graduates went on to college. 'It wasn't that Marvin's grades weren't good,' said Comedy. 'We were in the Honor Society both at William Syphax and at Randall, which meant having a straight A average. It was more to do with family pressure. His dad didn't want him hanging about with people like me because I was an unabashed fun-lover. It wasn't that I was bad, it was just that I didn't go for any of that foolishness that his dad talked about.'

At Cardozo Marvin fell in with a group of music-loving kids—Reese Palmer, Sondra Lattisaw, James Hopps, Vernon Christian and Leon MacMickens—who together formed a vocal group to practise during lunch breaks. For the first time black popular music, heard mostly on radio rather than on record, became an influence in his life. Particularly he liked the new vocal group sound, later referred to as 'doo wop', which was a rougher, rockier version of the harmonies that the Inkspots had perfected in the forties. Groups like the Dominoes, the Clovers and the Drifters were taking the strident vocals of gospel music and marrying them to a faster R&B sound. Records like 'Gee' by the Crows and 'Earth Angel' by the Penguins were heralds of the rock 'n' roll revolution.

'We called ourselves the DC Tones and we sang nothing but black music,' remembers Reese Palmer. 'We sang "Baby It's You" by the Spaniels, "Pain In My Heart" by the Dells, "A Girl To Love" by the Chords and songs like that. Marvin's father, of course, never liked what we did. If we played on the street corner, we were bums. If we sang R&B, it wasn't God's music. We could never do right by him.'

Even though they only performed locally, the group built up a reputation at Cardozo and music became part of Marvin's identity. He might not have been able to make the party scene, his conscience wouldn't allow him to prove himself in playground fights and his Sabbath rituals kept him off the gridiron, but in music he could express himself and become someone that others would notice and admire.

Frank Boulding, Cardozo's athletics coach, remembers having to chase the group out of the school building at lunch-times. 'They had a special area under a stairway just beyond the cafeteria where they liked singing because the acoustics were so good. They harmonized very well but sometimes their zeal and zest for singing would take them through the time for lessons and, as a teacher, I had to get them to class.'

Already a tall—five-eight—and handsome boy, with a broad grin and perfect white teeth, the two words most frequently used when friends describe Marvin at this stage are 'polite' and 'shy'. There was a kindness and natural humility that owed something to his church grounding and, like all the young people from the House of God, he was always immaculately dressed. The shyness stemmed from the strangeness of his background, which had made him unsure of where he fitted in. The House of God continually emphasized separation from the world, and this made him quiet and withdrawn. The Bible said that you were to be 'in the world but not of it', a difficult concept to grasp at fifteen. Marvin's way of being 'in but not of' was to become detached, an observer of the world, and yet a hesitant participant.

'He loved his mother and she was the main influence on his life at the time,' said Buddy Comedy. 'She was very loving and caring and so was Marvin. He would give you the shirt off his back if you needed it. He was always that way. He was a very, very unselfish guy.'

He enjoyed sport, but his father never coached him or even played with him and discouraged him from doing trials for the school teams because he feared it would clash with his church activities. Although Marvin never talked about it back then, it frustrated him that he wasn't able to prove his masculinity on the sports field and the frustration deepened as he grew older. He was never a member of any team that Frank Boulding coached.

'I remember that he couldn't do a hook shot on the basketball court because his dad just didn't allow him to get out as much as we could,' said Comedy. 'He was very athletic when he had the opportunity but he wasn't given the time to practise.'

His lack of sporting achievement didn't harm his sexual appeal. The girls loved his soft-spoken voice and his smart clothes. What may have appeared 'soft' to the guys seemed charming and debonair to the girls. He was never crude or rude and always took time to listen.

His main problem was that he felt he had been turned into a freak by his father's religious strictness. He longed to be like everyone else, with normal freedoms and expectations. He knew the House of God's answer. They would say that it was a necessary sacrifice and that spiritual growth comes through persecution. Didn't even Jesus once say, 'Beware when all men speak well of you'? Acceptance was a sign of error. Rejection was a sign of truth.

'It's quite a hardship on a child because he constantly has to prove to his comrades that he's as normal as they are,' Marvin once reflected. 'You have to do something rather bad or you're not accepted. You have to lose the stigma of being a child of God.'

Reese Palmer remembers that Marvin became more remote because he didn't have the inner freedom to throw himself into things. There was always the reproving figure of his father in the background brandishing a Bible and a belt. He had to weigh the acceptance by his peers against the disapproval of his father. 'He missed out on a lot of things because he always had to be home extra early,' says Palmer. 'If we went to a dance or something we would go in and then I'd look around and Marvin would be gone. What he would do was come in through the front door of the party and then go straight out the back door and down the hill to his house. He would go home early so that he wouldn't be chastised.'

To his friends he often appeared to be a conformist, but at home he was regarded as the rebellious child, the one who was willing to confront his father by ignoring his rules. It was as though he wanted to see what reactions were set off when laws were broken. How much punishment could he stand? Was it really all that bad to be defiant?'

'Marvin had a problem with authority,' says his sister Sweetsie. 'He would always do the more challenging thing. He would always want to flirt with danger.'

'His brother Frankie was totally different from Marvin,' remembers Geraldine 'Peasie' Adams, a neighbourhood friend from those days. 'Frankie would do anything his father said, but Marvin would retaliate.'

By 1956 Marvin was sneaking off to matinee shows at the Howard Theater, where Buddy Comedy had backstage access because the manager was an old schoolfriend of his mother. The Howard was, at that time, one of the premier showcases for black music on the East Coast— equal in importance to the Apollo in New York, the Royal in Baltimore and the Uptown in Philadelphia. Often an afternoon show would have seven or eight acts, and they'd be among the best in contemporary American black music.

'We would go to the Howard all the time,' says Reese Palmer. 'We would duck school, get in and meet the stars. We saw people like Clyde McPhatter, Jackie Wilson, the Spaniels, the Dells, the Platters, James Brown—you name them, we saw them. Marvin would get jealous of all those big-name black singers. He always wanted to be bigger than they were.'

2

The Call to Adventure

As a bird that wandereth from her nest, so is a man that wandereth from his place.   Proverbs 27:8

His father was restricting his development, and by 1956 Marvin knew that if he was ever going to grow up he was going to have to break away from this malign influence. His ambitions were regularly squashed and every expression of individualism was classified as sin. Mr Gay wanted Marvin to use his musical gift for the church, to succeed where he had failed, but Marvin didn't have the intensity of religious conviction that his father had experienced at the same age. He had no intellectual objections to the idea of God's existence and didn't dispute the wisdom of Christ's teachings, but he was uncomfortable with what he saw as the legalistic preoccupations of the House of God. Hadn't Christ criticized the Pharisees of his own day for the very same thing—for burdening the people with unnecessary rules and paying too much attention to outward appearances?

Living at home, there was no way to resolve the dilemma. Experimentation wasn't allowed. Doubts were forbidden. His father saw everything in clear black-and-white terms and couldn't be debated with. As a man who was secretly failing to live up to his own ideals he expected more of his children than he expected of himself.

Marvin was intelligent but not academic. He found study boring. He was fine with subjects in which he had a natural interest but everything else set his mind wandering. 'There were times when I swear that Marvin knew more than the teachers who were teaching him,' says Reese Palmer. 'That's probably why he wasn't interested. Some of the things they were teaching him he knew already. He was very intelligent.'

Even if he had been a great academic success at school he knew that it wouldn't provide an immediate escape from home. He began to think seriously about making it as a musician, waving farewell to Washington and taking to the road, maybe making enough money to send cheques home to his mother and improve her life. The only other option, a popular one at the time among blacks in the ghetto, was to join the armed forces. The US military had not yet been tainted by the scandals of Vietnam and there was no broad-based peace movement among the young. Russia was the biggest perceived threat to America's security, and troop levels were kept high to deal with a nuclear attack on mainland America or a conventional war in Europe.

In the summer of 1956, against his father's wishes, Marvin decided to quit Cardozo High School a year short of graduation and join the United States Air Force. 'He was already spending ninety per cent of his time singing in the hallways,' says Reese Palmer, who stayed on through twelfth grade. 'I guess there was nothing left for him to do but drop out.'

'He got to the point where he knew it was no longer worthwhile going to school,' says Geraldine 'Peasie' Adams. 'He didn't have any money. He didn't have a car. It was very discouraging for him. He had pride and he didn't want to live like that. Things weren't going too well for him at home and I think he just wanted to do anything to get away.'

It was clearly the move of a desperate man. Nothing could have been less suited to Marvin Gaye's temperament than a life in the military. Noted for his peacefulness and sensitivity, he had no particular aptitude for mechanics and, like his father, disliked being told what to do. He had also led a remarkably unworldly life. There had been no serious girlfriends, no drugs or alcohol, virtually no cinema or television, and no experience of living away from home. He chose the Air Force rather than the Army or Navy simply because he was a member of the Civil Air Patrol, a junior version of the Air Force, which met each week in the local community centre for drill practice and instruction on a Link Trainer. There was no thought of combat in the Civil Air Patrol: it was a matter of looking good, having fun and going places.

'We all had uniforms and it helped to get the attention of the girls,' admitted Buddy Comedy. 'Marvin and I were in the drill team, Ghich meant that we got to travel all over the country giving drill performances. There were regional competitions on the East Coast and then national competitions in places like Texas and Ohio.'

On 18 October 1956, at a United States Air Force recruiting office in Alexandria, Virginia, Marvin enlisted for four years' service. He passed a physical examination four days later and on 24 October was sworn in before enlisting officer Stephan N. Strauss, who sent him to the Military Training Wing of Lackland Air Force Base in San Antonio, Texas, for four weeks of basic training. Elvis Presley was at number one in the American singles charts with 'Hound Dog', Hungary had just been invaded by the Soviet Union and Dwight Eisenhower was just about to beat Adlai Stevenson in the American presidential election to begin his second term at the White House. Marvin later claimed that the recruiting officer had promised that he would be in Special Services and able to serve his time as an entertainer, although it's unlikely that he would have been offered this after such a basic examination. He certainly expected excitement in his career, and presumably thought that service in the Air Force would involve flying.

However, he underwent basic training in radio operation, mechanics, electronics and firearms but his scores were modest. As a mechanic he made only 25 per cent and as an electrician 20 per cent. Towards the end of the course he was given target practice with an automatic rifle and made 110, which was 19 points short of marksman status. Within days he realized that he'd done the wrong thing. He'd escaped from one tough regime only to find himself in another, even more inflexible one.

On 24 November he was transferred to Francis E. Warren Air Force Base in Cheyenne, Wyoming, for further technical training. Two hours north of Denver, Colorado, Marvin considered the area 'Godforsaken' and continued to resent the military routine. Seven weeks later, on 11

January 1957, he and other recruits on the course were formally promoted from Airman (Basic) to Airman (3C). However, the day after his promotion Marvin didn't prepare his barrack room for inspection; he was instantly demoted for 'dereliction in the performance of duty'. For a boy who had been brought up to respect authority and to obey commandments, this was defiance rather than insouciance. He was testing the capabilities of his new enemy, seeing how far he could push things. He wanted to get out, and if they wouldn't let him go voluntarily he'd prove himself so unmanageable that they'd be glad to get rid of him. It was a game he played frequently in later life.

From Wyoming he was posted to the 802nd Supply Squadron at Schilling Air Force Base at Salina, Kansas, where he became part of a four-hundred-strong team employed to organize the base's supplies of everything from food and clothing to gas. Marvin took a three-week holiday and reported for duty at Salina a day late. It was an ominous start and he was given an immediate dressing-down by his First Sergeant.

His first duty at Schilling was peeling potatoes for Food Supply, a job that he felt was demeaning. Military discipline rankled with him. He couldn't take orders from people who, he thought, were out to humiliate him, and he couldn't respect officers he considered 'pompous assholes'. Neither was he happy to be exiled on a base out on the plains of Kansas where the nearest town was a small community of 30,000 people, 98 per cent of whom were white. The only places of entertainment were a few 'clubs' that had opened outside the base to take advantage of the appetites of six thousand Air Force personnel, some of which had been designated 'off limits' because of prostitution, liquor violations and violence.

It was in one of these establishments that Marvin had his first experience of sex, with an overweight prostitute in a small upstairs room where he paid a few dollars for three minutes of action. He later referred to the brothel as 'a crummy little cathouse outside the base' which had 'four hookers for two thousand men'.

'About six miles out of town there was a black whorehouse,' remembers Jack Magyari, who served at Schilling AFB in the 802nd Supply Group at the same time as Marvin. 'It was called Patsy Prim's. It had a bar downstairs and there were girls upstairs.'

The thought of sex both fascinated and frightened Marvin. His father taught that sex was sacred, yet also referred to intercourse as 'doing the nasty'. The House of God, in its passion for holiness, believed that the utmost reticence was required even when speaking about sex.

'We are not common men but men of high standing, holding great responsibilities,' Bishop A. A.Smith had instructed the Church's General Convocation fifteen years before. 'Brothers should not accept the requests and pleas of women to attend them and should keep themselves in conditions that will win for them the highest respect, and conduct conversations and sermons so as to appear graceful and constructive in the ears of their listeners.'

But Marvin was not now in the mood to be graceful and constructive. He wanted to taste everything he'd been told was forbidden. 'She was waiting on the bed,' he told French journalist Patrick Zerbib when recounting the experience. 'She ordered me to take my shoes off and get undressed. "Please," I said, "not like that. I've never . . . " She was nice. I told her how shy I was, how all the girls preferred the older guys. She told me about her job. Then I had my three minutes and left.'

He immediately experienced a wave of post-coital remorse. There was something degrading about undisguised lust, yet there was also something alluring. He had climaxed quickly and it didn't seem a fair reward for all the anticipation. This was the beginning of his fascination with the dark undertow of his sexuality and with prostitution, which affected both his music and his deepest relationships.

Throughout the rest of April Marvin distinguished himself by reporting late for duty four times and once being found in bed during work hours. Later he claimed that he had been trying to convince the authorities that he was mad and told friends that he even wet his bed to make his superiors feel that he had a psychological problem.

'[Enlisting in the Air Force] was the worst thing I have ever done,' he admitted years later. 'It was one of the real horrors of my life. I had gone insane. That's what they told me because I was ready to go home and they said I couldn't because I was in the service . . . I lost all perspective. If they told me to get up, I'd lay down. If they told me to wash up, I'd throw dirt on myself. If they had threatened to shoot me I was mad enough to dare them. And it would have been okay dying then if I could hear just one of them say, "Wow, he sure didn't go for none of this shit, did he?' "

During May and June he complained of health problems and had appointments to see both a doctor and a dentist. Then, on 7 June, he was found in 'an unauthorized area' at three o'clock in the morning— most likely one of the off-limits clubs. He was promptly arrested by the Military Police and escorted back to the base.

By now it was clear to his superiors that he was of no use to the United States military. During his three months at Schilling Air Force Base he had been counselled several times about his behaviour; he required constant supervision and, according to official records, 'continually absented himself without permission'. The only remaining question was whether to give Marvin Gay an honourable or a dishonourable discharge.

On 10 June Major William B. Mayes, Commander of 802nd Supply Squadron, requested that action be taken 'to eliminate Airman Basic Marvin Gay Jr. from the United States Air Force'. It was agreed by Lt. Col. Gordon E. Heil that 'attempts at rehabilitation of Airman Gay have proved unsuccessful'. Marvin's captain, Thomas J. Warren, gave the reasons for his discharge as '(a) Lackadaisical attitude towards responsibility. (b) Indifferent attitude toward duty. (c) Easily influenced by individuals with whom he associates'. The final terse report, signed by Major Mayes, concluded that 'Airman Gay is uncooperative, lacks even a minor degree of initiative, shows very little interest in his assigned duties and does nothing to improve his job knowledge . . . He evidences a dislike for the service and indicated nothing that can show that he can meet Air Force standards . . . I am convinced that further retention in the service would be a waste of time, effort and money.' He was promptly given a discharge, 'under honourable conditions', and released to go back to Washington DC.

Speaking of the incident forty years later, Major Mayes estimates that Marvin would have been one of only fifteen to twenty airmen discharged in this way from the 802nd Supply Squadron during the 1957–8 period. 'Most, if not all, were separations by mutual agreement,' he says. 'The late fifties was a period of racial unrest in the

United States and the discharge of a black airman was a sensitive issue. Most separations were with the consent—in fact, enthusiastic support—of the airmen involved.'

Marvin was certainly enthusiastic. Yet at the same time he was apprehensive about returning to Washington DC, a failure in the eyes of his friends, to have to confront his father, who had so often told him that he would never amount to anything. In fact, he only stayed with his family a few days before moving out and staying with 'Peasie' Adams, who was now married and living in a nearby apartment block, where Reese Palmer, his old buddy in the DC Tones, also lived.

Four years older than Marvin, Peasie was like a big sister to him and, while her husband was away in the military, she sheltered him from his father by giving him a room to sleep in and food. She also acted as a go-between with his family. 'He just didn't want to stay in the same house as his father any more,' she says. 'He was no longer under his father's control. I knew his mother and she would give me money to pass on to him to make sure he always had something in his pocket. I used to go into their house through the back door to collect the money because Mr Gay didn't want anything to do with Marvin.'

Living in the same block was a young divorced mother named Sandra Lamont, whom Marvin began dating. After a few weeks he moved in with her and began his first serious romance. Friends noticed that while he was always shy and insecure around church girls, he relaxed in the company of women he knew to be sexually experienced. 'She was prettier than any girl Marvin had ever talked to,' says Peasie. 'She was tall, she had beautiful long hair and she was just a very nice girl.'

Reese Palmer, who had just graduated from Cardozo High School, was in the process of setting up another group. He had recruited a bass singer named Chester Simmons, who had been in the Rainbows, with Don Covay and Billy Stewart, and Simmons had in turn introduced him to James Nolan, a twenty-three-year-old baritone singer. Covay and Stewart became two of the biggest stars from that generation of Washington musicians, Stewart hitting it big with 'Summertime' in 1966, and Covay making his mark both as a recording artist ('Pony Time', 'Mercy Mercy') and as a songwriter for Aretha Franklin ('Chain Of Fools'), Little Richard ('I Don't Know What You Got [But It's Got Me]' and Solomon Burke ('I'm Hangin' Up My Heart For You') among others.

In the sixties Covay was instrumental in forming the soul stars' own 'rat-pack', the Soul Clan, with Solomon Burke, Arthur Conley, Ben E. King and Joe Tex.

Much to Marvin's annoyance, Covay would often claim in interviews that Marvin had also been a member of the Rainbows. Marvin, however, denied that he had ever appeared with them. The truth, he said, was that Covay had once auditioned him but had turned him down. The humiliation had made him vow that he would never audition again, a vow that he kept.

'Reese Palmer, Chester Simmons and myself got together and talked about forming a group and we said that we needed a fourth person,' says James Nolan. 'Reese said that he knew Marvin, who had just left the Air Force. He said that we should ask him to join as a tenor. Marvin became the fourth member and we became the Marquees.'

Within weeks of the group's formation they had a stroke of luck. A hairdresser friend of Peasie was dating Bo Diddley, the Mississippi-born creator of such R&B numbers as 'Bring It To Jerome' and 'Bo Diddley', who was then living locally at 2614 Rhode Island Avenue. Peasie managed to arrange a meeting between the singer and the group.

'Marvin started to come over and hang around at my house,' remembers Bo. 'I had a studio there and he would sing on some of the stuff I was practising with. He didn't do any of my recordings but he was on these tapes that no one ever heard. He had a nice voice and I thought that one day he would do something.'

Bo began to invite the Marquees to shows he was doing around Washington DC, Virginia and Maryland. 'Sometimes he would announce us to his audience,' remembers Nolan. 'Then he introduced us to the Okeh label, which was part of Columbia Records in New York.'

Reese Palmer had started writing songs during his final year at Cardozo and one of his most recent efforts was a novelty song called 'Wyatt Earp'. 'There was a slow song that we were doing in our set and at a certain point we would keep singing 'Earp, Earp, Earp' because at that time there was a well-known TV series featuring Hugh O'Brien. I developed this into a new song based on Wyatt Earp and we recorded a demo tape at Bo's studio.'

On the basis of this song Columbia offered the Marquees a contract, but there was a problem because Marvin was under twenty-one and needed his father as a co-signatory. 'Marvin's father wouldn't sign it and he wouldn't let Marvin's mother sign it,' says Reese. 'So I signed it for Marvin!'

The group travelled to New York and recorded 'Wyatt Earp' and its B-side, 'Hey Little Schoolgirl', on 25 September 1957, the day that schools were desegregated in Little Rock, Arkansas, with the aid of a thousand paratroopers. Bo Diddley came up to play on the session, along with his backing band of Jerome Green on maracas, Billy Stewart on piano and Mickey Taylor on guitars. A Columbia staffer, Joe Sherman, is credited as producer. During the same session the Marquees also backed Stewart on 'Billy's Heartache', his second single and a follow-up to 'Billy's Blues', which he had recorded in March 1956.

'I don't think Sherman was happy with Bo's arrangement or the band he had with him,' says Reese Palmer. 'The sound that Bo had was a DC sound. So they had us back a week or so later and cut a version with a New York band, which included Panama Francis, who had played with Duke Ellington, on drums and Sam "The Man" Taylor, who had played with Louis Jordan, on saxophone.' It was this second version that was released as a single. In the year when Elvis Presley had three of America's five best-selling singles ('All Shook Up', 'Jailhouse Rock' and 'Teddy Bear'), 'Wyatt Earp' didn't even make the lower reaches of the charts. Despite a jangling guitar solo the production was sluggish. It didn't call out for a second play.

'We had thought that by recording a novelty tune we would put ourselves over,' remembers James Nolan, 'but that year there were too many novelty songs out and so our single didn't go over big. It got a little airplay in the Washington DC area, and that was it.'

The commercial failure of the single temporarily thwarted the ambitions of the Marquees. They went back to Bo's and recorded five more demos—three written by Reese ('What Does She Use?', 'Borrowing Money All The Doggone Time' and 'Puff, Puff, Gimme A Drag') and two by Marvin ('Barbara', which took its music from the theme tune to the Perry Mason TV series, and 'Down In The Valley'). But Okeh was no longer interested in the Marquees: the tape was never returned and a brief recording career drew to a close.

'Marvin and I got depressed,' admits Reese. 'We never really had a chance. For some reason entertainers from the DC area seemed to be jinxed. We continued to play locally but we were no longer full-time musicians. We all had to get jobs.'

Chester Simmons became a roadie for Bo Diddley, James Nolan worked as a hotel bell-hop, Reese started shining shoes and washing cars, and Marvin went caddying on nearby golf-courses. At one time Marvin and Reese got a job together on the night shift at a commissary on Kansas Avenue where food was prepared for local Hot Shoppe restaurants owned by J. Willard Marriott. 'We had to work inside huge freezers getting the frozen food ready for the trucks and while we were working we would sing together,' says Palmer. 'One night we were in there singing our hearts out when the guy opened the door of the freezer. We didn't hear him come in. He clapped his hands and asked us to follow him.

'The first thing that crossed our minds was that he was going to turn us on to someone who would sign us up. He took us upstairs, where an older white guy came out and shook our hands. We really thought we were on our way to fame and fortune. Then the guy went into his office and came back and handed us our checks. That was it. We were out!'

Working in downtown Washington DC, Marvin became aware of overt racism for the first time. In the ghetto they rarely came into contact with the white world. Marvin had never had a white school-teacher and had no white friends. He was aware of the Alabama bus boycotts, which had taken place earlier in the year, and Martin Luther King's call for 'passive resistance and the weapon of love', but it hadn't stirred anything deep inside him. Then, one afternoon, he was at the People's Drug Store with Reese and a mutual neighbourhood friend, Wardell Belton. 'We were trying to get some food at the lunch counter but they put us out because they said it was an area for whites only,' says Belton. 'That was probably the first time that Marvin or any of us had really thought about segregation.'

In the ghetto there had been a general acceptance that being black meant you had to fight harder to succeed but there was no discussion of human rights, no political talk about overturning the social order and certainly no preparation for armed insurrection. 'Our world was basically on the other side of the tracks,' said Buddy Comedy. 'We were proud to be in the capital city of America but at the same time we couldn't go into its movie theatres or restaurants. We just thought that that must be the natural order of things. There were no local agitators to tell us that things weren't right. Our parents knew what the deal was. They understood segregation, and they and our teachers made sure that we were serious. We were growing up in a world that was hostile and in order to be equal to a white person we had to give one hundred and twenty per cent.'

Nowhere was this more true than in popular music. It began to bug Marvin that white men with undistinguished voices were getting recognition for performing black music while black singers were pushed to the second division. Of thirty-four acts that reached the American Top Twenty in the last quarter of 1958, only four were black. Pat Boone had already had as many hit singles as Chuck Berry, Little Richard and Fats Domino combined and his music was a recognizably watered-down version of R&B. There was nothing new in this. If anything, things were better than they had ever been, with white teenagers happy to defy their parents by listening to black music. Yet there was still the feeling that black artists would never get their dues, that they would be revered for their innovations but would never be wholeheartedly embraced.

'Marvin and I would sit and talk about this,' said Buddy Comedy. 'I would tell him that the number one male vocalist in America could not be a black man. The greatest singer of the time was Nat "King" Cole but you'd think that Frank Sinatra was, although Sinatra couldn't have carried Cole's underwear.'

Just as it seemed that Marvin would be condemned to an unfulfilled life of casual labour and thwarted show-business aspirations, things unexpectedly swung in his favour. On 29 December the celebrated doo-wop group the Moonglows arrived in Washington for a week-long residency at the Howard Theater. The group had been recording for Chance Records of Chicago since 1953, when they linked up with Cleveland disc jockey Alan Freed, the man credited with virtually creating rock 'n' roll through his promotion of black R&B. Freed had been running a classical-music show but, in 1952, discovered from a local record shop proprietor that white teenagers were showing an unusually high interest in black music. As a result of this

Freed started a radio show to exploit this interest and then a series of live concerts, which presented black artists to a predominantly young white audience.

After leaving Chance Records, the Moonglows had signed with Chess Records in Chicago in October 1954 and had a hit less than three months later with 'Sincerely', a song credited to Fuqua and Freed but actually written by Fuqua alone. The success of this record (it topped the R&B chart in January 1955, displacing 'Earth Angel' by the Penguins), coupled with the association with Freed, meant that the group's music was guaranteed airplay on Freed's influential *Moondog's Rock and Roll Party* radio show. They toured with the likes of Muddy Waters and appeared in the movie *Rock, Rock, Rock* alongside the Teenagers, LaVern Baker and Chuck Berry. The musical dynamos of the group were Harvey Fuqua, nephew of Ink Spots guitarist Charlie Fuqua, and Bobby Lester. They'd met each other in the 1940s while at high school in Louisville, Kentucky. After different changes in the lineup, they had settled with bass singer Prentiss Barnes, from Mississippi, guitarist Billy Johnson, from Connecticut, and tenor singer Alexander 'Pete' Graves, from Alabama. Lester had one of the most distinctive lead voices of the era and was able to bend notes with dexterity. Fuqua, besides arranging the harmonies and developing the trademark 'blow note' technique, was also, at twenty-nine, an accomplished songwriter.

The Marquees, who all admired the vocals of the Moonglows, had a vague connection with the group in that Chester Simmons had met them backstage at a Canadian concert when he was driving Bo Diddley. Marvin arrived one evening at the Howard Theater after the early show and met Harvey Fuqua, who was just leaving his dressing room to go out and eat.

'He was out there saying, "I love you guys. I'm in a group and we can sing like you guys,' " remembers Fuqua. 'I felt like I didn't have time. I had to go. But Prentiss Barnes stopped and talked to him and invited him into the dressing room so that he was there when I came back after eating. I didn't really want to be bothered but I said, "OK, let me hear your group. Why don't you go get them and bring them back?" That's what he did. When I heard them, I thought they were wonderful and that's when I decided that I wanted to grab these guys.'

What Marvin and the rest of the Marquees didn't know was that the Moonglows were breaking apart. Bobby Lester had a drug problem. Prentiss Barnes and Pete Graves felt they hadn't been properly credited as songwriters on the group's hit singles and complained that Fuqua was getting all the money. 'There were just a lot of disagreements in almost every area,' says Fuqua. 'There was tardiness, unwillingness to rehearse—several things.' There was also the fact that, commercially, the Moonglows had already seen their best days. Their strength lay in their harmonies—their influences were groups like the Ravens and the Five Royales—and the whole scene had changed under the impact of rock 'n' roll. They were all old men in comparison to current white chart acts like Elvis, Ricky Nelson and Buddy Holly, and even in comparison to new black singers like Sam Cooke, Jackie Wilson and Clyde McPhatter.

'Things were going as bad as hell for us,' says Prentiss Barnes. 'We could get anything we wanted but money. We didn't have no money but we felt like a million dollars. I never saw more than twenty-five dollars from *Rock, Rock, Rock* and *Mr Rock and Roll*. When Pete and I found out what was going on we just split up. We walked away from the Howard Theater.'

According to Graves and Barnes, they made the decision to leave. According to Fuqua, he'd already decided to ditch them. Whichever version is true, the outcome was the same. Fuqua contacted the Marquees and invited them to be the new Moonglows, with rehearsals to start almost immediately in Chicago. He said he would send a driver to collect them. Nothing happened immediately. January turned into February and there was still no word from Fuqua. It seemed as though yet another door to freedom was about to slam shut. Then, with no prior announcement, Fuqua arrived one morning in a nine-seater station wagon ready to take the Marquees away with him.

'We drove all the way to Chicago,' remembers Reese Palmer. 'We made one stop in Cleveland, Ohio, because there was a dance party TV show that Harvey had to be on. Then we left and headed for Chicago, where we picked up Chuck Barksdale of the Dells, who was waiting at a pool hall, and went on to an apartment that was owned by Chess Records.'

It was to be the most significant career break of Marvin's life.

Everything that was to come had its origin in this move. As Lawrence Berry, a contemporary of Marvin, remembers: 'Marvin was a good singer but Washington DC was full of good singers in the late fifties, from Van McCoy to Billy Stewart to the Clovers. I guess that if it wasn't for Harvey Fuqua Marvin wouldn't have got any further than the rest of us got. You could say that Harvey Fuqua really made Marvin.'

3

Meeting the Mentor

Hear instruction and be wise.
Proverbs 8:33

arvey Fuqua was a tall, avuncular man with slicked-back wavy hair and a slow, measured way of talking. Like Marvin's father, he was from Kentucky, but unlike Marvin's father he was a powerhouse of ambition who'd worked hard and become successful. His church background was Baptist and he'd started out as a child singing gospel songs with his cousins, who comprised an amateur group called the Fuqua Sisters, before teaming up with Bobby Lester. With Lester he had at first formed a duo, which made its professional debut in 1949. A year later they joined Ed Wiley's band for a tour playing jump and blues tunes, and at the end of it Fuqua landed up in Cleveland, Ohio, where he began working in gas stations by day while trawling the clubs by night in search of a musical education.

Ten years older than Marvin, Fuqua had already achieved most of what any black performer of the day could hope for. He had been a commercially successful recording artist ('Sincerely' had sold 250,000 copies), had toured widely in America (with, among others, the

Clovers, Sarah Vaughan and Muddy Waters) and had appeared in two movies (*Rock, Rock, Rock* and *Mr Rock and Roll*). More impressive, as far as Marvin was concerned, was that Fuqua was also deeply involved creatively as a songwriter, vocal arranger and keyboard player. In an era of manufactured stars who sang what was given to them in the style chosen by their producer, Fuqua was a man who knew what he wanted and knew how to get it. He also knew about business, having recently set up his own publishing company and taken on an A&R (artists and repertoire) consultancy position with Chess Records. He was the perfect mentor for nineteen-year-old Marvin.

Fuqua's age and his success gave him an air of authority and he knew exactly how to approach Mr Gay to tell him that the Marquees were about to leave Washington DC. 'His mother was more ready to have him go when I went to see them,' remembers Fuqua. 'Mr Gay said, "You gotta take care of my boy there." I said, "I certainly will, sir.' "

Fuqua did take care of him, becoming the sort of influence his father should have been: a strong, disciplined role model, who knew enough about the world and its pitfalls to guide someone through it without making them over-fearful. He was the first older man to take a deep interest in Marvin's life, to listen sensitively to his problems, encourage his talents and build his confidence. 'I felt that I had become a sort of father-figure to him,' admits Fuqua. 'This was mainly because of the way in which he acted towards me, and also because I didn't have any children of my own on the road and so he became like my son when we travelled. He would talk to me a lot about his problems. He was a troubled person.'

For three months, mostly during the evenings, Fuqua rehearsed his new Moonglows in the Chess-owned two-bedroom apartment, which was at the rear of a building on the corner of 47th and Woodlawn. They had to learn the group's entire back catalogue of thirty singles, complete with the distinct 1-3-6 and 1-3-7 harmonies. Meticulously, Fuqua broke the songs down into their component parts and drilled the group until its performance was note-perfect.

'I worked the hardest I have ever worked in my whole life because the Moonglows' harmonies were very different from the harmonies we'd been using in the Marquees,' says James Nolan of the rehearsals. 'Most of us could read music, but we had to learn all the Moonglows' tunes by ear—"Sincerely", "Ten Commandments Of Love", "See Saw". We had to learn everything.'

Marvin was an eager student and quick to pick up the tunes. He learned the other singers' parts as well as his own, and was clearly impressed by Fuqua's ability to conceptualize the harmonies and then teach them. It was a skill he himself used a decade later when he began to produce his own recordings.

'He wanted to know everything. He wanted to learn and he was on my case,' says Fuqua. 'I had one of the early Wurlitzer electric pianos which I took on the road with me, and even after we had finished the vocal rehearsals Marvin would want me to teach him some new chords. I would sit down with him and place his hands on the keys and go through them all, like you would if you were teaching a child. He took it all in without any trouble. In the end I used to let him do the rehearsals for me because he could sing all the parts. I didn't even need to be there.'

During the time they rehearsed in Chicago they also recorded at Chess Studios. Their first session, on 17 February 1958, was as backing vocalists, along with Etta James (Fuqua's girlfriend of the time), on Chuck Berry's singles 'Almost Grown' and 'Back In The USA'. Later they backed their old friend Bo Diddley on 'I'm Sorry' and Etta herself on 'Chained To My Rocking Chair'.

'We had already met a lot of the stars we idolized backstage at the Howard Theater when we were growing up,' says Reese Palmer. 'So it didn't thrill us as much when we came to record with Chuck and Bo because we thought we were stars as big as they were. That attitude helped us a lot in the coming years when we were on the road.'

As well as teaching them the Moonglows' back catalogue, Fuqua was introducing them to new material, such as the recently written 'Twelve Months Of The Year' and 'She's Alright With Me'. 'As we finished the new stuff we would go in and record it because we were living right near the studio,' says Fuqua. 'We must have recorded seven or eight tracks like that.'

Marvin's turn to display his talent came with 'Mama Loochie', the only track on which he was given a lead vocal. The song had been written by Reese Palmer for the Marquees but Fuqua changed the arrangement in the studio and Marvin improvised the lyric so that when the single was released it was attributed to Harvey Fuqua and 'Mildred Guy' (Marvin Gay). 'I didn't get any credit at all,' says Palmer. 'I didn't even bother to protest.'

'Mama Loochie' wasn't a hit but it displayed Marvin's ability to take a song and make it his own. He was already stretching and bending syllables, almost daring the music to finish before he did. He sang with easy confidence and control, his voice at times displaying the tone and range of Sam Cooke, the former gospel singer who'd recently had a national pop hit with 'You Send Me'. The song was lightweight—loochie rhyming with coochie at one point—but it gave Marvin the opportunity to find something, however remote, with which he could identify. The mama loochie was the perfect woman of his teenage dreams—the sanctified woman who 'cannot dance' but who nevertheless wins his heart.

The only other song from the session to be released as a single was 'Twelve Months Of The Year', a pedestrian list-song in the format of 'Ten Commandments Of Love' on which Marvin added a comically sounding spoken introduction and closing speech. He sounded as though he was about to crack up from the mock seriousness of the occasion.

After three months of rehearsing and recording, the Moonglows, or Harvey and the Moonglows as the new formation was known, warmed up with a week-long stint at the Regal Theater in Chicago, then took to the road for a four-month tour of the South with Percy Welch's band from Georgia to play behind them and Etta James as the support act.

Etta James, then only twenty-one, was a rarity: a black female rock 'n' roll artist who sang with the spirit of Little Richard. She'd made her mark in the R&B field with singles like 'Wallflower', 'Dance With Me Henry' and 'Good Rockin' Daddy'. For her solo act she had a backing vocalist, Abby Mallory, and a twenty-two-year-old dancer and fire-eater from New Orleans known as Toni Taylor ('Titty Tassel Toni' to the musicians), who performed an exotic interlude.

It was a gruelling tour with long distances between venues, two shows a night and rehearsals when they weren't travelling. The last shows often didn't finish until two in the morning and, because of the racial situation in the South, it was difficult to find accommodation for a troupe of black musicians. On the nights they couldn't find a cheap motel they were forced to sleep in their cars.

The tour swung down through Kentucky, where they played the Top Hat in Louisville, and then down through Tennessee and Georgia to Mobile, Alabama, and then out to the east coast of Florida. After playing the Palm Club in Hellendale, Florida, they took two weeks off in Miami before heading back west in the direction of Las Cruces, New Mexico, and then doubling back to Texas.

For Marvin it was a time of letting go the bonds of his childhood religion. After a lifetime of church attendance, Sabbath-keeping, Bible-reading and avoidance of the world with its dancing, drinking and swearing, he felt free to do exactly what he liked without fear of admonishment. The only visible signs of his House of God rearing were his impeccable manners and his avoidance of pork. If he had an uneasy conscience about jettisoning his past, he didn't show it.

'I never knew Marvin to even discuss religion when we were on the road,' says Palmer. 'I think his father had wanted him to turn out in his own image but Marvin didn't want to go that way.'

It was common for young people raised in the House of God to go wild once outside the old familiar structures. As one member told me, 'You hear so much about sin that you want to go and find out what it's all about. You figure that something that gets people that worked up must be wonderfully powerful and you don't just want to read about it, you want to do it.'

The appropriate Bible verse is found in Proverbs: 'Forbidden waters taste sweet.' Marvin had already experienced the thrill of doing the forbidden in the brothels of Wyoming and now he was ready for more. 'He would take chances,' says Fuqua. 'He became strong-willed about things he probably shouldn't have been strong-willed about and he was torn. It was a case of, "I'll do this although I really think I should be doing that.' "

In Chicago Marvin had smoked marijuana for the first time and had developed an affection for the drug that would last throughout his life. It suited his laid-back temperament, made him aware of tiny variations in sound when recording and seemed a pleasant alternative to alcohol.

'Marvin showed me how to roll a joint to perfection,' remembers Palmer. 'We'd never come across any drugs when we were living in the projects, then we met some guys in the neighbourhood when we came to Chicago and that's how I learned to smoke.'

In the atmosphere of the clubs they played, many of which, according to Reese Palmer, were nothing more than glorified barns, Marvin would lose his shyness. For the first time in his life he was surrounded by admiring women, whom he knew were available for uncomplicated lustful sex. Often they were married women looking for some relief from domestic boredom. Sometimes they were prostitutes, attracted by the dazzle of show-business.

Marvin fell in love in Jacksonville, contracted venereal disease in Atlanta and ended up in a ditch along the road with Toni Taylor after a vicious brawl that ended a short-lived affair. Once he was nearly attacked by an angry white man, who'd spotted him leaning over a road bridge looking at the legs of women drivers as they passed beneath.

'Women didn't *like* Marvin,' says Palmer. 'They *loved* him. Wives, girlfriends—they loved him. And when he sang, it just made matters worse. People accused Marvin of only being interested in "red-boned women", as we called light-skinned girls. It wasn't true, but he thought, to hell with it. He'd play it out.'

In Chicago he had romanced a woman called June, who lived with her husband and child in the apartment block where the Moonglows were being accommodated. When the husband, Lemuel, left for his day's work, Marvin would slip in and take his place in the marital bed. 'She was light-skinned and beautiful,' remembers Palmer. 'The husband found out that Marvin was messing with her. One night he got very angry and I heard loud noises at our front door. When I opened it the guy was standing there with a pile of house bricks, which he'd taken from a building site around the corner, and he was ready to batter Marvin's head in.'

In Roswell, New Mexico, three squad cars had descended on him as he and Palmer walked two girls through the street late at night. They were arrested on suspicion of having had sex with under-age girls. 'They tried to charge us but the girls admitted to the police that they hadn't told us their ages,' says Palmer. 'That's what got us off. White entertainers were never scrutinized as much as black entertainers. Everywhere you went in the South they were checking you out.'

Working divorcées were a particularly attractive proposition to travelling musicians because they could offer food and accommodation. Prostitutes would often give their services free. 'I think it was the glamour of a one-night affair,' says Palmer. 'The worst thing you could do on the road was to fall in love and Marvin always felt comfortable around these sorts of women. He could talk to them better than he could to a nice church girl and they were the type of girl hanging around at the clubs. If you were a nice-looking guy and you were in entertainment, you would get approached.'

Of all the Moonglows Marvin was closest to Fuqua and to Chuck Barksdale, whose tenure with the group was limited to this tour as he was already a member of the Dells. His relationship with James Nolan, who'd taken over Bobby Lester's role as lead vocalist, wasn't so good. In Chicago, during rehearsals, they'd come to blows because Nolan had a speech impediment, which made it difficult for him to enunciate some of the syllables. 'I think Marvin resented me because most of the tunes that the Moonglows did suited me much more than they did him,' says Nolan. 'Harvey had told me that my voice was the closest to Bobby Lester's and so I took his place. I think that made Marvin jealous. He didn't like the fact that I did all the lead singing and because of that he didn't like me.'

Just before an engagement in Atlanta in September, when the group was on a bill with Ray Charles, James Brown and the Five Blind Boys of Alabama, Fuqua visited his home town of Louisville, Kentucky, and returned to the tour with Bobby Lester, who was now singing with Bobby Lester and the Moonlighters. That night Lester appeared on stage with the group in a guest spot and sang some of the numbers he'd made famous as a Moonglow. The following day, 10 September, he accompanied the group on the long drive down to Corpus Christi, Texas, where they were to appear at a club with blues shouter Big Joe Turner, who'd recorded the original version of 'Shake, Rattle and Roll'. In Beaumont, Texas, on 11 September, the two vehicles containing the members of the Moonglows—Chuck Barksdale, Reese Palmer, James Nolan, Harvey Fuqua—along with Bobby Lester, Toni Taylor, Abby

Mallory and Etta James, pulled into a filling station on 11th Street for a quick service.

As they drove off at 10.30 a.m., an operator, who thought that the entertainers had been acting suspiciously, called the sheriff's department. They were then pursued down Highway 90 by two police cars and stopped just east of Dayton. The cars were searched and drugs discovered: a tobacco can containing loose marijuana, several joints, traces of heroin, a medicine dropper and three hypodermic needles. All ten performers were arrested and taken back to Beaumont.

It was most likely a racially motivated arrest. In Beaumont, back in those days, 'acting suspiciously' was a synonym for being black and driving a car. When John Steinbeck, the celebrated author of *The Grapes of Wrath*, passed through Beaumont a year later he, too, pulled into a gas station and the man who filled his tank looked at Steinbeck's dog, who was sitting beside him in the car, and said, 'Hey, it's a dog! I thought you had a nigger in there.'

'He laughed delightedly,' remembered Steinbeck, when he recorded the incident in *Travels With Charley*. 'It was the first of many repetitions. At least twenty times I heard it—"Thought you had a nigger in there." It was an unusual joke—always fresh—and never Negro or even Nigra, always nigger or, rather niggah. The word seemed terribly important, a kind of safety word to cling to lest some structure collapse.'

'It was embarrassing for me to be locked up for drugs because drugs was something I had never dealt with,' says Nolan. 'Marijuana was the hottest thing back then as far as drugs were concerned and I knew that a lot of the group were using it. We were taken and locked up in cells—the three girls in one cell and the rest of us in another. We must have been there for around five hours.'

Eight of the party were eventually charged with vagrancy and fined $27.25 each (including costs). To raise the money Harvey had to call his booking agent in San Antonio while Marvin spoke to his half-brother Micah and his aunt Zeola, who were now living in Detroit. It wasn't until 7.00 p.m. that the 'vagrants' were freed. Abby Mallory and Bobby Lester (charged under his real name of Robert Lester Dallas) were both held because drugs had been found in their personal luggage.

It was Lester who faced the most serious charge. He told the judge that the needles and the medicine dropper found in his suitcase were for the use of insulin as he was a diabetic, but his story wasn't believed. He was found guilty of possessing narcotics and of transporting them across state lines, and was sentenced to two years in prison. Mallory was freed without charge the next day.

Matters were made worse when the incident caught the attention of the media. It made the front page of the *Beaumont Enterprise*—'Two From Music Troupe Held In Narcotics Case'—where they were described as 'a Negro entertainment group', and later turning up as a news story in *Jet*, the nationally distributed black magazine—'Moonglows, Recording Stars, Jailed in Texas'.

'When the thing showed up in *Jet* it was plastered all over the United States,' says James Nolan. 'After that, everything started going downhill. If we turned up at a gig, the law would be there. They started following us around and what happened in those days was that if you had been involved with narcotics of any kind the booking agencies didn't want to use you. A lot of the gigs dried up. We did a gig in Houston and after that we couldn't get any more jobs in the South.'

'It affected us badly,' admits Fuqua. 'Things were terrible from then on. There were agents and cops at the gigs and we were being watched all the time.'

'We could probably have kept going for a little bit longer if it hadn't been for the drug thing,' says James Nolan. 'But the music scene was changing. Things were getting away from rock 'n' roll. What we were doing was beginning to die. We were being asked to do jazz-style material.'

Fuqua wasn't too concerned if the Moonglows had reached the end of an eight-year career because, ever since meeting Marvin in Washington, he had been planning a solo career for him. 'Marvin was a clone of me,' he says. 'The only difference was that he was much better. I was determined to do something for him from the first time I ever heard his voice. It was probably lucky for him that the group broke up when it did.'

The other Moonglows knew that Marvin and Fuqua were tight, and noticed that Marvin's confidence had seemed to grow midway through the tour, almost as if he had just been given some good news.

Barksdale can remember him announcing to him and Chester Simmons that he was going to be 'a big star' some day.

'Harvey left us one day to visit his family in Kentucky and we weren't sure when he was coming back,' says Palmer. 'I remember that on that day Marvin had a look on his face which said, "I'm gonna do better than this.' "

In the meantime Leonard Chess, of Chess Records, had hired Fuqua to help Anna Records, a fledgling Detroit label that it was distributing. It was owned by songwriter Billy Davis, a handsome man with a pencil-thin moustache, and his lover Gwen Gordy. Chess wanted a safe pair of hands to produce singles and promote new talent.

Fuqua and Davis already knew each other, Davis having co-written the Moonglows' hit 'See Saw' in 1956. Gwen Gordy was the sister of one of Davis's writing partners, Berry Gordy. Together they had written 'All I Could Do Was Cry' for Etta James, 'It's So Fine' for LaVern Baker and Jackie Wilson's classic rock 'n' roll hit 'Reet Petite', Davis writing under the pen name of Tyran Carlo.

Berry Gordy was already being talked about as someone to watch in the black-music business. With eight hundred dollars borrowed from a Gordy family fund earlier that year, he had formed Tamla Records and his first single, Marv Johnson's 'Come To Me', had made it to number six in the Billboard R&B chart. Not yet big enough to distribute his records nationally, he would put out Tamla singles in the Detroit area himself and license them to bigger companies for the rest of America. 'Bad Girl' by the Miracles, for example, went on the Chess label.

The Moonglows' final shows took place in the autumn of 1959 at the Twenty Grand club in Detroit. Better known for its car manufacturing, Detroit was a thriving music city, which had already produced the likes of Jackie Wilson, Sam Cooke, Della Reese, Hank Ballard, Little Willie John, Milt Jackson, the Miracles and Aretha Franklin. In a typical week during this time you could see Sam Cooke at the Flame Show bar, Louis Jordan at Haig's, Miles Davis at the Minor Key, and then go on to the Masonic Temple where Count Basie was in concert—although, if you were to read the *Detroit News* of the period, you would think that no black people lived in the city, let alone put on entertainment.

Detroit was a musician's paradise with highly competent house bands at all the major clubs with musical pedigrees going back to the great dance-band era of Benny Goodman and Lionel Hampton. Berry Gordy had been into all these clubs as a struggling writer selling his songs, and he had a vision of creating a record label that would tap into this great pool of talent and bring the teenage singers and writers out of the housing projects. More specifically he dreamed of a black-owned company that would extend beyond the narrow 'race' market that had traditionally been the preserve of blues and gospel labels. The time was right, he believed, for blacks to take control of their music and to use the rewards to build not only the black economy but black pride.

'Before Berry came along you didn't get into the record business unless you went with a big label,' says Mickey Stevenson, Berry's first A&R director. 'It was a terrible business for black people. We got ripped off. We were used in the same way that the Jews were used in the old days. Yet we had talent. Through Berry, the good Lord decided to put an end to it.'

Fuqua invited Berry Gordy, Billy Davis and Gwen Gordy along to the Twenty Grand to see his new Moonglows. 'We were excited about that because Berry had had some hot records out and we thought he could do something for us,' says James Nolan. 'We met him after the show but we never knew whether he liked us or not because Harvey didn't tell us.'

Fuqua wouldn't have told them anything because Chester Simmons, Reese Palmer, James Nolan and Chuck Barksdale didn't figure in his plans. There was only one person he wanted to continue to work with and that was Marvin. After the shows were over the rest of the Moonglows was disbanded and Marvin and Fuqua stayed on in Detroit.

The most significant introduction that night wasn't between the new Moonglows and the founder of Tamla Records but between Berry Gordy's older sister Anna and Marvin. It was a meeting that changed both of their lives and marked the beginning of his rise to fame.

'Anna loved Marvin from the moment she first saw him,' says Kitty Sears, a personal friend to both of them in later years. 'She truly loved him then and she still loves him today. She made him. He could sing before she met him but she took him and she made him. She's a great businesswoman.'

'The Twenty Grand,' says Anna Gordy. 'That's where I met Marvin.

I always say to Harvey, you brought Marvin to Detroit and you sicked him on me! I don't know if Berry came that same night but I know that he came along [during that week] and it all worked out because he loved Marvin's voice.'

Anna was then thirty-eight, just seven years younger than Marvin's mother, and yet she looked a decade less than her age, dressed in the latest fashions. Along with Gwen and their brother Robert she had run a photograph and cigarette concession at the Flame Show bar, which was one of Detroit's most sophisticated night spots and reputedly run by the Mafia. It was here that the girls began to meet the top musicians of the day, and Anna would often throw parties for them. 'It was through his sisters that Berry got introduced to some of the most power-ful people in the music industry,' says Bill Murry, who was the MC for the Moonglows' shows at the Twenty Grand. 'There were also a lot of Greek gangsters around in Detroit at that time, and Anna and Gwen found themselves living in what you would call the fast lane.'

Marvin already had family in Detroit. His mother's sister Zeola and her husband lived in Glen Court, and his half-brother Micah also lived in the city. Marvin stayed briefly with Zeola before joining Fuqua at the Highland Park home of another Gordy sister, Esther, and her hus-band George Edwards, who was a Michigan state representative.

In his autobiography *To Be Loved*, Berry Gordy overlooks the Moonglows' appearance at the Twenty Grand but remembers getting to know Marvin at the first Tamla Christmas party, which was held at the house they called Hitsville on West Grand Boulevard where he and his girlfriend Raynoma Lyles lived and worked. It had belonged to a photographer and had an apartment upstairs, offices downstairs and a cinder block extension that had once been a dark-room but which was now a studio affectionately referred to as 'the snake pit' because it was reached by a short flight of stairs down from the control room.

Marvin was in the snake pit, playing the piano, when Gwen urged Berry to come down. At first Berry was reluctant. It was, after all, a Christmas party, not a talent search. But, to please his sister, he went down and sat next to Marvin and asked him to play something for him. Knowing that he'd just left the Moonglows, he had expected something bluesy but instead Marvin began playing the old standard 'Mr Sandman'.

Berry was immediately attracted by the voice, which he found mellow and soulful. He would later say in his autobiography that it was at this moment that he knew he wanted to record him. He didn't want to get too excited because he didn't know how well they would get along but he told Marvin that he felt he had something special.

'He was fascinated with my voice,' Marvin would remember. 'He always said my voice was really something.'

4

Crossing the Threshold

Hast thou found honey? Eat so much as is sufficient for thee.

Proverbs 25:16

To Marvin, Berry Gordy epitomized cool. He dressed sharp, he was always surrounded by beautiful women, he was physically tough and he was a successful creative artist as well as a dynamic businessman. In Detroit there was already an aura surrounding Berry and his family. As far back as 1949 his family had been featured in *Color* magazine, which referred to them as 'America's Most Amazing Family'.

They were amazing at that time, according to the magazine, for the father's success in the construction and print industries, and the children's abilities in sport and music. 'Under the expert guidance of their parents,' the story read, 'the Gordy family, four boys and four girls, have all developed into healthy, unusually gifted men and women.'

The father, known to everyone as Pops Gordy, had started as a plasterer and had ended up with his own plastering and carpentry business, a general store and a print shop. Mom Gordy was equally astute in business, having studied at Wayne State University after her children had left home and then become a founder of the Friendship

Mutual Life Insurance Company. The Gordy family were exceptionally close-knit, looking after each other's interests and preserving the integrity of the Gordy name. 'They were the closest thing to a clan that any of us had ever encountered in Detroit,' said one friend, who later worked for Motown. 'You knew that if you spoke to Berry or to Robert you were in fact talking to Pops.'

By the age of thirty, Berry had been a professional boxer, a soldier in the Korean war, the owner of a jazz-record store, a cookware sales-man, a production-line worker at Lincoln-Mercury, a songwriter, and now he was a music publisher and the owner of a small record com-pany. He had a pleasant, outgoing personality, the ability to inspire others and a gritty determination to succeed. His plan for the Motown Record Corporation, of which Tamla was the first label, was clearly defined. He wanted to create music with the same efficiency that Lin-coln-Mercury made cars. Hitsville, the two-storey Gordy home and work space, would be the factory. The talented musicians, producers and writers that he had met over the years in the clubs of Detroit and the aspiring young performers living in the housing projects would be the workers, and hit records the product. As with any other produc-tion line there would be strict work hours, clocking-in facilities, time-and-motion studies and all products would have to be passed by Quality Control. 'I wanted a place where a kid off the street could walk in one door an unknown and come out the other a recording artist, a star,' he later said, and Marvin, although he had appeared on records as a Marquee and a Moonglow, recognized that as a solo artist he was still an unknown who needed to be discovered.

Marvin's personal goals had not yet been fully formulated. He wanted to sing, fantasized about becoming a black Frank Sinatra and realistically knew that show-business offered him his best chance of making serious money. 'It was just meant to be,' he said. 'I was meant to be in show-business. Some guys are meant to be doctors and I was born for this, and that's that.'

Since he was a child he'd had a recurring dream of being on stage in front of a huge audience. In interviews he dropped hints that wealth and success as a performer had been prophesied for him.

'I think his father may have given him what we call a "word of prophecy" back when he was a child,' says Polly Solomon. 'He mentioned more than once the idea that Marvin was going to make the family rich. There were times in the church when people used to prophesy. Not every week, but once in a while.'

The idea that he had been handpicked by God never left him. Even in the closing stages of his life, when he was filled with thoughts of doom, he would continually hark back to the idea that he had been chosen for a mission. This conviction was sufficiently strong to override his natural self-doubt and to survive the vicissitudes of his career.

Whatever his personal convictions about his divine election, he was an unemployed musician at the start of 1960 with a brief track record that wasn't impressive enough to open doors automatically. The best things he had going for him were the business interest of Harvey Fuqua and the increasing personal faith and support of Anna Gordy.

'When he first arrived in Detroit there was very little talk of him pursuing a solo career,' says Billy Davis. 'His real love was jazz singing. He didn't really like rock 'n' roll or rhythm and blues. His head was in a different place. We thought of him as a studio drummer and I didn't push him in any other direction and I guess Harvey Fuqua didn't either.'

Anna Records had its four office rooms and a small studio at 5139 St Antoine Street on the corner of Farnsworth. It was here that Marvin began to woo Anna, who was a limited partner in the company named after her, visiting her regularly in her office and following her, according to Raynoma Gordy, like a 'panting puppy'. He would confide in Raynoma, telling her that he didn't feel that Anna realized how serious he was. 'The age difference is meaningless to me,' he would tell her. 'I don't want some little girl. Anna is everything I've ever wanted in a woman.'

'Anna was very friendly and flirtatious,' says one friend, who knew them both at the time. 'She was very cute and yet very cocky. In terms of the street, fellows considered her to be a "player" and none of them could be bothered with her. She was very independent, not their type of girl. I think she was attracted to Marvin because she could dominate him.'

According to Harvey Fuqua the couple were an item within weeks of their first meeting. 'He was a good-looking guy,' he explains. 'She was a gorgeous lady. He must have thought to himself, I like her, she likes me, why not let's get together?'

By the spring of 1960 they were living together in Anna's apartment on West Grand Boulevard, five minutes away from the Hitsville studios. Few of their friends had thought that the relationship would go this far so soon. Anna was a sophisticated and sexually experienced woman used to dating rich and powerful men who would keep her in an appropriate style. In contrast, Marvin was a boy not long out of the ghetto who had no capital and no power. 'Maybe the attraction was in the fact that they were such opposites,' says Davis. 'The age gap didn't matter because Anna was such an attractive person and they looked good with each other. But they had their differences from very early on. They would often fall out with each other and he would leave her apartment and come and stay with me on Claremont until things were sorted out.'

Although Marvin's relationship with Anna brought him into frequent contact with Berry, it didn't guarantee studio time or a recording contract. He knew that he would have to hone his talents and develop new ones to compete with the other bright new talents lining up for auditions. He began songwriting on his own and with Fuqua, and improved his skill on the drums so that he could work as a session musician.

'Marvin wasn't working anywhere at the time and so we would just hang out together every day,' says Fuqua. 'He would just be with me and we would listen to records and tapes and rehearse people at the offices. If there was nothing on he might go out and see a movie or something.'

'He would help around,' remembers Billy Davis. 'I paid him money from Anna Records for helping in the studio, playing on demo records and doing background vocals. He played on a couple of singles that we did for David Ruffin. I think he played on the demo for "I'm In Love".'

Marvin knew that admission to the Hitsville inner circle came through making your presence felt and that he needed to hang out there to get work. The studio's increasing reputation in the local black community meant that young people were willing to work there doing any job, however menial, in the hopes of an unexpected invitation to add a handclap or a line of background vocal that could mark the beginning of a recording career. These things happened. Janie Bradford was working as a Hitsville receptionist when she coined the phrase that became the main lyrical idea in Berry Gordy's 'Money' (first recorded by Barrett Strong) and Berry gave her a share of the song. Martha Reeves was a secretary who took Mary Wells's place at a session to satisfy a union requirement that singers should be present during the recording of backing tracks. Berry was so impressed with the result that he put it out as the first single by Martha and the Vandellas. Motown specialized in plucking from obscurity.

'Marvin hung around the office as much as he could,' remembers Thomas 'Beans' Bowles, one of the original Motown session musicians. 'He would sit around in the A&R department, in the studio, on the porch or in the games room. There was always room and everyone intermingled. He was just learning the business. The studio was a twenty-four-hour-a-day thing.'

Marvin befriended William 'Smokey' Robinson, the twenty-year-old lead singer of the Miracles, calculating that, as Smokey was Berry's most valuable asset as well as his closest friend, a relationship with him could help advance his career. Smokey had been born in Detroit the year after Marvin was born in Washington. In 1957, shortly after leaving high school, he had met Berry, who helped write and produce the Miracles' first single 'Got A Job', a response to the Silhouettes' recent hit 'Get A Job'. When Berry formed his publishing company Jobete, later to hold the copyright of almost every Motown hit, Smokey was the first writer to be signed. He had driven with Berry to Owosso, Michigan, to pick up copies of Tamla's first release, Marv Johnson's 'Come To Me', and had recorded Tamla's first national hit single, 'Way Over There', in July 1960.

By the time Marvin met Smokey he was the closest thing to being a Gordy family member without being married to a Gordy. He encouraged Berry to take risks with his company, such as developing his own distribution rather than depending on United Artists or Chess as he had done for the early singles. In turn Berry inspired him as a writer and invited him to be part of the company's policy-making process. Smokey was the first Motown artist to be allowed to produce a fellow artist and the first to sing his own material.

Smokey nicknamed Marvin 'Dad' because callouses beneath toes on both his feet forced him to walk with an odd shuffle. It amused him that Marvin always seemed to be hatching what he called his 'big plans', quietly planning career moves as if he already had the whole world in his hands. Marvin would later drum on a Miracles' recording session and on 17 March 1961 he played in concert for them in Harlem on a bill that included Jerry Butler, Jimmy Reed, Bo Diddley and the Olympics. 'Our drummer got sick and Marvin happened to be in New York,' remembers Miracle Bobby Rogers. 'We were playing at the Rockland Palace, which was on 155th Street and 8th Avenue, and he sat in with us. He went on to be a great friend and hung out with us a lot back in Detroit.'

A week after this Miracles' show, on 25 March, Anna Records issued its last single, which was 'Ain't It A Mess' by the future soul star Joe Tex. The following month the label was acquired by the Motown Record Corporation. While Fuqua had been working for Anna Records his relationship with Gwen Gordy had developed from the merely professional to the romantic. He had replaced Billy Davis in her life and Davis knew it was time to move on. 'Harvey was a politician in many ways,' says Davis. 'He did whatever he had to do to get ahead. That's how Harvey always was. He looked out for Harvey in any way he could.'

During 1960 Fuqua and Gwen Gordy had registered the Hardye Producing Company (HPC), which had issued one single, and the gospel label Message, which had put out two. Now they borrowed ten thousand dollars from Berry to develop two new labels, Tri-Phi and Harvey, which they wanted to replace Anna Records.

Billy Davis had no trouble finding new work. He was taken back by Chess to oversee the Check-Mate label and he brought with him a cluster of Anna artists, including David Ruffin, later of the Temptations, and Lamont Dozier, later one of Motown's leading songwriters. Other Anna artists, such as Johnny Bristol and Shorty Long, remained with Fuqua and were signed to Tri-Phi, where they were joined by such new discoveries as the Spinners. The Harvey label picked up Junior Walker. All of these musicians, producers and writers later contributed to the outstanding success of Motown. The biggest of them all was Marvin but, strangely enough, he was the only one not to make a record during this period. He remained a background figure, helping out with drumming and cutting demos for Tri-Phi. Fuqua, who still managed Marvin, was saving him as the ace up his sleeve for when he sold out to Motown. 'I was reluctant at first to sign Marvin to Motown,' admits Fuqua. 'I hadn't wanted to sign him up to Anna because the company was a subsidiary of Chess. I wanted him to start with someone new. Plus, I thought it would look a little more impressive to Gwen, my wife-to-be, if I did things this way and went with Berry.'

When Fuqua did sell Marvin to Motown he only sold 50 per cent, keeping the rest for himself. This meant that he was still able to manage him even from within the Motown organization. 'Marvin was pissed with me,' he admits, still reluctant to reveal how much Berry paid out for his new star. 'He stayed annoyed with me for ever because we were supposed to be one for all and all for one. I didn't think it was unfair at the time, though. I needed the money.'

Marvin, who had taken to slicking back his hair, wearing pork-pie hats and smoking a pipe, had his mind set on recording music that was as smooth as his new image. At a time when his white contemporaries, like Mick Jagger and Rod Stewart, were feasting on urban and country blues he, like many other blacks, was trying to get as far away as possible from reminders of poverty and anguish. His taste was for the music of his teenage years, which seemed to be the ultimate in sophistication, taste and affluence—Tony Bennett, Perry Como, Mel Torme, and Frank Sinatra. 'He wanted to be a lover,' says Beans Bowles. 'He wanted to be a balladeer. He wanted to be a singer who crooned and cooed. That was the image he wanted to evoke. That was his ultimate goal.'

Berry Gordy wasn't convinced that this was the right way to launch Marvin Gaye. He had always been successful with a popular hybrid of R&B, which appealed to contemporary white teenagers. However, Anna persuaded him to let Marvin try out with an album of classic songs with jazz arrangements. There was, he conceded, an outside chance that a black Sinatra could make it in the more liberal atmosphere of the Kennedy era.

The only album Motown had produced to date was *Hi! We're The Miracles*. It hadn't sold well. Yet Berry entered the Marvin project full of enthusiasm, personally producing him on a set of American standards, including Cole Porter's 'Love For Sale', Irving Berlin's 'How Deep Is The Ocean' and Rodgers and Hart's 'My Funny Valentine'. The only contemporary songs were 'Never Let You Go', written by Harvey Fuqua and Anna, and Berry's 'Let Your Conscience Be Your Guide'. As a promotional single he recorded 'The Masquerade Is Over'.

'Berry recorded me as I wanted to be recorded, which was as a jazz singer,' Marvin explained later. 'I wanted to get into the top echelons of show-business without paying all of the dues.'

'Marvin really wanted to be different from any of the other artists that we grew up with,' remembers Mickey Stevenson, who had come to Motown as an aspiring singer himself but had become the company's first director of A&R. 'He wanted to have, for want of a better word, some "class" about him as opposed to the funk approach that R&B was taking at that time. He couldn't be James Brown because there was only one James Brown. He couldn't be Jackie Wilson because there was only one Jackie Wilson. He wanted to have a style that suited his voice and we agreed to that.'

'Let Your Conscience Be Your Guide', released in May 1961, was Marvin's début single and was released under the name Marvin Gaye rather than Gay. 'He was tired of people calling him "Mr Faggot" and "Mr Faggot Gay",' remembers Beans Bowles. 'He respected his father because he said his father respected God, but he didn't like the name.' The single sank without a trace and, two months later, so did the album *The Soulful Moods of Marvin Gaye*. Either Marvin Gaye wasn't ready for the world or the world wasn't ready for Marvin Gaye. It was a bitter disappointment and a test of his faith in himself.

'The look was right but the material was wrong,' reflects Mickey Stevenson. 'The material was wrong because the radio stations that played our records at the time were straight R&B stations and they were already into a particular musical sound. It wouldn't have worked for them to give their audiences such sophisticated material. There just weren't the number of MOR stations around that we have today.'

As Marvin brooded over his musical direction, Motown Records began to bristle with exciting new talent. Besides the Miracles with Smokey Robinson, there were now the Marvelettes, the Supremes and the Temptations. Some of the best of Detroit's session musicians were combining to forge the distinctive hybrid of pop, gospel and R&B

which would become known around the world as the Motown Sound. The hard core of these musicians, who remained largely anonymous to the general music-buying public, became known within Motown as the Funk Brothers. Some of them, like bass player James Jamerson, guitarist Robert White, drummer Benny Benjamin and keyboard player Earl Van Dyke, would play on almost every major Motown hit. Never credited for their riffs, and paid only in session fees, they were the unsung heroes of Motown.

Just as Berry had planned, Motown was functioning as a factory. Kids were rolling up with school-bags asking for auditions, the studio was pumping with sound day and night, and writers were clocking-in to construct songs like production-line workers. Artists were assigned to producers, everything recorded was checked for flaws, and finished tracks were tested on panels of local teenagers. The important thing was that it didn't feel like a factory. To the majority of those involved it felt like a family where everyone worked for each other, and all the activities were overseen by the strong but benevolent father-figure of Berry Gordy. For Marvin, like so many others, Motown provided the warmth, acceptance and encouragement lacking at home.

This family atmosphere was accentuated by the presence of other Gordy siblings. Loucye headed up the company's promotions, Esther ran International Talent Management, George became a songwriter, Robert an engineer, Fuller took over personnel, purchasing and company-policy maintenance, and their parents were always there to offer advice and encouragement. Although some artists were later to become disillusioned with Motown there was no discontent at the time because they were living the dream. Eighteen-year-olds from the housing projects didn't question the fact that the Recording Industry Association of America wasn't allowed to audit Motown's books or that as artists they would only be entitled to see them twice a year.

'Session musicians would get paid five dollars a session,' Marvin remembered. 'If you took eight hours on a session that was still five dollars. You sweated, played, ate, but you were young and your eyes were full of love, show-business and music. You were having fun and you were getting money for it. If you'd only got a dollar for it, it was OK because you were having fun.'

By 1961 Motown was fulfilling its early promise. The Miracles'

'Shop Around', written and produced by Smokey and Berry, went to number two in the pop charts, and then the Marvelettes, Motown's first all-girl group, became America's best-selling single with 'Please Mr Postman', on which Marvin played drums. 'I don't really recall how Marvin came to drum on that session,' says one-time Marvelette Kathy Anderson Schaffner. 'I think it was because the drummer who'd been booked didn't turn up and someone mentioned that Marvin played drums.'

Opinion is divided on his ability as a drummer. According to Bobby Rogers of the Miracles, he was 'very good', and Smokey Robinson describes him as 'first rate' but Uriel Jones, one of Motown's top session drummers, disagrees. 'He wasn't good,' he says. 'You've only got to listen to the records he played on. But he was good enough to add it to his act.'

What was unquestionably distinctive about Marvin was his demeanour. He was always immaculately dressed, gracious and well-mannered. While Smokey Robinson was forging a reputation for pulling impressionable young women around Motown, despite being married to his high-school sweetheart Claudette, Marvin appeared too shy to fool around. He was always at home when the offices were given over to wild 'swinging' parties. Women who weren't used to discovering a man who was so considerate and willing to listen found his charm quite intoxicating. He spoke in a seductively modulated whisper, punctuated with broad grins that showed his immaculate white teeth. By 1961 he had had only one tooth filled.

'He had a lot of the charisma and charm which you didn't always find in other gentlemen,' says Kathy Anderson Schaffner. 'He was a handsome man and the way he carried himself was very sexy. A lot of women wanted him. I can remember one girl from one of the groups who kept pestering him on the phone and he got very upset about it and came and asked me to help him get rid of her. We worked out a plan together. I was appearing at the Twenty Grand and Marvin was in the audience, and so I kept looking at him as if we had a thing going so that this girl would get put off. In between sets I would kiss him on the mouth and he would kiss me back. The girl was pissing mad at me but it didn't matter. She never bothered him again.'

Janie Bradford, Hitsville's original receptionist, met Marvin on his first day at Motown. 'I think my mouth kinda flew open when this tall handsome guy came in,' she says. 'He was a wonderful guy and that was to do with his whole aura, his very being. He was a perfect gentleman.'

On 8 January 1961 Marvin married Anna in Toledo, Ohio, with Harvey Fuqua as his best man. The choice of city was determined by the speed of the decision and in Ohio a civil wedding could be arranged at short notice. A reception was held later that day at the Twenty Grand in Detroit.

Two weeks later he released his second single, 'Mr Sandman'. It wasn't a hit but it displayed the meticulousness in Marvin's approach to making music. When he went into the studio he always knew exactly what was required, even though he often found it hard to articulate verbally. Not being able to read or write music, he would wait patiently until the musicians hit the song he could hear in his imagination. 'He had his own ideas right from the time he first came to Motown,' says Beans Bowles. 'That's probably what led to the conflicts he would eventually have with his producers. Right from the very beginning he knew what he wanted to get on tape.'

'He was a perfectionist,' agrees Kathy Anderson Schaffner. 'His idea was that the human voice is the best instrument we have and that we should use our voices to create as many sounds as we possibly can.'

Compounding the failure of his first two singles was a similar lack of public response to his next release, 'Soldier's Plea', which was put out in May. He was aware that some would say he had jumped the line for a contract because of his relationship with Anna. At the same time he knew that there would be no continuing marriage to Anna if he flunked it: her sister Esther counselled the young girls at Motown not to get involved with men who had no career prospects. 'You have got to marry someone out there who is doing something, has a promising career, making money,' she would say. 'If you pick a guy who don't have nothing, you're gonna end up the same way.'

Compromises were required if he was to have a hope of reaching the kind of audiences that Jackie Wilson and Smokey Robinson had reached, and he was aware of this. The music he loved was no longer making the singles charts. He was going to have to do something that had more of a rock feel to it.

'We were always trying to get him to sing some up-to-date songs,' says Bobby Rogers of the Miracles. 'When he recorded that Nat "King" Cole stuff, Berry told him it wasn't going to work. He told him that for things to work for him he was going to have to sing some other kind of stuff.'

'Stubborn Kind Of Fellow', an R&B song he'd written with Mickey Stevenson and Berry's brother George, was recorded in June. The guitarist on the session, Dave Hamilton, later told New York music writer Nelson George: 'You could hear the man screaming on that tune. You could tell he was hungry. If you listen to that song you'll say, "Hey, man, he was trying to make it because he was on his last leg.' "

In a way, the song was about Marvin, whose refusal to be driven by market trends was earning him a reputation as a 'difficult' artist, especially in a company whose whole *raison d'être* was to anticipate public taste and tailor product to fit. 'It was about his ideas towards his music,' admits Stevenson. 'We both had our particular fixations and he could be a stubborn kind of fellow.'

'Stubborn Kind Of Fellow' became a minor pop hit in America, reaching number forty-six in the charts, but a major R&B chart hit at number eight. It got him his first appearance on network TV on Dick Clark's *American Bandstand*, which he played on 2 October. 'We went round and saw the show at his home,' remembers Kathy Anderson Schaffner. 'We all died laughing when he came on because he was either chewing a piece of candy or a lump of sugar because he was afraid that his mouth would go dry. Once he had drawn our attention to it you could almost hear him chewing.'

At the age of twenty-two he was a minor pop star and Anna's faith in him had been rewarded. 'She was my motivator,' Marvin admitted. 'She knew how to get me going. In the beginning it was quite wonderful. I needed a strong woman.' Flushed with success he returned to the studio and recorded 'Hitch Hike', another R&B collaboration with Mickey Stevenson, this time using Clarence Paul as a third composer. Paul, who went on to become one of Marvin's closest friends and confidants, had become Stevenson's assistant in the A&R department and was also a writer and producer. Ronnie White of the Miracles had recently turned him on to a thirteen-year-old blind boy called Stephen Hardaway Judkins, whom Motown subsequently signed as Stevie

Wonder. Besides producing Stevie Wonder, Paul also played a big part in raising him.

'Hitch Hike', which wasn't released until the following year, capitalized on the recent trend for new dance songs kicked off in September 1960 by Chubby Checker with 'The Twist', which had since spawned such inventions as the Hully Gully, the Frug, the Locomotion, the Shake and the Mashed Potato.

'The idea for the song came out of playing the Regal Theater in Chicago,' says Stevenson. 'The kick-off moment was seeing people trying to get to the theatre by hitch-hiking. They would be lining the road with their thumbs out. Then I wanted to capture the feeling of enjoyment I used to see when I watched the audiences during the shows there.'

It supplied Marvin with a follow-up hit, but he still felt like an impostor. His rock voice, as he called it, was something he put on. It was an accent he faked. 'I love singing ballads and pop stuff but you have to keep the R&B people happy,' he explained to a journalist. 'I've been trying to appeal to other markets as I'd like to make it as big in this business as I can but a negro R&B singer's chances are slimmer. Only Ray Charles has made it and I don't feel that he's held in the same esteem as Frank Sinatra and Sammy Davis Junior. Although R&B, through young people, is making great strides, the older folk tend to stick to their pop singers and so their kind of music is more successful.'

Marvin drummed on Stevie Wonder's début single 'I Call It Pretty Music'. 'Beechwood 4-5789', a song he had co-written with Mickey Stevenson and Berry's brother George, had been a Top Twenty hit for the Marvelettes. Motown Records was becoming recognized as more than a local Detroit success story.

On 11 September Marvin recorded 'Wherever I Lay My Hat (That's My Home)' for Norman Whitfield, a tall, broad-shouldered boy who'd been hanging quietly around Motown, hoping for a break as a producer and writer. The song, co-written by Whitfield, Marvin and Barrett Strong, became an album track and then, seven years later, a B side. They didn't work together again for another five years until they created one of the greatest singles of all time, 'I Heard It Through The Grapevine'.

On the same day that Marvin recorded 'Wherever I Lay My Hat', producer George Martin was at the Abbey Road recording studios in London, England, recording three tracks with EMI's latest signing, the Beatles—'PS I Love You', 'Please Please Me', and the group's first British single, 'Love Me Do'. Although Abbey Road was over three thousand miles from West Grand Boulevard, a cultural shift was taking place that would unite the two centres of music. The sounds of Motown and the music of the Beatles were to become a major part of the essential soundtrack to the changes of the sixties, from the innocence of holding hands and dancing in the street to the disillusionment of standing in the shadows of love. Motown artists were not yet aware of the Beatles, but the Beatles were devouring Motown products. John Lennon had been singing 'Money' in concert since 1960, and he and Paul McCartney frequently cited the Miracles and the Marvelettes as an influence on their songwriting. Over the next decade many Motown artists returned the compliment.

Later Marvin saw something of himself in John Lennon and indeed there were parallels between them. Both men were unfulfilled as teen idols and embarked on journeys of self-exploration and political expression, which was reflected in their writing. Both were natural nonconformists, who placed artistic integrity above commercial success. Both had been rejected by their fathers and used their art to make sense of the confusion in their lives. Both died in their forties.

5

Tests and Trials

If thou faint in the day of adversity, thy strength is small.

Proverbs 24:10

In late October 1962 Marvin boarded a bus in Detroit along with eight other Motown acts for the long drive to Washington DC where they were to begin a week of shows at the Howard Theater under the title of the Motortown Revue. It was the start of a gruelling two-month tour, concentrated in the South and mostly made up of a string of one-night stands. Marvin was paid sixty dollars a week.

The schedule was mind-boggling. During a typical week in November they played consecutive dates in Atlanta (Georgia), Mobile (Alabama), New Orleans (Louisiana), Jackson (Mississippi), Spartanburg (Virginia), Durham (North Carolina), Columbia (Ohio) and Washington DC, travelling between venues in a converted school bus with hard seats and no bathroom facilities. Often the long distances didn't allow for overnight stays and they were forced to sleep either in their seats or on the overhead luggage racks.

Most of the artists had never been far from home before. Marvin had travelled for a few months as a Moonglow but never as a solo artist.

The Miracles and Contours had limited tour experience, but the Supremes, Marvelettes and Vandellas had yet to perfect a stage act. Bill Murry, from the Twenty Grand, who was the tour's MC under the name of Winehead Willie, had to teach them how to finish their songs in concert because on record they'd always been faded out.

The bill-toppers were the Miracles, still Motown's most successful act, and the then-unknown Supremes opened each show. Marvin, dressed in a grey mohair suit with a black bow-tie, came on half-way through the evening with the Vandellas as his backing vocalists. What everyone noticed was the effect his looks had on the women in the audience, which contrasted starkly with his private lack of self-esteem. He sang ballads like 'What Kind Of Fool Am I?' but also had to push his latest single, 'Stubborn Kind Of Fellow'. He was unsure whether he should project himself as a balladeer or as an R&B act.

'He didn't have a lot of self-esteem,' says Bill Murry. 'He didn't have the musical co-ordination of a black guy when he danced. He was more like a white guy. It took me two days to teach him how to get the actions right for 'Hitch Hike'. And yet, when it came to the music, he really knew his stuff. He could tell you if there was a single note out of place.'

For some stretches of the tour Marvin would forsake the cramped bus for a seat in the 'command car' alongside Beans Bowles, who had put the tour together and was now acting as road manager. It was Bowles's job to check on ticket sales, critique the shows and collect the box-office takings. During these long rides Marvin would seek the advice of the older man.

'When you drive with someone for six-hundred-mile journeys you become pretty close to them,' says Bowles. 'He was a disturbed man even at that point in his life. He was disturbed in whatever context you care to mention. He was disturbed about his father, he was disturbed about his relationship with Anna, and he was insecure about himself. I would say that, although he didn't show it, he was unhappy most of the time.'

His marriage to Anna had been explosive from the start. Both were attractive and opinionated, but Anna knew that as she moved into early middle age Marvin was only just out of his teens and already the object of a lot of female attention. Although she wanted him to

succeed, she could see how success could well cost them their marriage. At times their relationship descended into physical violence.
Clarence Paul claimed that the couple came to blows at their wedding
reception at the Twenty Grand. Session musicians can remember a time
when Anna hit Marvin across the head with the heel of her shoe so that
he had to wear a hat to hide the bruising. In these fights, as in the
fights of his childhood, Marvin usually remained passive. There was
not much he could do. If he retaliated he would destroy his future with
Berry, because the Gordys always looked after their own. Yet if he took
too much abuse he would be as badly off as he had been in his Washington childhood.

'She had control of him and he wanted to take control of his own
life,' says Bowles. 'Anna controlled everything and she could control
him because her brother had control over him. She could put pressure
on her brother and Marvin would be the recipient of that pressure.
That was his problem.'

The Motortown Revue was the first time that many of the younger
performers had been in the South, and therefore their first experience
of segregation. Days before the tour started, James Meredith had
become the first black student to enroll at the University of Mississippi
and he had to be escorted onto the campus by US marshals and pro-
tected from white agitators by the National Guard. In the same month
Martin Luther King had his first meeting with President Kennedy to
discuss civil rights.

'At that point in history segregation was the word in the South,'
says Bowles. 'You couldn't just sit down at a counter and eat. When the
bus stopped to be refuelled and we all got out, people thought that we
were Freedom Riders. They would stand in their doorways and stare at
us and behind those doors would be shotguns. Sometimes we couldn't
even find food. We'd pull into a place and when the owner saw us
arriving he would pull down the shade and say that he was closed.'

'We would have standing ovations at the shows and the audience
would be totally in love with us,' remembers Kathy Anderson
Schaffner of the Marvelettes. 'Then, after we'd packed up and left the
theatre, we'd have people trying to turn our bus over or shoot at us. It
was a frightening experience. Most of us had never encountered
racism in real life and it made us very aware of who we were and where

we were. It reminded us that although our performance had some significance it had no significance in affecting the hatred coming from people we didn't even know.'

For some it was the first time they had ever been refused entry to a hotel or had to use a blacks-only rest-room. At one motel in South Carolina, the white guests quickly vacated the swimming-pool area as soon as Diana Ross and her friends arrived in their swimsuits. In Macon, Georgia, a local service station refused to help with repairs when the bus broke down because there were blacks on board. In Birmingham, Alabama, where Nat 'King' Cole had been threatened by white supremacists only six years before when attempting to perform in what was his home town, the driver found bullets embedded in the Motortown Revue sign on the front of the bus.

'The outstanding memory for me,' says Bobby Rogers, of the Miracles, 'was when I went to a gas station to use the bathroom and was told that I couldn't use it. I had to go somewhere around the back of the building. It shocked me. I guess I had heard about racism before because my parents were from the South, but until then I had had no personal experience of it.'

Before the tour was half-way through there were complaints about the severity of the schedule, which involved two or three shows a day at each venue. It had been planned this way because Berry was finding it hard to get his acts on network TV and he wanted to prove to America that his company's hit singles could be backed up with live shows. But to pack in thirty-four cities and to conclude the tour with thirty-one appearances at the Apollo in Harlem was physically and emotionally debilitating. There would never be another Motown tour like it.

The most sobering side-effect of this pressure took place on 21 November when Beans Bowles was being driven in his command car from Greensville, South Carolina, to Tampa, Florida. The young driver, Eddie McFarland, a distant relation of Berry's, was so exhausted that he began to doze at the wheel and ploughed into the back of a truck. Both of Bowles's legs were broken and his shoulder was badly lacerated by his flute. McFarland died later in hospital. The rest of the party became aware of the tragedy only when they checked into their hotel in Tampa. Bowles was kept in hospital and Esther Gordy Edwards was flown in to take control of the tour. A pall of depression settled on the performers, which only lifted when the revue reached New York. Stevie Wonder, who'd just cut his first Motown single, was brought in to add some freshness and the whole thing was taped for the album *Recorded Live At The Apollo, Volume One.*

Although he was back in Detroit for Christmas, the pressure didn't let up for Marvin. 'Hitch Hike' was released the day after he returned and began to sell over the next few weeks, giving him his best showing yet in the American pop charts, at number thirty, as well as a high R&B chart ranking, at twelve.

A tour of thirty one-nighters came next, in which Marvin supported James Brown and the Drifters, who were in the charts with 'Up On The Roof', on a bill which also included the Crystals, soon to score with 'Da Doo Ron Ron', Doris Troy, Inez and Charlie Foxx and Jimmy Reed. This time Marvin had a personal road manager, Joe Schaffner, who was assigned to him by Motown, and the venues were generally bigger and better than the ones on the Motortown Revue tour. Schaffner was a solid, reliable man, who went on to work with other Motown acts, including the Temptations. He was able to take Marvin in hand and organize his schedule. 'Marvin started off almost bottom of the bill,' he says, 'and then James kind of moved him further up the bill until, by the end of the tour, there was only one act on between them.'

Although he had his own guitarist, Eddie Willis, and was still using the Vandellas as backing vocalists, Marvin relied on Brown's musicians to back him. Brown, whose most recent hit was 'Please, Please, Please', kept a close eye on Marvin, recognizing him as potential competition. If he saw that Marvin was wearing a white tuxedo he would wear an even fancier white tuxedo. If Marvin wore a red jacket, he would wear an even brighter red jacket.

Marvin's next single, 'Pride And Joy', which he wrote with Norman Whitfield and Mickey Stevenson, had been recorded seven months before its release in April 1963. It was a song of assurance to his increasingly jealous wife, for whom he had a genuine, deep love despite the often public disagreements.

'Most of the songs we did together became autobiographical either because of things happening in our lives or things happening around us,' says Stevenson. 'Love was beginning to slip into the picture for both me and him around the time that we wrote it in nineteen sixty-two.'

'Pride And Joy' continued Marvin's winning streak, giving him his best ever position in the R&B charts at number two, as well as his best pop chart showing at ten. He was now Motown's top solo artist and, in terms of chart success, second to the Miracles. Yet in the midst of this success he was still dogged by the ghosts of the past. ' "Pride And Joy" didn't change anything,' he admitted later. 'It was still a period of struggle for me and I have never viewed it with a lot of happiness. There was a lot of pain. I was young, I didn't know the business well and I was trying to find things out.'

Although his mother came to see him in Detroit his father remained at home. With the first real money that he had earned he bought his parents a new home on Varnum Street in north-west Washington. It was the first home that they had ever owned but whenever Marvin visited he made sure that his father was out.

Those he talked to about his family problems say that what he wanted more than anything else was recognition from his father. He wanted to be told by him that he had done well, but no such praise was ever forthcoming. Despite this, Marvin never voiced any hostility. His disappointment was always couched in deepest respect. 'Marvin told me that he thought it was important to keep at least one of the Ten Commandments,' says his half-brother Micah Cooper, who saw him regularly in this early Detroit period. 'He said that that was why he honoured his mother and father because the Bible said that, if you did, your days would be long.'

But his father's effeminacy and cross-dressing bothered Marvin: he worried that it might be an inherited condition because he knew that his own tastes were for soft fabrics and that his voice wasn't as deep as most men's. He confided that he was 'scared' by the possibility. According to those who met them, some of the other members of his father's family were even more outrageous than Mr Gay. They had the same soft voice and effeminate mannerisms. 'My eyes just popped out,' says someone who accompanied Marvin on a trip to Lexington during the seventies. 'To see all his father's family in one room together was a revelation. A couple of the unmarried ones seemed like real in-your-face fags. They wouldn't mind putting on a feather boa and sashaying around the room.'

There was also a lot of law-breaking in the Gay family. One of Marvin Sr's brothers, George, had been jailed for violent crime. Another, Clark, was later shot dead in a Lexington restaurant following an altercation. Out of the nine Gay boys, all except Clifton, Edward and Joseph would end up with criminal records. George's son, Robert Gay, who was two years Marvin's senior, was beaten to death with a plank by a fellow inmate while serving a four-year sentence for storebreaking in Eddyville Penitentiary, Kentucky. According to relatives, he was killed for 'not giving up his body'.

Perhaps as a reaction to his knowledge of these family traits Marvin accentuated his gentleness and his heterosexuality. 'He liked soft clothes,' says Beans Bowles. 'He liked the feeling and texture of things like silks but as far as I was aware there was never any indication of homosexuality. He was ashamed of his father's cross-dressing and everything.'

With three American hit singles in a row, there was no time to slow down. If he wasn't touring, he was either recording or writing. There was good-natured but intensely felt competition between Motown's writers to place their songs with hot artists, between producers to get allocated studio time and between performers to get their songs in the charts. Those who worked at Hitsville knew what their job security depended on. 'It was a family but it was a competitive family,' says Four Tops member Abdul Fakir. 'Everyone was competing with everyone else to do better than you had done on your last release or what you were going to do on your next. All the writers were competing. We bet the Temptations that we would beat them to number one.'

The Miracles had made the Top Ten in 1963 with 'You Really Got A Hold On Me', the first single to be written and produced solely by Smokey Robinson; Mary Wells had scored with 'Two Lovers', also written and produced by Smokey; Martha and the Vandellas with 'Heatwave'; and Stevie Wonder had made number one with 'Fingertips (Pt.2)'. Each hit increased the status of the writer, producer and artist.

Final mixes of songs were submitted to Quality Control, where Billie Jean Brown, a former student of journalism from Cass Technical

High School in Detroit, who'd started out writing Motown press releases while she was still at school, would listen to them and shortlist tracks to be presented at the product-evaluation meeting, the most important weekly event at Motown. Attended by producers, writers, artists and some carefully selected taste-makers, they were where destinies were shaped. Everything that passed Quality Control was listened to and then either okayed for release or consigned to the vaults.

'I would sit in the meeting,' says Mickey Stevenson. 'We would hear four or five tracks cut by Marvin and one of them would stick right out and slap you in the face. I'd just say, that's it! I didn't care who wrote the song. That's what made us grow as a company. Competition within the company, with love and care for what we were doing.'

'They had such a great roster of artists,' says Sylvia Moy, who wrote 'Uptight' for Stevie Wonder. 'If you had to write a release on somebody you had to compete with people right in the company. After the track was recorded it would be marked—given points for the track, the arrangement, the performance, the lyric. If you didn't get pass marks, your song wouldn't be released. If you were lucky you could salvage it by reworking it.'

Lamont Dozier, who had recorded for Anna Records as Lamont Anthony, had joined Motown as a songwriter and producer but didn't get a break until he teamed up with another former singer, Brian Holland. Together they had hits with Mary Wells and the Marvelettes. Then Brian's brother Eddie joined the team and in March 1963 they wrote 'Come And Get These Memories' for Martha and the Vandellas. Four months later they scored an even bigger hit with 'Heatwave'. From that point on Holland-Dozier-Holland became Motown's most powerful songwriting team.

'Brian was basically an engineer,' says Dozier. 'He played piano and he cut all the tracks. His brother Eddie, who really had the mentality of an accountant, taught himself to write lyrics so that he could be a part of what Brian and I were doing. I played piano and wrote lyrics. I worked with Brian on the music and with Eddie on the lyrics.'

All of Marvin's hits at this point had been produced by Mickey Stevenson but just as Martha and the Vandellas' single 'Heatwave' was released he cut his first Holland-Dozier-Holland song, a gospel-influenced track called 'Can I Get A Witness', produced by Lamont Dozier and Eddie Holland. 'It wasn't like I lost Marvin,' says Mickey Steven-son. 'What happened was this. I would be producing product with Marvin but if anyone else came up with a song that I thought was good for him then I'd let them produce their song with him. If Holland-Dozier-Holland came up with something great then I'd let them do it. My job was to come up with a variety of songs produced by the best producers in the company, take a listen to the result and pick the best song to go out at the time.'

Marvin felt Motown switched him from producer to producer. He felt reduced to the status of a puppet whose strings were jerked by office workers. It sowed the seeds of resentment. Berry's vision of a production team which cut records with the efficiency of an automobile production line didn't take into account the solitary, brooding artist with a streak of indignation. The only way that Marvin knew how to protest was to withdraw his services whenever he felt an executive decision wasn't in his best interests. 'I got into a lot of arguments,' he once recalled. 'I can remember an altercation with Brian Holland when I was supposed to record "I'll Take Care Of You". I just felt I wasn't ready to go down into the studio and Brian went and told Berry that I was being uncooperative and so Berry chewed me out pretty good. I got mad at Berry and we all had a vicious argument together. It was awful.'

'Can I Get A Witness', with its insistent beat doubled up with piano and drum, was an early prototype of the Holland-Dozier-Holland sound that was to work so effectively for the Four Tops and the Supremes. Appropriately enough, the title was taken from a familiar call that Pentecostal preachers made during sermons to whip up amens and hallelujahs of encouragement. In doing this, Marvin must have been aware that he was using the power of church music and church language for secular ends. 'We couldn't help but take from gospel,' says Dozier. 'The melodies from a lot of the songs we wrote were gospel-based because they were the only kind of melodies we knew. The flavour of what we were writing and the chord progressions we used were influenced by gospel music.'

Despite his initial hostility about being passed between producers Marvin felt comfortable in the hands of Holland-Dozier-Holland. 'They were serious producers and I could understand where they were coming from,' he said. 'I tried very hard to interpret what they were feeling and thinking about when they wrote the songs.'

In his autobiography *To Be Loved*, Berry Gordy recounted details of the product-evaluation meeting where 'Can I Get A Witness' was passed for release. As he remembered it, seven out of the eleven eligible to vote deemed that it would be a hit (producers weren't allowed to vote on their own product), most of them believing that it was Marvin's best single yet.

'Can I Get A Witness', which was another American hit, reaching twenty-two in the pop chart and fifteen in the R&B, was the beginning of a brilliantly creative period between Marvin and Holland-Dozier-Holland during 1964, which yielded the singles 'You're A Wonderful One', 'How Sweet It is (To Be Loved By You)' and 'Baby Don't You Do It'. However, after this run of hits, the Holland-Dozier-Holland team switched to the Four Tops and the Supremes, writing every Top Ten hit for both groups, including ten number ones for the Supremes.

For Marvin it was a time of learning, particularly concerning his vocal potential. 'I had to sing harshly but learn not to tear my throat out,' he explained. 'Sometimes I didn't make it. Holland and Dozier needed both roughness and softness in their music. They cut the songs very high and at times it was hard for me to control my voice. They said that they had to be cut high or else they wouldn't have sold like they did.'

The records that Holland-Dozier-Holland did with the Supremes were ultimately responsible for putting Marvin's career in the shade. Three of their 1964 singles—'Where Did Our Love Go', 'Baby Love' and 'Come See About Me'—made it to the top of the charts and Berry, who was now separated from Raynoma, began an affair with Diana Ross.

It was also in 1964 that the Beatles invaded America, ushering in a new era of pop music. Their first US hit, in February, was 'I Want To Hold Your Hand', and two months later they had six singles in the *Billboard* charts. For Motown, the group was good news because the Beatles shared a similar respect for clean harmonies, high production values and America's black musical heritage. The Beatles were keen fans of Motown records, and their raves about the Marvelettes, Stevie Wonder and Smokey Robinson helped create an interest in Motown among British music fans. They covered three Motown tracks on their first album, one of them written by Berry Gordy, and in January 1964, when British DJ Tony Hall asked the group who their favourite artists were, George Harrison listed Mary Wells, the Miracles and Marvin Gaye.

Marvin's first two singles, 'Stubborn Kind Of Fellow' and 'Pride and Joy', had been released in Britain on Oriole and the following four singles on EMI's Stateside label. None had made the charts, and on 17 November 1964, Marvin flew into London with Harvey Fuqua to promote his current single, also on Stateside, which was 'How Sweet It Is (To Be Loved By You)'. Although he didn't perform in concert he took part in two prestigious live television programmes, *Ready, Steady, Go!*—the hippest live pop show of the day—*Thank Your Lucky Stars*, mass-audience light entertainment, and the BBC radio programme *Saturday Club*. For most of Britain he was an unknown quantity, although there was a tradition of admiring black American blues singers and jazz musicians, and the British mod subculture was particularly enthusiastic about the Motown sound: the amphetamines they took in large quantities stimulated the central nervous system and made them more sensitive to the physical sensations caused by music. Pete Meaden, one of the key figures on the London mod scene and the discoverer of the Who, who died later of a drug overdose, once explained to me in detail the effect of Motown music on the mods.

'Motown were pulling out all sorts of stops in the studio,' he told me. 'Sometimes you could only hear the bass line going and then they'd push everything back up again and it was like a semi-psychedelic sound in 1964. Played very loud on those speakers in the Scene Club, which was a small room with concrete walls and concrete floors, it would bounce back at you and you'd be saturated with sound.

'Motown was a groovy company. They knew how to hit a person's bass responses. They'd hit you on your feet and up your legs with the bass and you'd physically react. They'd hit you inside with the bass drum and then in the head with the guitar and the piano. Sometimes a synthesizer would pick up on the top end. They were picking up on the whole body all the time and that's what mods were about. They were physical people.'

Melody Maker broke the news of Marvin's visit by describing him as 'the son of a Washington minister' who'd had an R&B hit in America 'but he also sings ballads and has written many of his own songs. He plays piano, drums and guitar.' Its review of 'How Sweet It Is' was hardly over-enthusiastic. The song had an 'insistent beat', readers were informed, and it was reckoned that Marvin's 'tantalizing delivery' might help it into the charts.

'It was purely a promotional trip,' says Peter Prince, who was then international manager for EMI Records, who distributed the Stateside label. 'Marvin was very excited about being in London for the first time. I remember we went down to the Pink Elephant, a club that musicians hung out in, and I drummed and Harvey played and Marvin sang. He wanted to try every pub, club and restaurant in town.'

One of the only people Marvin knew in England was Dave Godin, founder of Britain's Tamla Motown Appreciation Society, whom he had met the previous year in Detroit. Godin took him to nightspots like the Cromwellian club in South Kensington, where they saw Rod Stewart performing with the Hoochie Coochie Men, accompanied him on shopping trips and was by his side during the round of press and radio interviews. They visited Dionne Warwick, who was staying at the Dorchester Hotel in Park Lane, and in her suite they were introduced to the French singers Sacha Distel and Françoise Hardy, who were also in town for concerts.

'My personal view is that Marvin was overwhelmed by stardom,' says Godin. 'People think that if you become a star there is some inner programme that helps you to deal with it, but that isn't so. I think he was a very sensitive person. He had a good deal of shyness and even a kind of inferiority complex.

'I remember one incident, which was amusing to me at the time. He was just about to perform on *Ready, Steady, Go!* and I noticed that he was pushing his hand down his trousers and I asked him what on earth he was doing. He said, "Well, I've got to make sure that I show a little bit." He was putting his penis in the best position and he wasn't wearing any underpants. I think that was significant because sexually insecure men are very plugged into that symbol of their masculinity. I don't think he was gay or even bisexual but I do think he was an insecure heterosexual.'

The Rolling Stones were fellow guests on *Ready, Steady, Go!* plugging their new single 'Little Red Rooster'. Mick Jagger was anxious to meet Marvin and approached Godin, whom he knew as they had both attended Dartford Grammar School, to ask for an introduction. Godin, who didn't appreciate the Stones' appropriation of black American music, turned him down.

Also on the show was the Graham Bond Organization, a blues group notable for its illustrious alumni rather than for its commercial success. It contained two future members of Cream—Jack Bruce on bass guitar and Ginger Baker on drums—as well as saxophonist Dick Heckstall-Smith. 'Marvin always fancied himself as a drummer and during rehearsals he got behind Ginger Baker's drum kit and started crashing about,' remembers Peter Prince. 'Baker, who had no idea who he was, was infuriated. He was shouting, "Get this idiot off. Who does he think he is?" It was a real old bust-up.'

Not long after Marvin returned to Detroit, after a promotional visit to Paris, came the news that Sam Cooke had been shot dead in a seedy Los Angeles motel, the first major pop star to be murdered. The death disturbed Marvin because he was so often cited as Cooke's natural successor. He claimed that it made him feel 'extremely nervous' even to think about a soul singer who was shot to death. They shared similarities. Both were the sons of black American preachers, and had had to struggle with the choice between R&B and gospel. There was even a similar mellowness in their voices. Cooke had been an influential vocalist with the Soul Stirrers, and his gospel fans felt that he'd betrayed the Church by taking its music and modifying it for the secular market.

No doubt those who felt that Cooke had sold his soul to pop saw his death as a judgement. The man who'd left the Church for fame and money ended his life half-naked on a motel floor after being shot by a night manager. Apparently he'd attempted to rape a woman in his room.

In the immediate aftermath of the killing Marvin's name was floated as a possible candidate for the role of Cooke in a movie to be titled *The Sam Cooke Story*. Marvin, however, wasn't interested. There were too many parallels between their lives and the prospect of pretending to be Cooke horrified him. 'He almost had first choice to replace Sam Cooke,' said Motown's choreographer Cholly Atkins. 'He had his foot in the door. He was playing supper clubs and doing excellent, but it wasn't his bag.'

Berry wanted to capitalize on Marvin's romantic appeal by teaming him up with the cream of Motown's female singers. The first collaboration was with twenty-one-year-old Mary Wells, who'd recently had a huge hit with 'My Guy', and this produced the single 'Once Upon A Time' (produced by Clarence Paul) and the album *Together* (produced by Mickey Stevenson), both of which sold well. When Wells decided to leave Motown, following a generous offer from 20th Century Fox, Marvin was paired with twenty-four-year-old Kim Weston, the wife of Mickey Stevenson, for the single 'What Good Am I Without You'. Both girls were considerably younger than Anna, and the collaborations required intimations of romance, especially when the songs were performed on television. The cover of *Together* featured Marvin and Mary Wells gazing into each other's eyes with their foreheads gently touching.

According to those who knew the girls, their relationships with Marvin were always platonic. There was affection and respect, but never a hint of sexual involvement. However, that was not always the way his wife felt about it. 'Anna was very jealous of Marvin's singing partners,' says Kim Weston. 'She made her displeasure very obvious and that made him feel uncomfortable.'

It seems unlikely that Marvin was unfaithful to Anna during the first four years of their marriage. During his first headline tour, where he was supported by the Spinners and Hattie Littles, drummer Uriel Jones remembers Marvin for his sobriety. There were no late-night parties, no drunken binges, no one-night stands with adoring fans. He appeared self-disciplined, reflective, introverted. 'He kept himself to himself,' says Jones. 'He didn't go out. He always seemed to be deep in thought. He was a clean-living guy. When the job was over he would go straight back to his hotel room. He just wasn't a wild and crazy guy.'

His driver Joe Schaffner has similar memories. 'He could have had any woman he wanted at that time but he chose not to do so,' he says. 'Some men just have to have a lot of women. Jackie Wilson would have them in line waiting for him. But Marvin wasn't like that in the early days.' But Schaffner also knew that he was a man with a strong sex drive, who admitted to being a heavy masturbator. He collected pornography while on tours and had a good knowledge of specialist stores in all the major cities. 'He would buy stacks of these books,' remembers Schaffner. 'When we would go to Philadelphia, for example, there were certain stores he would go to. He would look at them and collect them. But buying pornography doesn't make you a pervert. We can think about a whole lot of things but it's a matter of whether we take those thoughts and put them into action.'

His image at the time was clean, and Motown required that it be so. Berry wanted the label to be upbeat, positive and happy—the 'Sound of Young America', as he was now referring to it. He knew that blacks had to work harder to prove themselves and that it was therefore important to avoid anything that would give white folk an excuse to condemn them. Beginning in 1964 he arranged for all of his stars to be groomed, to be given the class that was never handed down to them in the ghettos. They were taught to sing by Maurice King, to dance by Cholly Atkins and to conduct themselves properly by Maxine Powell, who encouraged them to have style and poise on stage and off. Her view was that one day they might be invited to perform in front of kings and queens and she wanted them to be ready. She wanted them to know how to dress, walk, curtsy, bow, talk, give interviews and all the rest of the things a performing artist is expected to do.

Maxine Powell was a small black lady, who had been training black models in Chicago since the mid-fifties. She was full of wise sayings, poems and slogans that would encourage her protégés to walk tall in the white world. Above all, she wanted them to be proud of who they were and to retain their natural dignity.

Marvin resisted such schooling. He told Maxine that he 'didn't need no charm school'. She replied that he certainly didn't need as much as most because his deportment was impeccable, but that he needed to improve his stage performance, which was stiff and lacked confidence. Reluctantly Marvin took a small part of the course.

'He was always kind and always a gentleman,' says Maxine Powell. 'He used to sing with his eyes closed and I told him that we would work on his posture to enable his body language to start to flow, to start to tell a story. We worked on those two things, and class. Don't forget, class is the main thing.'

6

Allies

Let thy fountain be blessed: and rejoice with the wife of thy
youth.   Proverbs 5:18

The years between 1964 and 1967 were golden ones for Motown.
The hard times of breaking in a label were over; the writers, producers and artists were on a creative high and the hits were
rolling in. Every month throughout those years there was an average of
two new Top Twenty American singles from one of the Motown labels,
whether it be Martha and the Vandellas and the Temptations on Gordy,
Marvin on Tamla, Jimmy Ruffin on Soul, or the Four Tops and the
Supremes on Motown.

The Motown sound established itself as an essential soundtrack to
the sixties, as important to understanding the mood of the times as the
'beat' music that emanated from Liverpool and London, and the psy-
chedelia of San Francisco. American soldiers listened to Motown in the
jungles of Vietnam, British mods listened to Motown as they danced
the weekends away at all-nighter venues, the Beatles listened to
Motown at home, and the newly fashionable discotheques of New
York, Paris and London throbbed with the Motown beat.

Although involved in making music that was part of a lifestyle revolution, Marvin was not a natural scene-maker. He preferred to be
with trusted friends, found small-talk difficult and was a surprisingly
bad dancer. He preferred to stay at home in his bathrobe and either
watch television or play music. 'In a way Marvin was a loner,' says
Sylvester Potts of the Contours, who was with Motown when Marvin
arrived. 'But even though he was a loner he surrounded himself with
good friends. He wasn't reclusive.'

Home had initially been an apartment in the Gordy building on St
Antoine and Farnsworth, where Anna Records had had its offices. Now
they were able to buy a larger property on Adeline, a street seven miles
north in an affluent suburb close to the Michigan State Fair Grounds
and the Palmer Park Municipal Golf Course. Smokey Robinson had
already bought a home nearby on Santa Barbara and soon other label
mates, including Stevie Wonder and members of the Four Tops, would
buy property in the area.

Early in 1965 Anna appeared to become pregnant and on 12
November it was announced that a son had been born. The child was
christened Marvin Pentz Gaye III at Bethel AME (African Methodist
Episcopal) Church on Frederick Street in Detroit, with Maxine Powell
becoming the boy's godmother.

But there were those at Motown who didn't believe that matters
were that straightforward. Anna, who was now forty-two, had for
some time been rumoured to be unable to have children and the suspicion was that the child had been adopted and the pregnant look faked.

Louvain Demps, whose mother had known Anna during her nightclub years, had backed Marvin on many of his records as part of the
Andantes vocal group. She knew, from what her mother had told her as
an old acquaintance of the Gordy sisters, that Anna wasn't able to con-
ceive but, like so many other musicians, felt that it would have been
inappropriate to ask too many questions of the Gordys.

'I knew that Little Marvin wasn't Anna's own child,' she says, 'but
just before he came along she went through this thing where she actually looked as though she was expecting. I noticed that she had put on
a lot of weight. She really did look like it.'

Those within the inner circle began to take it for granted that Little
Marvin, as he came to be known, was adopted. Some even knew that

the real mother was Denise Gordy, the fifteen-year-old daughter of Anna's brother George, although the identity of the father was left to speculation. This story appeared to be confirmed when Marvin told his biographer David Ritz that Little Marvin was adopted, although he didn't expand on the issue or identify the parents. In light of this new information the awkwardly phrased references on the *Here My Dear* album to the boy whom God had 'given' to him and Anna made more sense.

Yet in his apparent candour Marvin was still concealing the real truth, which was that although Little Marvin had been adopted into his family and Denise Gordy was the mother, he was the biological father. This was potentially explosive information, bearing in mind that Denise was under the legal age for sexual relations at that time, and he only shared it with a few close friends towards the end of his life and didn't even tell Little Marvin until he was midway through his teens.

'I knew the truth,' says Gerald White, who began touring with him as a bodyguard in 1977. 'Marvin ran everything down to me. I think that the Gordys arranged everything.'

'Marvin told me the story himself when I started to work with him,' says another former colleague. 'Regardless of what happened, Anna took that kid and raised him to the point that she is the only mom he knows. It takes one hell of a lady to do that.'

However, no one Marvin spoke to was told the precise nature of the liaison with Denise. It seemed incredible that Marvin would have risked his marriage and his relationship with Motown for a brief fling with his teenage niece. If it had been a foolish accident, why wasn't the pregnancy terminated and Marvin ousted from the family circle and dispatched into show business limbo? Billy Davis, who had been close to both Anna and Berry, reacted with incredulity at the idea that Marvin would have had an affair with Denise. 'I hadn't heard that,' he said. 'That one's spanking brand new on me. If Marvin had a child by George Gordy's daughter he would have been ostracised from the family.'

The truth, bizarre as it may seem, is that it was a planned pregnancy, that Anna wanted a child that had Gordy blood. Marvin did tell David Ritz that Anna was feeling insecure at the time and that they had both thought that a child would stabilise the marriage, that 'a child might bring us together', but he didn't explain how that was actually brought about.

Denise was the only unmarried Gordy girl of child-bearing age and she was asked if she would be happy to become pregnant by Marvin. She says that she had no apprehensions and was happy to oblige. 'My aunt was unable to have children and I had one for her,' she says. 'It was as simple as that. She's my aunt and I love her.'

Going through with the plan meant taking time off school and having to do home study. The baby was born in a private hospital in Detroit and was then handed over to Marvin and Anna to raise as their own. As far as Denise is aware, no official adoption papers were ever signed. She maintained a close relationship with Marvin, Anna and the new child and still considers herself to be 'very, very, very close' to Little Marvin. 'I don't think that Marvin and I really had a relationship,' she says. 'We were like family. I was like a surrogate mother.'

The Biblical parallel that comes to mind is not the adulterous King David and his lover Bathsheba but the patriarch Abraham and his maidservant Hagar. 'The Lord has kept me from having children,' Sarai tells her husband Abraham (Genesis 16:2). 'Go, sleep with my maidservant; perhaps I can build a family through her.' This union produced Ishmael.

A parallel such as this wouldn't normally warrant being dragged into the unusual lifestyle of a pop star, but Marvin had an unusually intense respect for the Old Testament and its 'men of faith' because of the Judaic bias of the House of God. Friends testify that Marvin would frequently cite the Old Testament to justify eccentric behaviour. He told Ritz that he named his son after his father in order to uphold tradition, adding: 'That's what we learned from the Old Testament.'

Andre White, his bodyguard and later his manager, remembers that he would frequently argue that polygamy was consistent with Biblical teaching, citing the case of men like King Solomon who had many wives. 'It was always a battle in his mind,' says White. 'He would think—what's wrong with it? He would justify his behaviour with certain things that the Old Testament said.'

Regardless of the unusual circumstances surrounding this conception and birth, Marvin and Anna loved their new son and Marvin strove to create the happy and stable environment that he'd never had himself. Over the next few years they took in two more illegitimate Gordy children—George, a second son of Denise's (not fathered by Marvin), and Parisee, the daughter of her sister Patrice. They became like a brother and sister to Little Marvin. Elgie Stover, a musician from Cleveland who was distantly related to Harvey Fuqua and had been a member of a vocal group called the Annuals, moved in as a personal aide to Marvin and a help to Anna in running the house and rearing the children. He offered Marvin relief from the pressures of work: he listened to his stories, laughed at his jokes, offered constructive criticism of his work in progress and cooked great barbecues. 'I became Marvin's right-hand man,' says Stover. 'I lived with the family. I cooked for them, fed them and helped bring up the kids. I was like a personal manager who took care of everything.'

The only other person working directly for Marvin at that time was Joe Schaffner, now married to Kathy of the Marvelettes. As well as being Marvin's driver, he helped with shopping, advised him on clothes, settled his accounts and managed his tours.

'He was worse than most people at managing his personal affairs,' says Schaffner. 'Money didn't mean that much to him and he was extremely careless with it, both in gambling and in giving gifts to people. He didn't place much value on money. Success is one thing. What you get for being successful is another. He would stay in his house for weeks on end. He would do a lot of music, play with his son, other kids would come by, friends would come by and we'd maybe go outside and cook a barbecue. His home became a gathering place. We would play cards and gamble. He didn't need to leave the house because everyone came to him.'

Marvin still played around with ideas for songs but he wasn't as prolific as he had been in the early days at Motown, when he had not only had a hand in writing his first three hits but had co-written 'Beechwood 4-5789' for the Marvelettes and 'Dancing In The Street' for Martha and the Vandellas.

Songwriting credits often gave a false impression. Writers were included because of favours or partnership agreements. Marvin's contribution to 'Dancing In The Street', for example, which was credited to Hunter-Stevenson-Gaye, was the title and Mickey Stevenson's credit

At William Randall Junior High School, Washington, DC, 1952.
Marvin Gaye *(left)* and his childhood friend Buddy Comedy *(right)*.

Harvey and the Moonglows, 1959. Harvey Fuqua *(foreground)* with, from left to right, Chester Simmons, Reese Palmer, James Nolan, Marvin Gaye, and Chuck Barksdale.

PHOTO: JAMES NELSON

When Marvin arrived at Motown in 1960 he wanted to emulate the smooth style of Nat 'King' Cole and rather disdained R&B.

October 14, 1967. Minutes after this photo was taken Tammi Terrell
collapsed in Marvin's arms. She would never sing on stage again, and it
marked the beginning of Marvin's retreat into himself.

PHOTO: HAMPDEN SYDNEY COLLEGE YEARBOOK

Photographed in Washington, DC, May 1972. The new, serious, spiritual image started around the time of 'What's Going On'.

PHOTO: BUDDY COMEDY

His mother, Alberta, remained close to him throughout his life. Strongly religious, she encouraged him in his career and often accompanied him on tour.

PHOTO: BUDDY COMEDY

Marvin's father *(left)* was jealous of his son's success and resented his becoming the family the breadwinner.

PHOTO: BUDDY COMEDY

Marvin with Bubby in Belgium, 1981.

came because he was Ivy Hunter's songwriting partner at the time even though he didn't work on this particular track.

'I was trying to write something at Mickey Stevenson's place over on Canfield Street,' says Ivy Hunter. 'Marvin was listening to me put the lyrics together and he said, "That sounds like dancing in the street." That's how he got his twenty-five per cent. What he meant was that it sounded festive and I had been trying to write a melancholy love song.'

Marvin worked best with writing partners: he never had confidence in his own unaided talent. Friends like Harvey Fuqua, Johnny Bristol and Clarence Paul brought out the best in him. He would start songs on his own but would rely on others to help him finish them or supply lyrical threads. 'He would play things on the piano at home and there would be people there who would say things,' remembers Joe Schaffner. 'They would start talking and he would start singing and quite naturally certain words would come up and they'd end up on the tape. Then, whenever the song was complete, whoever was there at the time would get credit for it. Marvin would always give credit.'

Marvin continued to admire Smokey Robinson, unique among Motown artists at the time for his autonomy. Smokey not only produced and wrote the Miracles records but was a vice-president of the company and an influential voice in the A&R department. Smokey could hone a fine lyric as easily as he could sing a great chorus. He was the all-rounder that Marvin wanted to become. Their relationship was cemented at Palmer Park, where Marvin and Smokey would play regular golf with Fuqua, Obie Benson from the Four Tops and Ronnie White of the Miracles. Marvin wasn't a great player but he was enthusiastic and loved to place bets with other golfers. He was known to lose anything up to twenty thousand dollars in an afternoon. Once he bet a man he had never seen before seven thousand dollars that he could beat him. The man won and returned the next day with a brand new Eldorado that he'd bought with his winnings.

Smokey's most successful song of 1965 was 'My Girl', a number that had been covered by the Temptations and gave Motown its first male number one. In the same year he took over Marvin's production from Holland-Dozier-Holland. The first song they did was 'I'll Be Doggone',

written by Smokey with fellow Miracle Warren 'Pete' Moore and guitarist Marv Tarplin. It became a pop hit and Marvin's first number one
in the R&B charts.

A lot of Motown songs took clichés from conversations and
reworked them until they didn't sound like clichés. Smokey had done
this successfully with songs like 'Shop Around', 'You've Really Got A
Hold On Me', 'My Guy' and 'The Way You Do The Things You Do'. 'I'll
be doggone' was a phrase that occurred to him as he watched Marv
Tarplin working on the riff that was to underpin the song of that title.
There was a similar story behind 'Ain't That Peculiar', Smokey's next
song with Marvin, which duplicated the success of 'I'll Be Doggone' in
both charts. 'We were together every day as the Miracles,' says Bobby
Rogers. 'Marv Tarplin had come up with another riff while we were on
tour in England and Smokey said, "Hey! Ain't that peculiar?" and I'd
said, "Yeh. Peculiarity." We were just joking around but Smokey put it
right there in the song he was writing.'

There were to be two more songs with Smokey—'One More
Heartache' and 'Take This Heart Of Mine'—neither of which did as
well in the American charts. Yet at the same time that he was making an
impact on the R&B charts and gaining a reputation as a sweet soul
singer he was still clinging to his ambition to be the black Frank Sinatra. 'Smokey saved me during a time that I was being non-productive,'
Marvin said later. 'I was writing strong but I didn't have a great deal of
confidence in my pen because the giants were around—people like
Holland–Dozier, Norman Whitfield and Smokey. Smokey saved me at a
time when I needed some records.'

In November 1964 Marvin had released a collection of show tunes
under the title *Hello Broadway* and a year later, following the death of
his idol Nat 'King' Cole, Harvey Fuqua, Hal Davis and Marc Gordon
produced *A Tribute To The Great Nat 'King' Cole*, cover versions of
twelve songs such as 'Unforgettable' and 'Mona Lisa', which Cole had
made famous.

Marvin still considered R&B to be beneath him while recognizing
that he needed to perform it to get established. Some people saw this,
along with his neat looks, his soft voice and his shyness, as a form of
snobbery. This was something of which Marvin's father and his brothers had been accused, but they said it was an expression of dignity and

self-respect. 'He knew he was in the position he was in because of the success of his R&B singles,' says Joe Schaffner, 'but at the same time he wanted to incorporate ballads and show tunes. His heart was really in that kind of music. He wanted to sing things that really had some slide and glide. I think this is the reason that people said that he wasn't a performer. He never adapted to the R&B choreography because that wasn't what he wanted to do.'

He tried to win over his audience by wearing tuxedos in concert and by doing supper-club performances. When he was in New York he would visit a clothing store where Nat 'King' Cole had shopped to buy the same suits and shirts. In San Francisco he flummoxed an audience by offering an evening of classic songs from the forties with only a seven-minute medley of his own chart hits.

He recorded an album of duets with Kim Weston. It was titled *Side By Side* and given a catalogue number, Tamla 260, but was never released. Weston became increasingly unhappy with the way her product was being held up at Motown and to appease her one of the tracks cut with Marvin—'It Takes Two'—was rush-released. It reached number four in the R&B chart, and fourteen in the pop charts. 'I was put with Marvin after Mary Wells left the company,' says Kim. 'There had been talk about me working with him while she was still there but it was when she was gone that Mickey put us together. We recorded for over two years but Motown stopped releasing any product. That disturbed me. "It Takes Two" didn't become a hit until after I'd left.'

Marvin's most successful pairing was with Tammi Terrell, a twenty-year-old from Philadelphia who had been a member of James Brown's revue and who had been spotted by Berry Gordy in 1965, when she was touring with Jerry Butler. Born in Philadelphia as Thomasina Montgomery, she had started out at the age of nine in talent shows before singing with Steve Gibson and the Red Caps and then signing as a solo artist to Scepter Records at the age of fourteen. 'Even though we were put together by the company, Tammi was one girl I really wanted to work with,' Marvin once admitted. 'I liked Tammi. She was pretty, she was nice, she was soft and she was misunderstood.'

Berry brought her to Motown, where she recorded two singles written by Harvey Fuqua and Johnny Bristol, 'I Can't Believe You Love Me' and 'Come On And See Me', before being put together with Mar-

vin in December 1966 to cut a song by a new songwriting team, Niko-
las Ashford and Valerie Simpson, who'd met each other in a New York
Baptist church in 1963 and had written Ray Charles's great R&B hit
'Let's Go Get Stoned'. The song they had written for Marvin and
Tammi was 'Ain't No Mountain High Enough' and it was passed on to
Fuqua and Bristol.

'As soon as we heard the tape of the song we thought of Tammi and
Marvin,' says Johnny Bristol. 'When they cut it, we were jumping up
and down in the studio. We knew that we had a hit.'

The remarkable fact is that the two singers had never met each
other before their first recording session and Marvin had never before
heard her voice. There was an instant musical bond, which turned
into an emotional bond. Observers thought they must be lovers,
even though Tammi was deeply involved with David Ruffin of the
Temptations.

Mary Wells had been a safe proposition. She was no sex kitten and
the pairing only lasted for one release. Kim Weston was already married when 'It Takes Two' was recorded. Tammi Terrell, on the other
hand, looked good with Marvin and had a track record for dating powerful male vocalists. Yet, despite the affection in and out of the studio,
Marvin always denied that there had been an affair. He argued that she
was too independent for him. His friends believe that there was a deep
and genuine love between them but that this had a lot to do with the
protective role Marvin undertook.

Tammi had been battered both physically and emotionally by past
relationships and Marvin was the considerate gentleman who showed
her the sort of affection she needed to put herself back together again.
He was the first man she had met who had showed her concern and
tenderness and who was there for her when she needed him. 'Knowing
Marvin, I think that he was more like a protector or a big brother to
Tammi,' says Louvain Demps. 'I think he probably tried to advise her
how to do something better for herself. That's the way he was. That's
the man I saw.'

This view is confirmed by almost everyone who knew them both.
'They worked together and Marvin felt a great deal of affection for
her,' says Joe Schaffner. 'Tammi had led a wild life and she was one of
those people who attracts a wild bunch. Marvin was kinder, warmer

and more gentle than these people. He gave her the courage that she could change things and that she could do well.'

'I don't know whether it went into a sexual relationship,' says Marvin's second wife Jan, 'but I think he loved her very deeply. He loved her more than just as a fellow artist.'

Elaine Jesmer, a Los Angeles-based publicist, who worked with the duo in 1967, sensed that Tammi had the upper hand. 'I think that she had Marvin by the short hairs,' she says. 'He didn't know what to make of her but he was fascinated. She loved it and she played around with him. She was very, very much in love with David Ruffin, but she would have screwed with Marvin if she could. In her mind, she was going to be a bigger star than Marvin. So, when they were both on stage, Marvin couldn't relax.'

When 'Ain't No Mountain High Enough' was released in April 1967, the single went into the pop Top Twenty as well as reaching number three in the R&B charts. Marvin and Tammi began touring together, playing colleges, universities and exclusive clubs. By this time the five-year-old marriage between Marvin and Anna was strained. Neither of them felt they were getting the attention from the other that they deserved. Marvin told a friend that when he had approached Anna to make love one night she stormed out of the bedroom and into the garage, returning with his golf clubs, which she threw on the bed beside him. 'Make love to them,' she shouted. 'They're what you're married to.'

The outbursts became more public. Joe Schaffner can recall a press conference in the Summit Hotel, New York, where a female journalist made a play for Marvin in front of Anna. 'This woman was all over him,' remembers Schaffner. 'When we got downstairs and walked to the car Anna started arguing with him, accusing him over this girl.'

They both played the game: Marvin claimed that Anna had been unfaithful to him and that he had caught her in a hotel bed with a lover; Anna accused him of having affairs on the road.

'Anna was a Gordy, she wasn't just a Gaye,' explains Elgie Stover. 'The Gordys were stronger than the Gayes. She was Berry's sister and, as such, she carried all the popularity. As far as proving that she had an affair . . . She was accused of going with a guy called Williams who was in the clothing business but Anna had several friends like that. I wouldn't say that she was having affairs with them. She believed in underdogs. She tried to help them. But these things led to arguments. Marvin would have tantrums. Sometimes he would just go off. You never knew what had upset him but most of the time it would be Anna. They would have rows. It could be about something that he thought she was doing because she came in late or was out all night.'

According to Joe Schaffner, Marvin got his biggest kicks from voyeurism rather than from illicit affairs. He always avoided potential entanglements. He liked the company of prostitutes because they provided a sexual charge without encumbrance. But even with prostitutes he liked to keep his distance, preferring to talk sex with them, be massaged or arrange for a private show. 'Prostitutes protect me from passion,' he once admitted. 'Passions are dangerous. They can cause you to lust after other men's wives.'

'These girls gave him the most relief because they didn't want anything from him,' says Schaffner. 'If they could take their clothes off for him and parade around he would ask them to do that. If you didn't know how to ask someone to do certain things, these girls could help you because they did it on a natural everyday basis. It was their profession. Marvin would just watch. He would look at them and they would maybe have sex between themselves. It was no different from going to a place where you pay money. It was just that they were standing in his hotel room and doing it. He was an observer. After he found out that he could just ask these girls to do stuff and they'd do it, he stopped buying all his pornography books.'

In January 1967 he worked on seven tracks that he had commissioned from arranger Bobby Scott. Lushly orchestrated, they reflected his continued determination to be his generation's Nat 'King' Cole. All he had to do was to add his vocals, but he was never happy with the result. His voice, in his opinion, didn't have the depth of experience to match the emotions of the songs. He needed to suffer more before he could tackle them. He wouldn't attempt this for another decade.

The next month he began work on 'I Heard It Through The Grapevine', the song that most rock critics feel drew out his greatest single performance. 'If you know anything about Marvin's personal life at that time you'll know the emotions that were evoked for him by that song,' says Beans Bowles. 'When he sang it he was relating to a personal experience. There may not be any names in it but it related to something in his life.' The song was composed by Barrett Strong, the artist who'd given Berry his first Tamla hit in 1959 with 'Money', and Norman Whitfield, who by now had written 'Needle In A Haystack' and 'He Was Really Sayin' Something' for the Velvelettes, and 'Ain't Too Proud To Beg' and 'Beauty Is Only Skin Deep' for the Temptations.

'It was a song I first thought of writing when I was in Chicago working for Veejay Records,' says Strong. 'I'd always heard people use the phrase "I heard it through the grapevine" but I had never heard anyone use it in a song. I thought it was a great line. I moved back to Detroit after I heard the Temptations do "My Girl" because I realized that Motown were now doing my style of music and I discussed the idea of the song with Norman. I had a little groove on the piano and we went ahead and did it. We used pretty much the same beat that I'd used on "Money". It's a beat that everyone is familiar with and everyone can feel. Norman co-wrote it with me, I came up with some music fills and he produced it.'

The song was a plea by a wounded lover who discovers from a third party that his partner has rekindled an old flame. It's a song of both loss and betrayal, of loneliness and humiliation. The music—a low, swampy beat with a sinister tambourine shake by Jack Ashford and tom-toms by Richard 'Pistol' Allen—amplified the theme of rumour and insinuation. James Jamerson's bass line seemed to simulate the stabbing thoughts of a troubled conscience. The opening bars became some of the best known in pop.

The track was worked on again for four days in February 1967 and completed on 10 April. When Berry heard it, he liked it but thought it was too innovative and didn't fit in with Marvin's image of the time as a romantic winner. Instead he argued that Marvin should release the Holland-Dozier-Holland track 'Your Unchanging Love', and the tapes of 'Grapevine' were put into the Motown vaults ready for possible use on a future album. Frustrated but still determined, Whitfield cut the song again on 15 June, with Gladys Knight and the Pips. Released in September it made number two in the pop charts, selling over two million copies. A version by the Miracles was released in 1968 on their album *Special Occasion*.

While Berry's reasons for not releasing it were made clear, Marvin said later, 'Berry canned ['I Heard It Through The Grapevine'] because he didn't have a lot of faith in it. Or maybe he canned it because I was acting ridiculous at the time. That happened a few times. I would have done the same thing to someone if they were giving me trouble.'

Billie Jean Brown admits that as head of Quality Control it was she who blocked its immediate release because she believed that the production of Marvin's version was too advanced for 1967. She felt that a more accessible version was needed. 'I didn't think that Marvin had the right groove as a first time for that song,' she says. 'That was the way I felt at the time, and I got away with it. I still believe that part of the reason Marvin's version got the attention it did in order to become as big as it did was because it was so different to Gladys's version. She had paved the way.'

7

Enemies

Ponder the path of thy feet, and let all thy ways be
established.   Proverbs 4:26

Nineteen sixty-seven is best remembered for the Summer of Love,
a time of flowers and incense, love-ins and peace marches, com-
munes and hallucinations. The Beatles released their most ambi-
tious album yet, *Sgt. Pepper's Lonely Hearts Club Band*; Timothy Leary,
the Harvard professor turned LSD prophet, encouraged college-aged
young people to 'Turn on, tune in and drop out'; and the new music of
bands like Pink Floyd, Jefferson Airplane and the Grateful Dead was
taking pop in ever weirder directions.

But for Marvin it was a very different kind of summer. The difficulties of his marriage seemed to be mirrored in the turmoil of the outside
world. On 24 July Detroit exploded into flames with some of the worst
race riots ever witnessed in America. Paratroopers from the 84th and
101st Airborne Divisions were brought in and, when it was all over,
there had been 7,000 arrests, 43 deaths and 1,200 homes and busi-
nesses destroyed.

The riots appeared to be a bad omen for Motown. On West Grand

Boulevard they could literally smell the smoke and hear the sound of gunfire. Berry Gordy was in Las Vegas with the Supremes, who were performing at the Flamingo Hotel, and security guards had to be brought in to protect Hitsville. After he returned, an anonymous threat was made to firebomb the company and Berry decided that it was time to move to a large office building at 2547 Woodward Avenue in the downtown area. According to almost everyone, this was when the spirit of Motown left Motown. The move heralded the beginning of the wranglings, firings and desertions that bedevilled the company well into the next decade.

Whilst none of the artists would have been where they were without Berry's guiding vision, and certainly he had the right to develop his company in the way he saw fit, some of the artists felt he exercised too much control. These young stars now regarded themselves as creative artists, rather than song-and-dance folk, and they demanded the freedom to develop and experiment. The mood of the times brought about a shift from naked commercialism to free expression. Sometimes, as with the Beatles, the two came together without any evidence of compromise.

'Berry wasn't keen on his artists doing too much writing or producing,' says Kathy Anderson Schaffner. 'This affected Marvin because he was multi-faceted. He was gifted as a writer, producer, singer and musician. If he had started producing his own stuff it would have cut someone else out.'

'Berry Gordy was like a dictator,' says producer and songwriter Hank Cosby, who worked with Marvin on several projects. 'You did things his way because that's the way he wanted things done. Looking back, it couldn't have happened any other way because we would have had too many heads trying to run things, but it created problems for the artists.'

The first major losses had come with the departures of Kim Weston and Mickey Stevenson. As a vice-president, Stevenson had wanted stock options in Motown but had been refused; he was also upset at what he saw as Berry's failure to promote his wife's career effectively. Then Holland-Dozier-Holland, whose work had come to define the Motown sound and who had achieved almost fifty Motown hits over four years, became disgruntled. This culminated in them going on strike in the summer of 1967. Motown sued them, they countersued and both cases were eventually settled out of court.

To make matters worse, while this dissatisfaction broke out Berry was in California, planning how to make an even bigger star of Diana Ross. Having done everything he could in music, he was keen to get into films and had bought a two-storey house in Beverly Hills from the comedian Tommy Smothers. The Detroit operation was left in the hands of lieutenants. A white executive, Ralph Seltzer, became the head of the creative division. Beans Bowles was dropped from the session pool for getting too involved in local politics; Florence Ballard was sacked from the Supremes; Clarence Paul took his songwriting talents elsewhere; and Harvey Fuqua and Gwen got divorced.

Other Motown artists were buckling under the pressures that came with success. Bass player James Jamerson and drummer Benny Benjamin of the Funk Brothers were both suffering from substance abuse and turning in less than perfect performances. The Temptations lost David Ruffin and Eddie Kendricks. Paul Williams, also of the Temptations, was having drink and money problems, which eventually drove him to suicide.

'There were people who started having mental problems when they reached the age of twenty-one and found that the money they had expected to be accumulating in their escrow accounts just wasn't what they had thought it would be,' says Bill Murry.

'Everything changed when I left,' says Mickey Stevenson. 'Then it became business, business, business, but not a caring business. The formula that had made it work was gone. Not that I was the only formula, but in the music department I was the formula. Berry picked me to be the formula.'

Marvin was seeing his long-time allies disperse—Harvey to a lucrative deal with RCA, Mickey Stevenson and Clarence Paul to MGM, choreographer Cholly Atkins to Las Vegas—and he knew he couldn't walk away so easily. He was tied to the Gordys through blood and marriage. It went against his obstinate spirit but the price of leaving was just too high.

Berry had recently given him the use of his ranch-style home at 3067 West Outer Drive while he moved his Detroit base to an even bigger Italian Renaissance-style house on Boston Boulevard. Marvin loved this new home on Outer Drive. With its sunken living room and deep carpets it was his first taste of real luxury, yet because it belonged to Berry it increased his sense of dependence. His feelings towards Berry were ambivalent. He respected him and believed in his vision for Motown, but at the same time resented being controlled. He would tell friends that he felt as though he was being manipulated and that if he had been with any other record company he would have walked out.

Like Holland-Dozier-Holland, he was unhappy with his publishing deal with Jobete and later cited it as the reason behind his meagre output as a writer. Royalties on records were no better. At the time, group members such as Martha Reeves, of the Vandellas, were being paid as little as 1.3 per cent of the price of each single and it was only in 1965 that Motown began to pay the basic union rate to its session musicians.

'I'm probably as prolific as any other songwriter,' Marvin declared in 1976. 'The problem for me has always been a political one with Motown. I just don't let my songs go. I still have songs I wrote in the fifties and sixties which I refuse to record even though they would probably be smashes. My publishing deal with Motown isn't flexible enough for me to afford to let them happen.'

Martha Reeves was one of the first Motown artists to confront Berry Gordy over royalties. In common with many of her colleagues she felt that while she had helped the company become a world-beater she hadn't prospered proportionately. Marvin didn't rebel but he became more obstinate.

'His wife was still business because she was a Gordy,' says Ivy Hunter. 'The family was very tight-knit. It appeared to me that he loved Anna very much and so it wasn't for lack of love that things started going wrong but there were tax problems and then there were problem problems. Success brings problems and he was a sensitive guy.'

It was an extra concern that Berry's interest in Marvin's career waned as he concentrated on Diana Ross. Berry wanted to cut her free from the group, and had already renamed it Diana Ross and the Supremes in anticipation of a solo career that he hoped to extend from Detroit to Las Vegas, from Broadway to Hollywood.

Marvin became troubled. 'He was very depressed because he was broke,' says Elgie Stover. 'There were times when he didn't want to live and I would have to talk him out of it.' He once locked himself in an apartment with a gun, telling everyone that he was going to shoot himself. Pops Gordy, whom he respected deeply, had to coax him out. At other times he would suddenly absent himself from Outer Drive for days on end and Anna wouldn't know where he was.

'I was at my lowest ebb during this period,' he later admitted. 'I really didn't feel like I was loved. Because I didn't feel loved, I felt useless.' Music became his main consolation. It provided an outlet for his joys and anguish.

'His relationships were reflected in his music,' says arranger Paul Riser, who worked on a lot of his material during this period. 'He was a real sensitive person. He would get upset very easily and then he would come back to his music and that's where he would find his peace of mind.'

Increasingly, his other form of relaxation was drug-taking. He had been smoking marijuana since 1959 but he was now supplementing it with cocaine, which became more readily available in Detroit after the riots. 'Back in those days,' remembers Ivy Hunter, 'you could get a small vial of pharmaceutical-quality cocaine for fifty dollars and it was as far removed from the kind of drugs you get on the streets today as you could imagine.'

'He would freeze coke on his gums,' remembers Elgie Stover. 'He would never freebase or anything like that or even snort it in 'hose days. He would dip his finger in and rub it on his gums and then maybe go out for a round of golf. That's the only way I ever saw him use coke.'

His view was that narcotics were okay in moderation and he felt he possessed a strong degree of self-control. There could be nothing immoral about drug-taking because it was against the self rather than against others. Only God had the right to judge his actions. 'If I choose to do something I do it with full knowledge of what I'm doing,' he explained later to *Rolling Stone* journalist Ben Fong-Torres. 'I do it with the knowledge of my body and its capacity. I'm a very careful person. I always have been. I was a very careful teenager. I like grass but I don't like booze. I've only been drunk once in my life.'

The success of 'Ain't No Mountain High Enough' would be repeated in a string of hits with Tammi Terrell projecting a happy, idealistic view of love—'Your Precious Love' and 'If I Could Build My Whole World Around You' from the Johnny Bristol–Harvey Fuqua-produced album *United*, and 'Ain't Nothing Like The Real Thing', 'You're All I Need To Get By' and 'Keep On Lovin' Me Honey', produced by Nickolas Ashford and Valerie Simpson for *You're All I Need*.

Ashford and Simpson were ideal collaborators for Marvin and Tammi. Both men were writers and performers, who had recorded their own work, and they shared a background in church music. On the demo tapes Valerie Simpson's voice was so close to Tammi's that all Tammi had to do was duplicate what she heard.

Marvin and Tammi were presented as the ideal young couple, happy to be in each other's company, devotedly gazing into each other's eyes. Motown historian David Morse described it as being a 'symbolic marriage which conveyed a vision of harmony and trust . . . The rapport they achieved was not merely musical but seemed to express a genuine warmth and affection. As on the stage, the art lay in playing a role with such fidelity that it did not appear to be one.'

On 14 October 1967 Marvin and Tammi turned up for a Homecoming Concert at Hampton Sydney College in Farmville, Virginia. They arrived early in the afternoon and Tammi, who wasn't feeling well, spent the hours before the concert lying on a couch in the office of the college's athletic director while Marvin and the musicians played poker in the locker rooms.

When the concert started at 8.00 p.m. over four thousand people were crammed into the gymnasium. Marvin stepped out and performed his solo hits and was then joined on stage by Tammi. 'She sang maybe two songs if I remember rightly,' says Bill Selden V, one of the concert organizers. 'Then, as she began the third song, which was "Ain't No Mountain High Enough", she started to collapse right next to Marvin and he caught her before she hit the ground. The whole place went quiet. One of the band members stepped forward and helped to carry her off.'

She was taken back to the athletic director's office and the college physician, Dr Ray Moore Jr, who lived on the campus, was called in to examine her. His recollection is that when he saw her it seemed as though she had fainted or been overcome by the heat in the gymnasium. He wasn't too worried by what he saw. 'She had normal vital signs,' he says. 'With the party spirit that was going on that evening I thought she had just overdone it or had maybe taken some mood-ameliorating drugs. I didn't detect anything more serious. I advised her to take it easy. In other words, not to go on with her assignment.'

Bill Selden made an announcement to the waiting crowd telling them that everything was fine and that Marvin would soon be back on stage. Within thirty minutes, while Tammi remained resting upstairs, Marvin bounded back on stage. 'He put on an absolutely tremendous show,' recalls Selden, 'and then as soon as it was over they weren't on the campus for more than ten minutes. They didn't even change out of their stage clothes or take a shower. They just went down, packed up and headed off into the night in their vans with Tammi.'

Tammi's collapse was not reported in the local paper, nor was it mentioned in the college magazine when it ran a photograph of the concert in its next issue. It didn't seem that important. 'Nobody thought that this was life-threatening or that it would be the last concert that she would ever give,' says Selden. 'Nobody thought that was the way it was because we were all college students and we just didn't think that way.'

For Tammi it was the first serious indication that something was wrong with her brain. She had experienced severe headaches before but she had never lost consciousness. A hospital check-up revealed the awful truth: she had a brain tumour. Over the next few years she had a series of operations that sapped her strength and vigour. The once vibrant singer with the long dark hair was reduced to a shaven-headed figure in a wheelchair weighing only 93 pounds. She lost her sight and some of her motor functions. Motown paid her medical bills after she returned home to be with her parents in Philadelphia.

Tammi's illness had a profound effect on Marvin. Some believe it produced a sense of loss that he never overcame. There were rumours that her brain had been damaged through violence in her past, when she had kept wild company. Once, it was said, she had been attacked by someone with a hammer. Another time she had been pushed down a flight of stairs. Some believed that she already had a steel plate in her head. Bill Murry can recall arriving at the Howard Theater in Washington to set up for an act and discovering that Tammi had been so badly beaten the night before that her parents had to come to collect her.

These stories caused Marvin to ponder on the complexities of human relationships, where love and hate can be so closely related; where tenderness can be followed by brutality. He found it ironic that he and Tammi were celebrated for their invocation of perfect love when both of them had been abused either by lovers or carers. But, as rock critic David Morse pointed out, Marvin managed to synthesize apparently opposing passions involved in love. Tenderness was evident in the songs with Tammi but also the determination to protect himself from being mistreated. 'This only makes him seem more of a man,' wrote Morse, 'for his independence is exerted in a just cause.'

With Tammi no longer able to tour, Marvin had an excuse to cut down on his already sparse live schedule. Taylor Cox, who, as a director of Motown's International Talent Management, was responsible for booking him during this period, recalls that a combination of stage-fright and downright laziness prevented Marvin from realizing his full potential as a stage performer. 'He could have worked heavily but he didn't,' says Cox. 'He just didn't want to take up the offers that came in. Sometimes he would agree to do something and then he'd call at the last minute and tell me that he didn't feel like going. The thing is, it takes a lot of preparation to take up an engagement. You have to choose the songs and rehearse with a band and that requires quite a bit of work. Marvin was not known for his love of work.'

His period with Tammi was one of his busiest as a performer. Yet even as he sang these bright, optimistic songs on record and on stage, he was drawing on darker thoughts for his own solo recordings. Whether deliberately or not the material he chose for his next album, *In The Groove*, was to do with disappointment, betrayal and loneliness, a reflection of what was happening in his personal life as well as in America, and to black Americans in particular.

Although Motown was slow to react to the changing mood of America in the aftermath of the Kennedy assassination, there were subtle adjustments. Records like 'The Happening' and 'Reflections' by the Supremes and 'Cloud Nine' by the Temptations responded to the psychedelic revolution just as the Four Tops' 'Standing In The Shadows Of Love' and 'Seven Rooms of Gloom' reflected the deepening pessimism that resulted from the failed idealism of the early sixties. Marvin sympathized with the hippies and peaceniks who were challenging the morals of white middle-class America. Like them, he was a drug-taking, peace-loving idealist, who hated big business, military discipline and unquestioning obedience, but he wasn't yet perceived as such a person. His Motown image was still that of a polite, handsome black man, who believed in fidelity, success and family life.

His religious upbringing boosted his nonconformity and prepared him for the stands he would eventually take. He had been taught to obey the dictates of his conscience rather than the commands of men, to speak what is true rather than that which flatters. He had been warned of the dangers of money, the love of which was the root of all evil, and had been reminded that the greatest gift of all was not the voice of an angel but love. There was something in the new youth movement that fanned the embers of his religious beliefs.

When Martin Luther King was assassinated on 4 April 1968 Marvin had been deeply affected. It seemed to him that America was going crazy, that the country couldn't accept a man who was truly good and honest. In common with the Four Tops and the Supremes, he didn't comment directly on the situation but began to record songs that touched on the darker side of life. Between the massive peace march on the Pentagon and the King assassination, he was recording the Frank Wilson song 'Chained' and Ivy Hunter's 'It's A Desperate Situation'. The greatest song of desperation on *In The Groove* was 'I Heard It Through The Grapevine', which Norman Whitfield had to fight to get included. It became a hit primarily because one Chicago disc jockey, Phil Jones, selected it as his favorite track from the album and played it on his night-time show. 'The listeners went crazy,' he said later. 'I put it on the air and the phones lit up.' Because of this interest, Motown released it as a single. It went on not only to top the charts but to sell four million copies and to become, in the opinion of many respected music critics, the best single of the rock era. Dave Marsh memorably summed up the brilliance of the recording when he commented, 'The record distils four hundred years of paranoia and talking drum gossip into three minutes and fifteen seconds of anguished soul-searching.'

The incredible thing is that Marvin himself seems to have thought so little of it and to have cut it only to please Whitfield. 'I wasn't keen on recording it,' he said. 'But Norman had this whole new arrangement worked out and it came out pretty good . . . I simply took Norman's direction as I felt it was a proper one. Had I done the song myself I wouldn't have sung it at all like that.' When interviewed by *Melody Maker* after it had topped the British charts, he seemed to talk about it as if it was a sop to the young people who liked R&B but a bit of distraction from his real calling as a balladeer. 'I can't see why it should be such a big hit in Britain but it's marvellous news,' he said. 'I've given up the idea of trying to become two people—a split personality. I love singing ballads and pop stuff but you have to keep the R&B people happy. I was schizophrenic in a sense. I knew what I wanted but I didn't know how to get it. I'm just going to try and give the public what they want now.'

The success of 'I Heard It Through The Grapevine' increased the pressure on him to tour. He compromised by agreeing to do sporadic dates—a week at Mr D's in San Francisco, appearances at San Diego University and the Las Vegas Convention Center, a guest spot on *The Joey Bishop Show*.

The horn player Preston Love was with Marvin when he started a short tour on 2 April 1969. As he recounts in his book *A Thousand Honey Creeks Later*, 'When he arrived [from Los Angeles] my fellows and I were in the locker room of the university arena preparing for the concert. Even before he greeted us as he usually did, Marvin began to pace up and down the room with his head down and a concerned expression on his face. I asked solicitously, "What's the matter, Marvin?" He moaned, "Oh, just think, I'm *thirty* years old today." The fellows burst out in laughter, but Marvin was deadly serious.'

Although he was not yet identified with the emerging counterculture he was admired by the same people who liked the Grateful Dead and the Doors. He played the outdoor Miami Pop Festival, where he told the audience, 'I'm high, just like you are. I'm high on music and loving it,' and in June 1969 he was scheduled to appear on the bill at another outdoor show at Devonshire Downs in the San Fernando Valley along with the Jimi Hendrix Experience, Don Ellis, Taj Mahal, Joe Cocker and Spirit.

Most artists in his position would have jumped at the opportunity of reaching out to a younger, hipper generation but Marvin didn't care. His only concern when he arrived at Los Angeles International

Airport to take part in the concert was to see whether he had been correctly billed.

'We picked up a copy of the *Los Angeles Times* and there was an advert that stated Jimi Hendrix would be playing and it listed five or six other acts who would be appearing,' remembers Joe Schaffner. 'Then, it just said, "and others". There was no mention of Marvin's name and so he said, "Well, if I'm not good enough to be listed among the names then I'm not doing the show." He asked me to make reservations back to Detroit and that's exactly what I did.'

His failure to turn up for shows became notorious. Sometimes these cancellations were because of his inability to get himself together on time or because he didn't want to break off from watching basketball on TV, but at other times there was a matter of principle involved. When he found himself booked into Harlem's Apollo Theater for three shows a day for seven days he decided, at the last minute, that he would only play the evening shows. 'It came time for us to leave Detroit,' says Schaffner, 'and he decided to go to the golf course. At the very time when he was due on stage in Harlem he was teeing off! He played nine holes of golf, then set off for New York. That was it. He wasn't going to do the early shows. He changed a lot of things about what promoters could ask you to do. In that case he pioneered the idea that artists were only going to do two shows a night. When he later started producing himself he helped other artists in being able to get that sort of freedom built into their contracts.'

His only solo album recorded and released in 1969 was *MPG*, an unfocused record involving contributions from twelve different producers, including Ivy Hunter, Smokey Robinson, Mickey Stevenson and Norman Whitfield. Even though it made the best showing yet in America of any Marvin Gaye album, it increased Marvin's feeling that he was no longer anyone's special project.

His next album, *That's The Way Love Is*, produced by Norman Whitfield in late 1969, was the last time he would accept a producer assigned to him by Motown and record what he was told to. He had decided that he would exercise control over his own career.

Later in life he made contradictory statements about his songwriting and record-producing. At one time he claimed to be insecure as a writer, at another that he stood 'head and shoulders above everyone else' and was writing 'smashes' that he didn't want Motown to have. In one interview he claimed that it was while recording 'I'll Take Care Of You' in 1967 that he 'started seriously thinking about producing myself', in another that he had been too busy concentrating on his vocal performances until 1970 even to consider production.

The truth seems to be that just as in the military he had resented being told what to do, he resented Motown's regimentation. He felt he was as talented as his producers and that many of them had learned from him. At the same time he was reluctant to make the final break, to discover himself as an artist.

Yet, he felt blessed. He maintained his belief that he was a chosen person. 'God loves me and I love God,' he said. 'I try to do his work as I feel I am supposed to and I do it to the best of my ability. As a result he blesses me.' This conviction was vital to the next stage of his career. It provided him with the courage to make the move, and the assurance that when he made it there would be something to say.

8

The Inner Cave

The glory of young men is their strength.

Proverbs 20:29

The catalyst for some of the biggest changes in Marvin's career was Tammi Terrell's death on 16 March 1970 at Philadelphia's Graduate Hospital after losing her battle against the brain tumour. At her rainswept funeral, four days later at Jane Memorial Methodist Church, Marvin wept openly before the three thousand mourners. Gazing at her body in the bronze-coated coffin he began to talk to her as if she was still alive, recovering just long enough to deliver his own eulogy praising her courage and optimism.

Coincidentally, the day of the funeral marked the American release of the final Marvin and Tammi single, 'The Onion Song', but what only Marvin and a handful of others knew was that the female voice on the record, already a hit in Britain, was not Tammi's. Her part had been sung by Valerie Simpson, who had also sung the previous single 'What You Gave Me', and Marvin had gone along with the deception because Motown told him that this way Tammi would continue to receive royalties even though she was too ill to sing.

To Marvin, Tammi's death was more than just the loss of a friend: it was the loss of a belief in the pure love that they had come to represent through their songs and performances. In a later interview he hinted that part of his reason for detaching himself from the music industry was because of what he believed it had contributed to her demise. 'It influenced my decision not to perform,' he said, 'because I understand the bottom line of her death—which is something I wouldn't like to discuss.' In the months following the funeral he refused to leave his home.

'It affected me tremendously,' he admitted later. 'So much so that I didn't perform for a couple of years. I had such an emotional experience with Tammi and her death that I didn't imagine I'd ever work with another girl again. I loved her very much.'

With the exception of two one-off concerts he did not return to the stage until January 1974, the same year that he recommenced his duets, this time with Diana Ross, the first female singer he had chosen personally to record with.

'I think Tammi's death triggered something in my boy,' his father told *Rolling Stone*. 'He troubled up and I would call and ask him, "Marvin. Why aren't you working?" He would say that he was tired of his music, but his excuses didn't satisfy me. It just didn't sound like him. I have to attribute the fact that he wasn't working to the girl's death. It took something from my boy.'

Uncannily, his new lifestyle began to parallel the life his father had lived in Washington DC when Marvin was growing up. He would spend long hours brooding in his bedroom and began to pay less attention to Little Marvin and his cousins. He stopped wearing the classy suits that had been an integral part of his image for so long and began dressing in sweatshirts and gym shoes, and disguised an emerging bald spot with a knitted hat. He also grew a beard for the first time in his life, an unprecedented move at the time for a black pop star. It was as though he was using this self-imposed lull in his career slowly to put to death the old Marvin, the 'Sound of Young America' Marvin who was always smartly dressed, clean-shaven and smiling for the camera. He wasn't yet sure what the new Marvin would look like but knew that he was going to have fun finding out. After years of emulating white musical styles and adopting white fashions, he was becoming more conscious of his identity as a black American, reading the work of political activists like Malcolm X and Dick Gregory with whose sense of outrage he identified.

There were other important elements in this transition period. He was moved by current events such as the trial of Lieutenant William Calley for ordering the massacre of innocent Vietnamese women and children in the village of My Lai, and the deaths at the hands of the National Guard of four students protesting against the war at Kent State University, Ohio, yet he realized that his music was detached from these great cultural upheavals. He was playing in the orchestra while the *Titanic* went down.

'I had wanted to do something that would disturb people and make them think at the same time but something wouldn't let me do it,' he confessed. 'I was upset at the problems and conditions in the world. I was upset by the war in Vietnam. I wanted to come up with something that could be translated into any language and still retain its meaning.'

He'd felt this discrepancy most intensely when he recorded the album *That's The Way Love Is* with Norman Whitfield in the summer of 1969 when the Woodstock Festival was taking place in upstate New York. Most of the tracks were routine love songs, unaffected by the social changes of the era, but Dick Holler's song 'Abraham, Martin and John', previously a hit for Dion, eloquently mourned the assassinations of the great American political idealists Abraham Lincoln, Martin Luther King and John Kennedy. The night that he recorded the song the studio was dimly lit and an unusually reverent mood pervaded the session. 'I felt sincere when I recorded that song,' he said later. 'It may well have started me thinking about social problems and the world situation.'

He was taking his first tentative steps as a producer by recording a number he'd written with Anna, 'Baby I'm For Real', with the Originals, a vocal quartet who'd previously recorded for Berry's Soul label and had performed at Motown as backing vocalists since the early days. 'It was a mutual friend of ours by the name of Richard Morris who first suggested that we do the song,' says C. P. Spencer of the Originals. 'It wasn't even on tape at that time. Marvin had to play it to us on the piano. But he already knew exactly how he wanted each voice to sound and it took us a couple of months to put the track together in the studio.'

This production marked a significant departure for Marvin. It showed that he was at last prepared to fight against the restrictions placed on his artistic capabilities. It also made him aware of his own talents in arranging voices, something he had done rarely since teaching the Moonglows their harmonies back in 1959. 'I was getting tired of all the pressures, tired of all the fights I was having with Motown's administration,' he said. 'I was also tired of being in the hands of other producers. I started telling them that I wanted to produce myself. I'd never actually tried to learn production but I'd seen so many producers at work that I just picked it up.'

His belief in himself was vindicated when 'Baby I'm For Real' went to the top spot in the R&B charts and to number fourteen in the American pop charts in November 1969, eventually selling over a million copies. 'That really showed Motown that it was absurd putting me with a producer,' he said later.

These new experiments were made easier by Motown having shifted its central operation to Sunset Strip in Hollywood. It had even opened up recording studios in Los Angeles, which it called MoWest. Its biggest new act, the Jackson Five, hadn't even had to start out in Detroit. They had been moved to California from their hometown of Gary, Indiana, and their first single, 'I Want You Back', had entered the charts at the same time as the Originals. The session musicians who could afford the move dutifully made their way out to the West Coast.

'Baby I'm For Real' was followed up in April 1970 with 'The Bells', a track credited to Marvin, Anna, Anna's niece Iris and Elgie Stover, and 'We Can Make It Baby' by Marvin and Motown employee James Nyx. Stover and Nyx, neither of whom had ever had any great songwriting success before, were to play a significant role in the making of Marvin's next album.

On 14 January 1970, Marvin and Joe Schaffner had flown from Detroit to Las Vegas to catch the final performance of Diana Ross and the Supremes at the Frontier Hotel. In accordance with Berry Gordy's plan, Diana was to leave the group to concentrate on her career as a film actress and solo recording artist. She would be replaced by Jean Terrell and the group would be relaunched as the Supremes. It was a big night out. Smokey and Claudette Robinson were there, so were television personalities Dick Clark and Steve Allen. Ed Sullivan sent a congratulatory telegram, which was read out from the stage. During the singing of 'Let The Sunshine In' Diana picked an embarrassed Marvin out of the audience and had him sing along. 'I'm your biggest fan,' she gushed. 'You know that.'

The day after the show Marvin and Joe left for Los Angeles, where Anna was already staying with Berry on one of her increasingly frequent extended shopping trips. Schaffner realized that the couple were drifting apart. They were leading almost separate lives, even though they still shared a home in Detroit and the upbringing of a son. 'Things started to get strained at that point,' he says. 'We stayed in Los Angeles throughout January and February, and I remember it was a terribly rainy season. The weather was gloomy, the mood was gloomy and Marvin and Anna became a lot more distant from each other. His relationship with Motown was difficult because there were things he wanted to do and the company wouldn't allow him. He was becoming defiant. He said that he knew what he wanted to do and what he was going to do. Anna was telling him that he should do what he was told to do because it was her brother's company. She was trying to defend him. There were conflicting allegiances. There was her brother/sister relationship with Berry and her husband/wife relationship with Marvin. Anna was caught in the middle.'

When Marvin returned to Detroit after Tammi Terrell's funeral in April, Al Cleveland, a staff writer for Motown, passed a song to him that he thought might make a good follow-up single for the Originals, who were still high in the charts with 'The Bells'. Co-written by Obie Benson of the Four Tops, the song was called 'What's Going On' and detailed some of the horrors that were confronting contemporary America—the very things that Marvin knew his own songs had overlooked. It had been put together by the two writers at Benson's apartment and Benson had hit on the hook line one afternoon while driving past Lake Michigan. 'What's going on?' was a familiar black greeting, but as a song title it had ambiguity. It could be a greeting, a serious question or simply a statement of fact—this is what's going on. The subject matter had arisen from their discussions as Benson worked out the melody on his acoustic guitar.

'That song was supposed to have been ours,' confirms C. P. Spencer. 'He did that work with the intention of recording it on us but as he started to do it he realized he was falling in love with the song himself. We were on the road at the time so people on the session began to suggest that he do it himself. It was the best thing that could have happened because that turned out to be his signature tune.'

Recorded over five days in June and July 1970, the single 'What's Going On' was a breakthrough track for Marvin. The session, arranged and orchestrated by David Van De Pitte, who had first worked with Marvin on the Originals singles, was loose and spacy. The party atmosphere, created by bringing in Bobby Rogers of the Miracles, football players Lem Barney and Mel Farr of the Detroit Lions to rap some scripted one-liners, such as 'What's happening, man?' and 'Everything is everything', set the record in a specifically black context. This was no longer just the 'Sound of Young America', this was the sound of black America, and for the first time Marvin sounded as though he was speaking in his own voice.

The feeling was much more indebted to jazz than anything Marvin had done before and bore no relation to the feel-good sound of his hit singles. The saxophone break that kicked off the track, played by veteran session man Eli Fontaine, was done as a warm-up exercise but kept for the final version. Similarly, the multi-tracked vocals were laid down so that Marvin could choose which to keep for the master tape; he decided to keep both, a move which influenced his future vocal style. Marvin was clearly in a mood to experiment and to agitate. He didn't care any more about keeping the rules. He once summed up his attitude as 'To pursue what makes you happy in life' because to do this is 'a brave and wonderful thing. I don't care what people say.'

Unfortunately, Motown wasn't as excited about the track as Marvin was. They thought that the mix was too confusing, and didn't really want to release a single that was so overtly political. It wasn't Berry's style to stir up trouble. 'This is the worst record I've ever heard,' he reputedly said to the company's sales vice-president Barney Ales. 'How could you release that?' It remained unreleased for six months while Marvin refused to record anything else in the meantime.

'Berry just didn't feel that it was material that reflected Motown,' says Joe Schaffner. 'It wasn't universal enough. It was a ghetto thing. It was very political at a time that Berry was promoting American music—music that sounded good, that everyone could dance to and appreciate and that had no real message.'

'I don't think the objections to it were ever clearly articulated at the time,' says Billie Jean Brown. 'I think that the general feeling was just an "it's not what you do" kind of thing. I don't think that there was any deep philosophical objection to the record.'

During the summer and autumn of 1970, with 'What's Going On' still on hold, Marvin continued his personal transformation. With no duties either in the studio or on stage he began to evaluate his life and rebuild his self-esteem. He read books of popular psychology such as the transactional analysis bestseller *I'm OK—You're OK* by Thomas A. Harris and the cult classic of 'spiritual wisdom', *The Teachings of Don Juan: A Yaqui Way of Knowledge* by Carlos Castaneda, which had been published recently in a popular edition.

The Teachings of Don Juan purported to be the account of a meeting between an American graduate student in anthropology and an old Yaqui Indian who passes on to him ancient secrets of sorcery and reveals the hidden powers released by various plants and seeds. 'At a very early stage in my apprenticeship,' writes Castaneda, 'Don Juan made the statement that the goal of his teachings was "to show how to become a man of knowledge".'

'I would like to become a man of power and knowledge,' Marvin told Geoff Brown of *Melody Maker*. 'I would like to use it in a good fashion to better the world's conditions, to have people understand that if they don't achieve powers they can at least get on the trail and try because what is life except to know oneself and so to become a superior being . . . ?'

He also spent time praying and meditating, trying to recapture the feeling of happiness he had known as a child in his father's church when he had what he would call his 'moments with the Spirit'. Less anchored to the teachings of any church, he was now becoming open to anything that presented itself to him as 'spiritual'. 'I turned within and prayed for help and guidance,' he told British journalist Mick Brown in 1981, when asked about the period surrounding 'What's Going On'. 'Then I said, the heck with all of them. I can do it myself . . . '

Although he would speak a lot of God and being blessed by God, he was rarely spotted reading the Bible during this period. His beliefs were closer to the gnostic idea that a direct experience of God was available to a spiritually aware élite who had no need for the structures, rituals and disciplines of the Christian Church. This, of course, suited Marvin's temperament. 'Institutionalized religion is good for the masses but I have a special God who looks over me,' he once said. 'He is the same God that people worship institutionally but I feel I have a special link. Anyone can have a special link if they assert themselves.' Again it was possible to see a parallel with his father, who wanted either to be recognized as a prophet in the House of God or nothing at all. Neither man could accept being an ordinary person in an ordinary congregation. Their lifetime fight was to be known as special, gifted and anointed.

In addition to tending to his spirit, Marvin began to pay attention to his body after years of neglect. His sporting ambitions had been thwarted as a child and now, at the age of thirty-one, he planned his comeback. He cut back on his drug consumption and took up running and weight-lifting. He built a gym at his home and hung out with boxers at the gymnasium of the King Solomon Baptist Church.

He also befriended two Detroit-based medical doctors, Robert Sims and James Wardell, whom he'd met while playing golf at Palmer Park. He would talk to them about his experimentation with cocaine, marijuana and heroin, and was particularly interested in the precise chemical effects of each drug on the brain. He would ask them for advice on fitness and diet.

'I tried to encourage him to run and exercise from a fitness standpoint,' says Robert Sims, 'but he really had a burning desire to be an athlete. He used to try to race me for money over a hundred-yard dash. I'd been a track man and a basketball player at college. He could never have beaten me at anything but he'd always want to try. He'd bet on anything. You name it, he'd bet on it.'

To outsiders it might have appeared that Marvin was simply

improving his fitness, but those close to him realized that he was determined to prove he was at least equal to his professional sporting friends. In his mind he felt he could play football to such a high standard that he would be offered a trial with the Detroit Lions or box effectively enough to win a professional fight. His booking agent, Taylor Cox, saw it as evidence that Marvin would only work hard at something if he thought it would confound everyone. Fulfilling expectations wasn't enough motivation for him. Everyone knew he could record hits and sell out concerts, so the challenge was extinguished. No one believed he could become a sporting champion in his thirties, so he put all his resources into proving them wrong. 'He was a peculiar guy,' says Cox. 'At any given time he would get something in his head and would really work at it. He was dead serious about being a boxer and then about joining the Detroit Lions. He was so serious about these things that he actually thought he was going to do them.'

'After I'd sung on "What's Going On" Marvin felt that he was good enough to play football and score a touch-down,' says Lem Barney, who had started his professional career with the Lions in 1967. 'He had never played organized football before then but he was taken with the idea that he could be a walk-on in a professional game. I told him the procedure that you had to go through before you could even get a trial with the Detroit Lions and he began working out and gaining weight until he looked like a facsimile of a football player.'

In the end it was impractical for Marvin even to train with the team because of the likelihood of serious injury. No one would insure him. In his mind he was 'as good as, or better than' the professionals he was playing alongside but the truth was that he was just another enthusiastic amateur chasing after the cheers of a crowd.

'Joe Schmidt was the head coach for the Detroit Lions at the time that Marvin came out,' says Barney, 'but he really only ever had one proper work-out with the team because Joe didn't want him to get injured. The risk was just too great.'

When he realized that a career in football was not beckoning, he transferred his enthusiasm to boxing, working with a local trainer and sparring at the gym with Michigan-based middleweight Tommy Hanna, whom he would later go on to manage. 'We were friends before we became business associates,' says Hanna. 'I taught Marvin to box.'

The desire to build himself up physically was seen by some as an attempt to assert his independence and his authority. It was a constant worry to him that he was lacking in overtly male characteristics and he was terrified of turning into his father, an arrogant but essentially weak-willed man. He felt inferior to his brother Frankie, who had seen active service in Vietnam, and also to his half-brother Micah, who had been a welterweight Golden Gloves boxer and narrowly missed representing the USA in the 1960 Olympic Games due to a criminal conviction. 'My wife says I'm running around trying to prove that I'm a man,' Marvin admitted later. 'She's probably right. I happen to think it's because I'm a sports nut.' If he was trying to be a man, the man he was most likely trying to be was Berry Gordy, who had made his mark as a boxer before entering show-business.

'He definitely wanted to be like Berry,' says Elgie Stover, who, during this time, had to prepare special food for Marvin to increase his bulk. 'He was married to Berry's sister and he knew that if he and Anna ever got into trouble then Berry would buy her a house. So Marvin could never win! He could never buck against the Gordy family. He tried to build the Gaye family up so that it would become as strong as the Gordy family, but he didn't have the power.'

He built up the power he did have—physical power and artistic power. He wanted to become that unusual combination of brute strength and artistic sensitivity. 'When he first came to Motown he was like what we would have called back then a ninety-pound weakling,' says Hank Cosby. 'His wife used to boss him around. Then when he started working out he went up from maybe a hundred and sixty pounds to over two hundred pounds and it was all muscle! It was a big difference and it changed his personality and changed his way of thinking. His wife couldn't boss him around any more. She jumped on him one time and he manhandled her a bit. He let her know that he was a man and that she was not going to be doing it any more.

'Marvin is one person who I actually saw change right before my eyes. He mentally changed. He physically changed. His whole attitude changed. From that point on he really started to do things.'

9

The Supreme Ordeal

Open thy mouth, judge righteously, and plead the cause of
the poor and needy.   Proverbs 31:9

In January 1971 Berry relented and 'What's Going On' was released
as a single. The impact was overwhelming. The critics welcomed
Marvin's change of direction and the sales vindicated his stand. It
went to the top of the R&B charts and hit the number two spot in the
pop charts. 'Within a day of its release distributors were calling me
back,' says former Motown marketing executive Phil Jones. 'It was a
monster.'

Because Marvin had refused to record anything until 'What's Going
On' was released, the single wasn't part of an album already in progress
but its success gave him the leverage he needed to record more songs in
the same vein. He was about to embark on the project that would take
all the loose threads from his past and weave them into something powerful and brilliant, the album that after all these years would be the
expression of his deepest soul. Here he would find a resolution of his
spiritual conflicts and a vindication of his musical vision.

Al Cleveland, now living in Los Angeles, and Obie Benson had assumed that they would be involved with the subsequent album—they had discussed ideas of a concept based on the single—but when they contacted Marvin they found that he was already writing his own material and intended producing it all himself. The old Motown practice of giving the album to the writers of the hit single was all over as far as Marvin was concerned.

The most amazing discovery, in the light of the album's revered position in the pantheon of pop, is how haphazardly *What's Going On* was put together, how the thematic and almost operatic quality was more a result of chance encounters and a hot moment in his life than it was a calculated effort to come up with a grand artistic statement or to produce a black *Sgt. Pepper.* The bulk of the songs had been written by Marvin at home, mostly with the help of Elgie Stover or James Nyx. The subject matter, like that of the single, was what was in the air at the time. Rather than having a fixed theme in mind, Marvin was concerned to avoid subjects he had already covered extensively. Around a dozen songs were discarded because they didn't seem right for the project. 'The whole album basically came out of the newspaper,' says Stover. 'We knew that we had to be different and that's the reason you don't hear anything about girls and boys on it. That was the furthest thing from our minds at the time. We wanted to show the people that there are more things to be concerned about in the matter of love than going to bed with someone.'

When the album's orchestral conductor and arranger, David Van De Pitte, first heard the songs they were in the form of rough piano and vocal demos that Marvin had recorded in his living room. Sometimes the songs had completed lyrics, sometimes not. Very often he could envisage sounds that he was unable to translate and he relied on Van De Pitte to bring into being the music that was locked in his imagination. There were none of the musical bridges that eventually linked the tracks.

'He had decided that he was going to make a different sort of album,' says Van De Pitte. 'He just didn't give a damn. He was at a point in his career where he didn't really want to record for Motown any more. He was unhappy and thought that, for a change, he would do exactly what he wanted to do and to hell with everything else. He was hoping it would be released but had a suspicion that it wouldn't be.

'Right off the bat there was a whole different feeling about the material. The chords were entirely different from anything they were using at the company at that time. It was related to both gospel and R&B but the extensions on the chords made it very jazzy. He was obviously going to do exactly what he wanted to do. He'd been listening to a lot of Miles Davis, Lester Young and Hank Crawford.'

He'd also been listening to James Taylor's album *Sweet Baby James*, which had produced the hit single 'Fire And Rain' the previous November, and Taylor's light vocal style had inspired him to be more relaxed at the microphone. Throughout the sixties he had strained to sing what he perceived as the rock 'n' roll style of Motown. Now he wasn't going to feel pressurized to shout. He was going to sing more like he spoke. 'Fire And Rain' may have influenced Marvin in other ways. It was one of the first pop songs to deal with the struggles of a heroin addict and also one of the few to make the charts that mentioned the name of Jesus. References to God and Jesus were traditionally taboo in pop but this was breaking down with singles such as 'Mrs Robinson' by Simon and Garfunkel (May 1968) and 'Spirit In The Sky' by Norman Greenbaum (March 1970).

The most significant departure with *What's Going On* was that Marvin was involved in every song both as songwriter and producer. He was shaping the product from beginning to end. Elgie Stover and James Nyx both witnessed the album develop during long songwriting sessions on West Outer Drive.

When he came to write the sleeve notes Marvin credited Stover as having been 'instrumental in provoking my thought process'. Although he worked primarily as a lyricist on the album, he claims that he also suggested the moods of some of the songs and encouraged Marvin to sing his own backing vocals, a departure in studio procedure at that time. 'I would sing things through for him in the studio,' says Stover. 'I'm not a singer but I've got a feeling and Marvin would pick up on the feeling I was suggesting and turn it into a song. I would suggest a melody, or a feel, or a direction and Marvin would go with it. Before I got into R&B I was into opera, where a lot of double melodies were used, and I suggested that Marvin tried some of these. I was around a lot of opera singers in Cleveland and that's where that idea came from. You'll notice that there's a very high, operatic feel to some of the tracks.'

James Nyx, a 'gentleman and a scholar', according to the sleeve credits, worked strictly on lyrics. In common with Elgie Stover, he was an unusual collaborator—a fifty-seven-year-old man with no track record as a songwriter, who had spent his years at Motown either as an office clerk or a switchboard operator. 'I'd always written poetry, and several people had said to me that I should try writing songs,' says Nyx. 'So I was messing around with lyrics and Marvin called me on the phone and asked me to come out to the house to work on some material. He seemed to like me. He liked to listen to me talk about politics and stuff like that. He was interested and would ask me lots of questions.'

Typically Marvin would take a lyric, sometimes one created at his suggestion, and work it up into something that was very much his own. 'I would write the basic story,' says Nyx, 'and he would put in what he wanted and take out what he wanted.'

The words of 'What's Happening Brother', the second track on the album, developed the theme of a troubled America suggested by 'What's Going On' but this time from the point of view of a soldier returning home from Vietnam. Marvin's brother Frankie had spent three years in Vietnam as a radio operator. Their cousin, Corporal Marvin Gay, of Lexington, had been killed there in November 1968 after only five months of active service with the First Marine Division. He was twenty-one. More recently, Marvin had appeared in a made-for-television film, *The Ballad of Andy Crocker*, produced by Danny Thomas and Aaron Spelling, in which he played the part of Dave, the combat buddy of a soldier who returns to America and finds that everything at home has been transformed for the worse. One of the songs on the soundtrack referred to him having won a medal but being unable to go back home. The film was screened in November 1969.

' "What's Happening Brother" was basically Marvin's idea,' says Nyx. 'I wrote it but I knew exactly what he was trying to do. I think the idea of Frankie coming back from Vietnam was in his head because it was in his conversation a lot.'

'Flyin' High (In The Friendly Sky)' alluded to drugs and contained lines about the attraction of danger that would become apposite to Marvin's eventual demise, but the song wasn't written with Marvin's personal drug habits in mind. 'Drugs weren't as bad in his life back then,' says Stover. 'That was a song about heroin because that was going on in the streets at the time that I wrote it. Marvin already had some music written, which Berry's brother Fuller had submitted some lyrics for. It was a song called "Sad Tomorrows", which was later released as a B side. We took the same music and rewrote the song. We had thought of calling it "Stupid Minded" but I finally came up with the title from a United Airlines commercial, which was then running on television.'

'Inner City Blues', which indicts America for a catalogue of sins including the Vietnam war, heavy-handed policing, poverty, inflation, crime and high taxes, was originally written by Nyx under another title. Significantly Marvin added the line 'makes me wanna holler', which Nyx considers to be 'the best thing he did with that song because it said everything in just a few words'. Then the title was discovered in a newspaper article. 'I said to Marvin, "That's a great title because it's not a real blues song but we're crying about the situation." We'd had several titles but we needed something appropriate. At that time the subject matter was very controversial for a company like Motown to be having anything to do with. I knew what we were doing would be controversial. In fact, I did suggest to Marvin that we take out the line "trigger-happy policing". It was one of my lines and it was a nice phrase but it hit a raw nerve.'

The music of 'Inner City Blues' came from a suggestion offered by Elgie Stover. 'A lot of the stuff on that album was inspired by old groups,' he says. 'The music for "Inner City Blues" we took from an old Drifters' song. It doesn't sound anything like it but the only way I could communicate my musical ideas to him was to take another song that was similar to show him how I thought it should feel.'

What made the album different from any other 'protest' or 'message' album at the time was the religious feeling that pervaded it. There was anger, but it was tempered with love. God was invoked on almost every song. Cornel West, director of Princeton University's Afro-American Studies Program and professor of religion, would later claim that Marvin 'evoked the love ethic of Jesus Christ as the basis for negating and transforming the world. If we learn from the book that Jesus left us, we can rock the world.'

'Wholy Holy' and 'God Is Love' were the two most explicit gospel songs on the album, the first written with Obie Benson and Al Cleveland, the second with Elgie Stover and James Nyx. (Stover says that although Anna Gaye is credited on the song she had no creative input.) The message of both songs is almost identical—Jesus offers forgiveness but commands us to love each other as a response to His mercy. It is only as we accept this offer of salvation that the world will be renewed. The lyric of 'God Is Love' was written by Nyx, who, while of 'no particular faith' himself, admits that he carried out 'quite extensive reading on religious things and the nature of the mind'. Again, the little flourishes that Marvin added to the lyric were memorable and telling. It was he who added the song's opening lines: 'Don't go and talk about my father/God is my friend.' Did he mean to contrast the loving fatherhood of God with his own father or was the father of the first line the God of the second? 'I really don't know,' says Nyx. 'It was just there. I had assumed that he was calling God father. I had written it one way but when he got through with it it came out another way. It made me look at it different when I learned how bad his relationship was with his own father.'

'Save The Children' was a vision of the desolation of the world, possibly inspired by his readings in the book of Revelation. Later in the decade he became obsessed with the idea of a final global conflagration, regarding himself as a prophet come to shake mankind out of its apathy. He had been raised to believe in a physical return to earth by Jesus Christ, an event alluded to in 'Wholy Holy', and that this coming would be preceded by such signs as wars, earthquakes, famines and religious persecution.

But there were other stimuli in the form of Little Marvin and the one-year-old Parisee Monyel Watkins, the daughter of Denise Gordy's sister, whom Anna had agreed to raise. Dr James Wardell, who'd befriended Marvin the year before, believes that the line 'If you wanna love, you gotta save the babies' was in part prompted by his own specialized work in saving the children of pregnant drug addicts. 'I started the Eleanor Hudson Recovery Program in nineteen-sixty-nine and we have the highest salvage rate in the country,' he says. 'He loved children and he was very interested in the work I was doing, and would ask lots of questions about it.'

Five years later Marvin said that the song was an attempt to get through to men who had become hard-hearted about the destruction they were bringing on the world through their greed. 'I figured that the only object I could use was children,' he said. 'Having been a child himself I felt that the hardened man might perhaps say, "Well, I'll save what I have been." I was appealing to feelings of fairness.'

'Mercy, Mercy Me (The Ecology)' was the only song written unaided by Marvin, and it fused the familiar gospel refrain with a contemporary rebuke about the state of the land, sea and sky. Environmentalism was only just reaching the public consciousness and it had barely been mentioned in pop before. 'Berry Gordy didn't understand the word "ecology"',' Earl Van Dyke once remembered. 'It had to be explained to him.'

'Right On', written with conga player Earl DeRouen, was a funky version of the Sermon on the Mount, which reiterated Marvin's fundamental belief that only love can defeat hate. As with his other songs on the theme, he distanced himself from the counter-culture by stressing the 'Love for God' along with 'Love for your brother'. 'Right On' was the final song chosen for the album. 'After we accepted that,' he said, 'we closed the album off.'

Other songs were written during the period that weren't chosen but, as their titles suggest, they were similar in outlook: 'Product Of Society', 'Solidarity' and 'Word Power', written with Obie Benson, and 'Ghetto Soldier', 'Respect Due' and 'When I Get To Heaven', written with James Nyx. 'We threw out about ten songs,' says Stover. 'They just didn't fit.'

According to David Van De Pitte the chosen songs were recorded in the sequence in which they appear on the album except for 'God Is Love', which had already appeared as the B side of 'What's Going On'. The rhythm tracks and vocals were all recorded at Hitsville, known as Studio A, and the brass and strings overdubs were done at the larger Studio B, which Motown leased from Ed Wingate's Golden World recording company. The rhythm tracks were all completed in two days, on Friday 19 March and Saturday 20 March. Elgie Stover says that the tapes were then taken to California by Marvin and his personal engineer Steve Smith. 'That's when he added that operatic synthesizer and started using those machines with the high pitches. We were out there to do a film called *Chrome and Hot Leather* which Peter Gunn starred in.'

Because Marvin couldn't read music, Van De Pitte had to write all the lead sheets and suggest new ideas where Marvin had imagined solos that weren't possible on a particular instrument because the notes simply didn't exist. Musicians on the album recall Marvin asking them for the first time to re-create sounds that he could imagine but which he couldn't explain. 'I don't know why, but we couldn't hear what he could hear,' says Louvain Demps, a backing vocalist on the album. 'The things he wanted us to sing, some of them we just couldn't imagine. It was like he had to actually sing it to us before we could understand. He knew exactly what he wanted but we weren't able to pick up on it right away. It's like the notes of a piano—there are some passing tones and they make the whole thing, but if you don't have a real sharp ear you don't understand what it is.' Marvin later told *Crawdaddy* magazine that *What's Going On* was an attempt to unlock areas of music that hadn't been unlocked before, to touch on new dimensions of sound that had previously been unimaginable. 'These can't be the only notes in the world,' he argued. 'There have got to be other notes some place, in some dimension, between the cracks on the piano keys. Why isn't there another horn or another saxophone? Why can't you have five or six saxophones, and another trumpet, or another kind of texture, and different colour?'

'Primarily we worked out the album as we went along,' says Van De Pitte. 'The ideas flowed as we went from tune to tune. Then it became, "Let's hook this one to that one and hook that one to this one." Because of the overall topic of the album the tracks just ran into each other. Everything seemed to fit together naturally.'

For the musicians it was a relief to be working on music that differed from the normal Motown sound. 'It was a total departure from what was happening,' says trumpet player John Trudell. 'It was a milestone in the field of soul and pop.'

'Most of the session musicians came from jazz backgrounds but they never got a chance to play that sort of stuff at Motown,' says Van De Pitte. 'It was mostly pretty square rock 'n' roll type chords. That's all there was. Here we were using some extensions and things like that. It wasn't really far out but it provided a great sense of relief to these guys.'

Louvain Demps remembers the atmosphere in the studio being almost religious. 'I think he was on a spiritual high,' she says. 'If I could talk to him now I think he might tell me that he had been fasting at the time because I know that when you are fasting you are open to God.'

This wouldn't have been at all unusual. Ten years later, when asked by Nelson George about the possibility of doing a similar album for the eighties, Marvin said that a project like that would require 'fasting, feeling, praying . . . lots of prayer'.

It was Marvin's consistent belief that the album was divinely inspired. He once told Smokey Robinson that he wrote the album with God and told a journalist: 'It was a very divine project and God guided me all the way. I don't remember a great deal about it. I can't. I was sort of in another dimension, enwrapped in something, and I don't have a great deal of recollection about the project.'

Even the album's packaging was different from anything he or Motown had ever done before. It was the first Motown album to print the lyrics, and one of the first to credit musicians by name. There was a collage of family photos inside the gatefold sleeve, mainly showing children, and a personal message from Marvin thanking his family and friends for their love and encouragement. He recommended that his listeners embark on a search for God and learn to obey the Ten Commandments in order to combat hatred and evil. He closed the exhortation with a prayer of thanks to Jesus, thereby specifically rooting his spirituality in the Christianity of his childhood. This was a brave thing to do in 1971 and a further indication of Marvin's determination to be his own person.

The cover shot itself was a distinct break from the idealized images of his previous albums, where he had been portrayed either as a lover, a gentleman or a superman. It showed him bearded, the collar of his black patent raincoat turned up, droplets of rain resting in the tight curls of his hair. The subliminal message was: Take me as I am. Trust me. This is the truth about who I am. This is what's going on.

'That picture was taken in his back yard on West Outer Drive,' says

Joe Schaffner. 'It was raining that day and Marvin refused to go to the photographer's studio. So the photographer came on over to the house. Marvin said, "We can do it right here in the house or we can do it outside." The photographer said, "But it's raining." Marvin said, "I don't care. We can do it wherever we want to do it." So he put his coat on and went outside and that became a classic photo. He did things his way and it came out all right.'

Berry was initially cautious about releasing the album for the same reasons that he had been cautious about 'What's Going On'. It was too unusual for Motown. He told Marvin, 'Don't you understand? Women all over the world love you. You're the sexiest star we've ever had and you're going to ruin all that by doing a protest album? It's not only crazy, it's uncommercial.'

David Van De Pitte believes that it was only pressure from Anna that convinced Berry to release it. 'I think they allowed Marvin to do his own thing assuming that he would be turning up with more of his usual fare,' he says. 'I don't think that they realized that he was such an unhappy camper. What he showed up with made Berry furious. He didn't want to release it but fortunately Anna had a lot of clout.'

Anna recalls Marvin playing her the finished tapes at home and she responded immediately with, 'Baby—that's it!' He asked her what else he could do. 'I told him, nothing. There was nothing more he could do. That was it! I had never heard anything like it.'

Yet, despite Anna's enthusiasm, there was a battle to be fought at Motown. 'Quality Control threw it in the trash,' says Elgie Stover. 'They all thought it was garbage. Marvin had to bet his life to get them to release it. The bet was that Berry would pay Marvin a certain amount of money every day if the album was a hit.'

Marvin was more cautious in his explanation: 'There was not the total confidence in it that most record companies have when they release a project on an artist. This was because it was different and innovative. They felt that they were taking a chance. I used to have spiritual battles with Berry over it. He would come up with an objection and I would say, "God'll take care of it. Trust me," and that sort of thing. I would be telling him all the time and we would have those sort of debates.'

One of the biggest problems for Motown was that the album had been conceived and executed without reference to the powers that be who traditionally monitored every project every step of the way. Marvin had, in effect, become his own A&R director, producer and Quality Control. 'Marvin had departed from the formula that Motown had created for him,' says Beans Bowles. 'They didn't want him to do that. He had been going to local clubs and hearing people like Wild Bill Moore. Everybody always laughed at Wild Bill but, like Duke Ellington had done, Marvin picked people for their mood and sound. He picked things that meant something to him and he put them in the context of this new album.'

'I think that the biggest battle over *What's Going On* was getting Marvin to let go of it,' says Billie Jean Brown. 'None of us heard it. He hid himself away. I think initially Berry tried to talk Marvin out of it but when Marvin refused to change his mind there was no room for reservation. Either it was done or it was not done. Once it went out, Motown was totally behind it.'

Released in May 1971, the album was a critical and commercial hit, the first Motown recording to storm the album charts at a time when albums were beginning to overtake singles both in commercial importance and in cultural significance. Elvis Presley was remembered for his singles, but Led Zeppelin would be remembered for their albums. Singles would now be released as trailers for albums rather than ends in themselves.

What's Going On topped the R&B charts and rose to number six in the pop charts. Reviewers were taken by surprise. 'There are very few performers who could carry a project like this off,' wrote Vince Aletti in *Rolling Stone*. 'I've always admired Marvin Gaye, but I didn't expect that he would be one of them. Guess I seriously underestimated him. It won't happen again.'

The beauty of the album was in its seamlessness, the way that the moods of the songs were contrasted so that the listener was never taken up too high or brought down too low. Despite the intensity of the subject matter—almost all the key issues of the day were referred to, from police violence to nuclear war—it never resorted to posturing or haranguing. The overall effect was uplifting, inspiring and humanizing. Marvin's artistic achievement was to unite the apparently disparate elements of his life and art in one triumphal project. In this recorded series of moments, he resolved the conflict between his radical political instincts and his sanctified church background, between his love for the sweet vocals of the pre-rock 'n' roll era and his knowledge of gutsy R&B, between his appreciation for strings and his love of funk and jazz. Here, also, he resolved the conflict between his desire to be a star and his need to be an artist.

The only important aspect of his life that was not added to the mix was sex. Although he'd been able to look at America's social divisions through the lens of Christian teaching, he lacked the confidence to do the same with his sexuality. Possibly he was worried at what he might discover. His religious understanding, shaped by the House of God, had been dualistic. The Church was separate from the world, religion was separate from politics, gospel was separate from pop and the spirit was separate from the flesh. Slowly, and without the advantage of a wise tutor, he was trying to integrate what had been presented to him as opposing choices.

The House of God, while having no official proclamation on pop music, took the line that all music should be used for obvious praise of God. This did not include praise for things made by God—love, family, nature—or criticisms of ungodly systems. As one elder of the Church put it to me: 'If you do music in the secular arena, who are you praising? Who are you benefiting?'

Marvin must have seen the album as a vindication of his choice to enter show-business. At a time when his father had lost both his congregation and his prophetic gifts, Marvin had gained the ears of the world and was being hailed as a great spiritual voice. *Cashbox* voted him Male Vocalist of the Year while *Billboard* gave him its Trendsetter award.

'Marvin didn't go to church that often because he didn't have a clear conscience,' says Joe Schaffner. 'He felt that if he went it had to be with a purpose and in good faith. He didn't feel his life was very important. He was always trying to please his dad, who was jealous of his success because he'd never had any. I can remember Marvin buying him a new Cadillac, which he enjoyed driving around Washington, but he would never tell his friends and neighbours that Marvin gave it to him.'

Each of the three album tracks released as singles made the Top Ten pop charts and number one in the R&B charts. *What's Going On* looked set to make Marvin serious money, both as a recording artist and as a songwriter. Accolades came in from contemporaries he respected, like Stevie Wonder, Smokey Robinson, Lionel Richie and Barry White.

He had irrevocably changed things at Motown as more and more artists clamoured for control over their output. Stevie Wonder was the first to benefit, being given a new deal that offered him unprecedented creative freedom and higher royalties. His next recording was *Music Of My Mind*, a synthesizer-based album with no obvious singles. 'Stevie gained from that fight,' Marvin said later, 'and the world gained from [Stevie's] genius.'

Marvin basked in the new-found respect and attention, and found his self-confidence being rebuilt. When he heard that Sammy Davis Jr was likely to be signing with one of the Motown labels, he set about writing songs he hoped his hero would record. Inspired by songwriters like Gershwin, he wrote songs that displayed his mood of optimism. He spent $45,000 of his own money on studio time and session musicians to have the backing tracks recorded, but learned later that Motown didn't even pass on the material. 'When you get a lot of pats on the back,' he reflected later, 'it makes you go on these ego trips. I was only the instrument in *What's Going On*. All the inspiration came from God Himself.'

It was a belief he repeated frequently. He felt that the album was wiser and more perfect than he could ever be. His brother Frankie Gay says, 'One of the most profound things that Marvin said to me was that he could learn from his own records. He once said to me, "I'll be learning for a long time because I listen to these words over and over again and I get chills over my body. I know where they come from, but they're not mine." I liked that humility about him.'

10

Reward

Whoso comitteth adultery with a woman lacketh understanding: he that doeth it destroyeth his own soul.

Proverbs 6:32

*W*hat's Going On not only gave Marvin the financial stability and
artistic independence for which he yearned but bestowed on
him a prestige that meant more to him than chart positions. He
was starting to be revered as a significant black figure, able to frater-
nize with civil rights leaders and politicians. The National Association
for the Advancement of Colored People gave him their Image award for
being 'the nation's most socially significant entertainer'. Jesse Jackson
said of him: 'Marvin is as much a minister as any man in a pulpit.' In
January 1972 he was chosen to be the host at the first Martin Luther
King Birthday Commemoration concert in Atlanta, Georgia, but
backed out at the last minute, explaining later that he had 'a psychological hang-up about performing live'. He hoped to be nominated for a
Grammy in 1972, but wasn't. Carole King's *Tapestry* won in the album
category, and Lou Rawls was voted best R&B male vocal performer.

When *Rolling Stone* reporter Ben Fong-Torres visited Marvin at home in February 1972 he found him upset that he'd been overlooked by the Grammys. Although he claimed not to follow chart positions he clearly relished the respect of his peers and various trophies and awards littered his den. 'It's human to get hurt if you feel you deserve something and you don't get it,' he explained. 'I've swept several awards this year but I really want the Grammy. Not that I'm not happy with the others. I'm just . . . cocky . . . or selfish, maybe that's the word.'

The resulting *Rolling Stone* feature, a six-page spread with photographs by Annie Leibovitz, was the first time Marvin had emerged from behind his Motown image. 'He was incredibly relaxed,' remembers Fong-Torres of the interview, which took place over two or three days and included a visit to a gymnasium where Marvin's boxer Tommy Hanna was training. 'For one thing he was stoned, and that helped a bit. He hadn't done any major interviews with the rock press before and I think he felt very much at ease once he realized that I knew his music. He expressed his every fantasy. He didn't yet know how to edit himself. His candour was almost child-like.' He spoke frankly of his experimentation with drugs (alcohol, cigarettes, uppers, downers, heroin, cocaine and marijuana), his religious experiences as a child, his fears as a performer and his premonition that 'in the back of my mind maybe I know that I won't live long'.

The reference to a possible early death was in a rambling and apparently unconnected answer to a question about whether there had been a particular turning point that led to the creation of *What's Going On*. What he seemed to be hinting at was his need to create something that fulfilled his vision of what music could be, before it was too late. Mortality was, in this sense, a spur to creativity.

He spoke to Fong-Torres of an album that he was already working on, which would be his follow-up to *What's Going On*. He said that he had started six months ago because he had so much 'creativity to burn' and that it would be an even more explicit album. His hope was that it would 'lead a million people out of despair'. He even played some of the tracks. Fong-Torres reported that they sounded 'strange' with Marvin singing in a rough tenor voice about travelling a road on one track and sounding like a fifties R&B act gone loony on another. 'I'm just patiently waiting,' Marvin said. 'I'm dangling and saying, "Hey, if you

just give me a chance to do my thing, I can really do something different." They hear it and say, "That's too different," or "You can't do that
because it just isn't done." '

In Washington DC, 1 May 1972 was nominated Marvin Gaye Day,
and Marvin was invited to take part in a day of celebrations that would
start with a reception at his old school, Cardozo High, and culminate in
a gala concert at the Kennedy Center, attended by local dignitaries
including the city's Mayor, Walter Washington. At first Marvin was
reluctant to accept. He felt that Washington DC had done little if anything for his career—all his successful moves had been made outside
the city—and, anyway, he still wasn't happy to fly or to perform on
stage. It was only pressure from his mother that persuaded him to
relent.

The night before, he called Louvain Demps, who would be singing
with him, and poured out all his worries. He said he was anxious about
returning to live performances and they agreed that if he should lose
his nerve in concert he would turn and look at her and everything
would be okay. 'He told me he was afraid,' she says. 'He talked a lot
about God and his feelings. It was like talking to someone who really
knew that there was a God and knew that they were here for a purpose,
but who wasn't sure what that purpose was. When life got hard he ran
away from God instead of running to him. I remember telling him that
the thing he was trying to achieve with drugs he already had it inside
him, but that if he carried on with drugs it would push him so far out
he wouldn't be able to get back.'

His current single was 'You're The Man—Pt. 1', an angry song
about black American poverty. Recorded in March and April, it
sounded as if it could have been from the collection of 'more explicit'
songs that he had discussed with Fong-Torres. An album titled *You're
The Man* was scheduled for release and given a catalogue number
(Tamla 316), but was then cancelled. Marvin explained later that the
long gaps between album projects in the early seventies came as a
result of Motown's internal politics. 'I wasn't motivated,' he told Lon-
don-based DJ Paul Gambaccini. 'My royalty statement didn't motivate
me to do another album.' When Gambaccini suggested that the sales of
What's Going On should have been a motivation, Marvin said, 'My
statement didn't show tremendous sales so it slowed me down for my

next project because I was sitting around incensed, mad and angry. When I get that way I don't do anything. That's my only weapon.'

With the aid of cocaine and marijuana, Marvin made it through Marvin Gaye Day in Washington DC, warning 1,300 gathered students at Cardozo of the dangers of drugs, accepting the key to the city from the Mayor, attending a VIP reception with his mother and father, driving in an open-car motorcade and finally performing the whole of *What's Going On* in concert along with a medley of his sixties hits.

He was to have stayed in Washington for the weekend only, but his old childhood friend Buddy Comedy—who, like Marvin, had become politically radicalized—persuaded him to stay on. For the next few days Comedy, along with his brother, both of whom had been acknowledged in the sleeve notes for *What's Going On*, encouraged him to continue making political statements in his music. 'On that album he was talking to all black people,' says Comedy. 'We could decode what he was saying. We didn't need music critics to explain what Marvin was saying. We knew. But the music business doesn't want a black man talking about what's going on. They want a black man talking about sex. We told Marvin this, and he said it was stuff that he had already been thinking about but no one had called him on it before. He said he had a lot of leeches around him. He offered me a job but I couldn't take it because I knew that my place was at home with my wife and kids. He offered me forty thousand dollars to go on the road with him because he said that he was now surrounded by thieves and that almost everyone he knew wanted something from him.'

In the light of the voice he had found with *What's Going On* his next recording project was a strange choice. He agreed to write and produce the soundtrack for a 20th Century Fox 'blaxploitation' movie called *Trouble Man*, which starred Robert Hooks, a co-founder of the Negro Ensemble Company, as a private eye who helps the poor with his profitable commissions from the underworld. Mostly instrumental, the only words on the album were drawn from black street talk and were a long way removed from the hymn-like lyrics of 'Wholy Holy' or 'God Is Love', although Jesus was acknowledged in the sleeve notes. Composing all the music, and playing much of it on piano and Moog synthesizer, he came up with a work of haunting beauty, which suggested the menace of night in a dangerous city. 'I've had *Trouble Man* within me for a long time,' he said. 'It took a serious piece of negativity to bring it out.' Marvin was riding on the new wave of black self-confidence that had produced *Shaft*, soundtrack by Isaac Hayes, and *Super Fly*, soundtrack by Curtis Mayfield.

Marvin's fascination with the things of the spirit was matched by his curiosity about the strange appeal of the sinful, which was probably strengthened by the prohibitions of his childhood. Friends comment that he was frequently attracted to the weird and bizarre, and although often too frightened to participate, he liked to get a close look. Trouble provided a vicarious thrill. 'Marvin was a good guy but he always liked hoodlums,' says Elgie Stover. 'He liked the golf hustlers and the dope dealers. He liked to be around them and he liked to talk a little slang. He talked like he would like to be a thug but he never could be. He admired them a lot. He wanted to be a gangster but he could never have been a gangster.'

When *Trouble Man* was released in November 1972, Vincent Canby, the film critic of the *New York Times*, noted that there had already been twenty films open that year in New York directed specifically at a black audience. These included *Buck and the Preacher* (black Western), *Sounder* (black social commentary), *Lady Sings the Blues* (black biography) and *Blacula* (black horror). 'I find it difficult to believe,' he concluded, 'that anyone connected with *Trouble Man* believed that the film would do anything else except make money.'

The soundtrack has proved the most enduring part of the project, on sale long after the movie has been forgotten. It gave Marvin a toe-hold in Hollywood, something he had long fantasized about. In the sixties there had been talk of him starring in bio-pics of recently deceased black singers, including Nat 'King' Cole, but nothing ever came of these projects. Similarly his own ideas of a screenplay based on *What's Going On* had come to nothing. The screen appearances he made had been inconclusive. *The Ballad of Andy Crocker* was only shown on TV and his first cinema release, *Chrome and Hot Leather* (March 1971), in which he played a Green Beret who avenges the death of a girl murdered by a gang of bikers, was described by Roger Greenspun of the *New York Times* as 'a stupid motorcycle movie', which had 'absolutely nothing to recommend it'.

All the major Motown stars had now moved out to Los Angeles and while working on *Trouble Man* Marvin had started renting a small apartment at 8850 Cattaraugus Avenue in Culver City, close to the Santa Monica Freeway, but true to his stubborn nature he resisted cutting his ties with Detroit. The city had been good to him and he quite liked the idea of working there now that there was no one left to control him. Yet he realized that to enjoy his success he was going to have to go to California.

The summer of 1972 marked the beginning of his separation from Anna. When his work on the film was over he continued living in Culver City while Anna took a house in Beverly Hills, at 1004 Benedict Canyon Drive. 'That's when the battles began,' says Joe Schaffner. 'It was over what they were going to do, why they were going to do it and how they were going to do it. He didn't really want to do anything and was living this strange life, almost like a hermit.'

Marvin explained the split as a result of Anna's insistence that he shouldn't spread his sexual favours around. 'She was too possessive,' he said. 'I have to be free. She overreacted with jealousy. That tore me up inside. If I had been riddled with guilt I could have understood her reaction. But I don't have a guilt problem.'

Making himself even more evasive, he began to spend time at a cheap hotel in the Crenshaw district of East LA, where he went to escape. He picked up his relationships with former Motown colleagues Mickey Stevenson and Clarence Paul and began socializing with football star Jim Brown. He is remembered as living a relaxed and anonymous lifestyle during this period: partying with ordinary black families in South Central, working out with his boxers Lee Mandingo and Tommy Hanna, playing basketball and football. 'He didn't want to go back on stage,' remembers Dickie Cooper, a songwriter and one-time member of Lionel Hampton's Hamptones who was introduced to Marvin by Clarence Paul. 'He didn't want to be part of the celebrity scene. He used to practise football with my nephew at Hamilton High School just to keep in shape, and he would ride around in the little old red truck which made him look like something out of *Sandford and Son*. He didn't want anyone to know who he was. He was terrified that someone would recognize him and ask him for his autograph.'

Motown, keen to capitalize on the success of *What's Going On*, tried to coax him back into the studio. He only relented after becoming reacquainted with Ed Townsend, a singer and songwriter turned producer who'd had a pop hit in May 1958 with 'For Your Love'. Townsend, who had recorded two albums with the Nelson Riddle Orchestra, had first met Marvin in the sixties when both men were touring performers. He had gone on to produce artists as varied as Brook Benton, Connie Stevens and the Shirelles and his song catalogue, which dated back to 1948, contained over a hundred songs. 'I had written a song and a friend of mine, Larry Clayborne, had mentioned me to Marvin, and Marvin had said that he'd really like to see me again,' says Townsend, who at that time was living in New York State. 'I went to Marvin's apartment in Culver City and I played him several of my songs, including "Let's Get It On", "Please Don't Stay" and "If I Should Die Tonight", on a piano that he had standing by his bed. He then told me that he would sing these songs if I would agree to produce him. I told him that if he meant it he should call Motown and tell them that that's what he wanted to do. So he picked up the phone and spoke to Ewart Abner, the new President of Motown Records, whom I had first met when he was with Veejay Records, and he said he thought it would be a great marriage.'

The album, which Marvin began recording in February 1973 at MoWest Studios in Los Angeles, was an unexpected departure both from *What's Going On* and from *Trouble Man*. Drawing its energy from the raunchy title track, it would become one of the most erotic and seductive albums of the pop era, an opera of bedroom delights. The coyness of the Tammi and Marvin days was stripped away to reveal the spectrum of sexual passion from the moral anxiety of 'Just To Keep You Satisfied' to the freakish pleasures of 'Come Get To This'. 'It wasn't planned as a thematic album,' says Townsend. 'It just happened. I had this thing I used to say to Marvin which was "Keep your hand on the tit and the clit and you've got a hit!" He would laugh about it and yet he understood what I was saying. You write about something erotic and sexual and people will buy it. He never seemed at all cautious about going in this direction.'

Townsend had written 'Let's Get It On' as a recovering alcoholic just out of a rehabilitation centre. 'To me the song was more about the business of getting on with life than it was about the sexual side,' he says. 'It finally took the form of a sexual song because Marvin could take the "Star Spangled Banner" and make it sound like it meant "let's go to bed".'

To Marvin the title alone was 'a smash' but what eventually catalysed its erotic potential was the arrival in the studio of Janis Hunter, the teenage daughter of an old friend of Townsend. A beautiful coffee-skinned girl with large eyes and a nose covered in freckles, she fell instantly in love with Marvin and he recognized her as the girl of his dreams. The product of a short-lived affair between an Irish-American girl, Barbara Hunter, and the Cuban jazz musician Slim Gaillard, Jan had been raised in the Fairfax district of Los Angeles by her mother and her stepfather, Earl Hunter. When she met Marvin she had only just turned seventeen and was still at high school.

'Jan just sat there and Marvin liked what he saw,' remembers Townsend. 'She was a very attractive girl and she liked him and he liked her. I told him, "If you take her home you must go by and ask her mother if you want to take her out.' "

He did ask her mother, and he did take her out. Over the coming weeks the mutual attraction developed into a love affair, the repercussions of which were felt on almost every song on the album. Even though some of the songs had already been written, they were reinterpreted in the light of his new relationship. He was now dedicating his art to her. 'If I Should Die Tonight' had been written about a movie star whom Townsend had once idolized and then met. 'Originally Marvin had told me that he could never sing that song because he had never felt that way,' he says. 'Then, after he had met Jan he said, "Ed. You know that song? I can sing it now.' "

'Keep Gettin' It On', extracted from a spontaneous ten-minute improvisation, contained ad libs directed at Jan, and his own songs, like 'Come Get To This' and 'You Sure Love To Ball', were unabashed celebrations of the fresh sexual excitement in his life. 'All of the songs are sex songs actually,' he told Dennis Hunt of the *Los Angeles Times*. 'They're not love songs.'

'He'd just come out of *What's Going On* and was recognized as this guru, this master of thought, this spiritual being, and then he turns up with 'You Sure Love To Ball' and people really didn't understand,' says Jan. 'A lot of it had to do with us meeting and exploring each other. There's no way of knowing whether that album ever would have come out in the way it did if he and I hadn't had the kind of relationship we had.

'He had shocked people with *What's Going On*, and with something that he was very fascinated by—sex—he shocked the world again. The album said things that he had always wanted to say that were taboo, they were things you weren't supposed to put on a record. I think that for years he fought these things and then finally said, "Fuck it, I'm gonna sing about the things I want to.' "

Although he sang his erotic songs with confidence, the album's sleeve notes were an apologetic defence of loveless sex. In them he argued that although sex and love worked together well, they could also be totally divorced from each other. Sex didn't require love to validate it, just as love didn't require sex. If two adults agreed to get it on with each other, he couldn't see why any fuss should be made about it. The fact that he felt the need to add this explanation suggests that he harboured traces of guilt. In the lyric of 'Let's Get It On', he reassures his partner that if the spirit moves them to have sex, then there's no need to worry about whether it's right or wrong. It sounded like a justification of his adultery on the grounds that the spirit isn't bound by laws.

Jan was different from Anna in almost every way. She was thirty-four years younger for a start, inexperienced in the ways of the world, in awe of celebrities and willing to bend to Marvin's every whim. Where Anna fought back and often humiliated him, Jan was adoring and obedient. She was, he felt, an appropriate trophy for him at this time in his life.

'I considered myself a child at the time,' says Jan. 'Our relationship personified this thing he had about exploring the forbidden. He was drawn to danger. I was a total babe in the woods. I didn't know what was going on. It was try this, try that. I'm gonna take you here. I'm gonna take you there. My whole life changed and it's never been the same.'

The major obstacles right from the start were the age gap and the fact that Marvin was still married. The ramifications of an open affair were, initially, too horrendous to contemplate. As the album built, the intensity of his feelings for Jan became obvious to everyone in the studio. The songs all appeared to be soul-wrenching confessions of utter devotion and the underlying fear of eventual loss. The one song that referred to Anna, 'Just To Keep You Satisfied', was a farewell song, which mentioned her jealousy and their arguments. Appropriately it was the final song on the album.

Dickie Cooper remembers that Marvin was concerned about the immensity of the decision that he knew he was going to have to make. 'I can remember him sitting on a couch in his apartment and asking my advice,' he says. 'He said, "Dickie. What do you think about a man who is thirty-four years old who falls in love with a girl who is only seventeen?" I said, "Are you talking about you and Jan?" He just laid back and burst out laughing. He was talking about himself in the third person.'

By the time *Let's Get It On* came out, in August 1973, Jan had dropped out of high school and was living with Marvin in his $160-a-month apartment in Culver City. The album climbed to second place in the pop charts and the single reached the top spot in both the pop and R&B charts. The success seemed to confer a blessing on the relationship.

'Marvin went into seclusion at that point and Jan was the only person that he was seeing,' says Joe Schaffner. 'It was a relationship which grew out of anger and pain. She was a young girl and able to do things for him that an older person couldn't do. She made him feel a certain way. From that, love grew. They were very close and very united.'

In September 1973, Motown advertised the success of *Let's Get It On* with a billboard on Sunset Strip, which announced that the album had sold over a million copies during its first month of sale. Bill Murry happened to be working with Edwin Starr at the Whiskey A Go-Go and noticed the sign. 'I ran into Marvin in Hollywood the next day,' says Murry. 'Marvin was a bit troubled because he asked me if he could borrow some money. I said, "Marvin. You've got a million-seller. You should be lending me some money!" He asked me what I meant and I told him about the billboard. Well, he got in his Jeep and drove up there, saw the sign, went to Motown and requested a million-dollar advance as part of a renegotiated deal. The next thing was, he bought himself a recreational vehicle and no one saw anything of him for weeks.'

In November an album of duets with Diana Ross, which he had

recorded while working on *Let's Get It On*, was released. It seemed a backward step after all the groundbreaking work of *What's Going On* but Marvin saw it as a way of appeasing Berry Gordy and consolidating his power with the company.

There was never any great love between Diana Ross and Marvin, although they both admired each other's voice. Their working methods were so different—Marvin liked to smoke dope in the studio and lie on a couch while singing—that the album's vocals ended up being recorded separately. Marvin told Jan that she didn't need to fear that he'd have an affair with Diana because he found her 'too skinny'.

Early in 1974, after Jan had had a miscarriage, Marvin bought a home for them on Everding Road high in Topanga Canyon, a rugged, isolated part of the Santa Monica mountains. The A-frame house stood on the crest of a hill and the only approach to it was from a dirt track. He loved the idea of anonymity and of being surrounded by raw nature. It was here that he planned to deepen his relationship with Jan, away from the prying eyes of the media. He loved waking up to the sight of trees, rocks and the distant blue of the Pacific Ocean, and drew artistic inspiration from the untouched world around him. 'Early in the morning he used to like to turn on his reel-to-reel tape-recorder and record the birds singing,' says Dickie Cooper. 'He told me that he could get ideas for melodies from the sounds of birds singing.'

He began work on an album with the arranger of *What's Going On*, David Van De Pitte, this time with Van De Pitte co-writing and co-producing most of the tracks. They worked on the songs side by side on the piano and Marvin sketched out the lyrics. 'It had a similar feel to *What's Going On* but it wasn't hinged together with a single theme,' says Van De Pitte. 'It was very jazzy and we had people like Herbie Hancock playing on it, but before we had time to do the vocals Marvin just disappeared in his camper. He went off into the desert unexpectedly and announced that he wasn't going to finish it. So the album was never titled and was just shelved.

'Motown were upset at Marvin because they needed product from him. They had called me out to California and put me up for at least two months specifically to get it done. It cost them a fortune and they never got anything back for it.'

Marvin knew that he was going to have to face up to his fear of performing. Professionally and economically it made no sense for him to sit at home while his albums sold in their millions. Touring would raise fresh revenue as well as stimulate album sales. Jan encouraged him to think about going back on the road. 'He absolutely hated performing at that time,' says Elaine Jesmer, who was continuing to work for him as a publicist on a freelance basis. 'He was essentially shy and going out on stage was like murder for him. He didn't even like promoting his records. He did interviews, and I would make sure he turned up on time for them, but everything was done grudgingly.'

Candidly, Marvin explained to the journalist Dennis Hunt his horror of getting up in front of a crowd. 'Part of it is a crazy ego thing,' he admitted. 'I want to be liked and I would hate it—I mean really hate it—if the audience didn't like me. It's really a hang-up.'

The concert that heralded his comeback as a touring act was mounted at the 14,000-seater Oakland Coliseum on 4 January 1974, with a band that contained Crusaders Joe Sample and Wilton Felder, Motown bassist James Jamerson and a forty-six-piece orchestra. Ashford and Simpson, the writers and producers of his great hits with Tammi Terrell, opened the show. It was during this evening, recorded as the album *Marvin Gaye Live*, that he made his first public declaration of love for Jan when he dedicated a newly written song ('Jan') to her, explaining that she had asked him to write it for her and referring to her as 'darling'. What had for almost a year been a private affair became public knowledge in an instant.

In his own mind he had to justify his behaviour. Just three years before he had been the great family man and spiritual leader. Now he was an adulterer and producer of erotic music. 'People are supposed to say, "If he's giving up the Supreme Goodie, then he must be a good man," he told *Rolling Stone* reporter Tim Cahill after the Oakland concert. 'Why shouldn't a religious man have the Supreme Goodie and be an even greater man?'

It wasn't long after the Oakland comeback that Jan discovered she was pregnant again. Although Anna had been separated from Marvin for almost eighteen months she now felt publicly humiliated. After all, they were still legally married and Marvin had a son for whom he was responsible. On 1 April she had a preliminary half-hour meeting with Louis Blau at the Wilshire Boulevard law offices of Loeb and Loeb to discuss divorce.

In May 1974 Marvin went to Kingston, Jamaica, and played two benefit concerts for the Trench Town sports complex, the first of which, at the Carib Theater, had Bob Marley and the Wailers as his support act. The invitation had come from Stephen Hill, a well-known Jamaican impresario who'd been bringing American acts to the Caribbean since the fifties. Marley was such a storming success with his home crowd that Marvin worried that he would be an impossible act to follow. Stephen Hill's son, also called Stephen, remembers Motown's Ewart Abner approaching him in the foyer and asking him to get Marley off stage or risk a cancellation. 'I told him, "Abner, if you want to take him off, you can do it. But I ain't gonna do it. They'd kill me,' " he says. 'I think Marvin was a little nervous because Bob was going down so well and if you haven't played for a long time you don't want to be going on after somebody has really got the audience all worked up.'

A well-educated and well-spoken man, Stephen Hill Sr made an impression on Marvin and was invited to be his manager as he relaunched his career. Hill moved out to Tarzana, California, and set about re-establishing Marvin as a live performer. Three months later Marvin embarked on his first tour of the decade, a twenty-city tour with a band, backing singers, dancers and a twenty-piece orchestra. During the tour, on 4 September, Nona Aisha Gaye was born in Washington DC. It almost caused Marvin to cut short the tour, but he held on until it finished in November, when the family reunited and moved into an apartment at 612 South Barrington Avenue in Brentwood.

While on the road Marvin had read *Number One With A Bullet*, a novel written by Elaine Jesmer which had used him as the model for the central character, Daniel Stone. Jesmer had used her experience of working with Motown to create the story of Finest Records, run by the powerful Bob Vale. The book's stories of lesbianism, adultery, greed, drug-taking and corruption got the reading public guessing who was who and spurred Motown into hiring America's leading libel lawyer to try to prevent its publication. When the screen rights were bought up by Paramount, Motown also tried to prevent it ever being made into a film. 'Motown went nuts,' says Jesmer. 'They killed the movie and I think that they bought up a whole lot of copies of the book.' Although Marvin never again spoke to Jesmer, he was quietly proud of his fictional counterpart, his only complaint being that the novel didn't go far enough.

Now that Marvin was with the woman that he loved and had a good home in an affluent part of Los Angeles it seemed that everything was at last going well for him. He was enjoying good sales and critical success, and he had control over his own career.

11

The Central Crisis

He that trusteth in his riches shall fall.

Proverbs 11:28

In November 1974, *Ebony* magazine ran a story on Marvin and printed a photograph of him with Jan. Slim Gaillard saw it, called his son Mark in San Francisco and urged him to check it out. Mark Gaillard had never met his half-sister. 'When I saw the picture of Jan I realized that she looked exactly like my own sister,' says Mark Gaillard. 'I contacted her through Motown and then, quite soon afterwards, we all met up and had a real good time. Eventually Marvin invited me to move down to LA, where he'd just become the owner of a new studio.'

The Marvin Gaye Recording Studio, at 6553 Sunset Boulevard, had been purchased for Marvin's company, Righton Productions, as an advance on future royalties. Custom-built with dark wood panelling, the studio had its own jacuzzi and a private apartment with a king-size waterbed. Mark Gaillard was hired to manage the building, help out on recording sessions and keep undesirables away. 'He had an accountant who found out that he was owed some more money by Motown,' says Gaillard. 'Rather than give him the money Motown decided to buy him a recording studio. They probably figured that if anything went wrong it was easier to repossess a studio than to try and recoup cash, plus, if he had a studio of his own, it would be easier for them to get him to record.'

It was becoming increasingly urgent for Motown that Marvin record new material. In five years he had produced only two albums of original songs in the studio, and with the reduced commercial clout of such Motown stalwarts as the Four Tops and the Temptations, along with the break-up of the Miracles and the Supremes, Marvin was becoming an even more vital asset to them. After the débâcle with David Van De Pitte, Motown was cautious about putting Marvin with another songwriter or producer, yet recognized that he seemed to work better when stimulated by a co-worker. Then Berry Gordy heard a track called 'I Want You', written by Leon Ware and Diana Ross's brother Fred 'T-Boy' Ross, and became convinced that Marvin could do something with it.

Ware and Ross had written it as part of an album they were hoping Motown would release but were happy if Marvin wanted to cover the title track. Marvin heard the whole album, was captivated by the sound and the sentiment, and invited Ware over to Brentwood, where he made him an offer he couldn't refuse. He told him that if he let him record 'I Want You', he could be the album's songwriter. Ware cleaned his own vocals from the tapes and prepared himself to produce Marvin. 'We took my voice off and put Marvin's voice on it along with his spirit,' says Ware. 'The lyrics were already very sensual but Marvin would often change them as he was recording. He brought his own attitude to the songs. Fate had brought us together.'

I Want You took Marvin deeper into the erotic territory he'd already touched on in *Let's Get It On*, but this time there was no attempt to dress it up in an apology for righteous sexuality. There was no evocation of the language of the House of God and no message of gratitude to Jesus in the sleeve notes. 'I didn't know where to take the album conceptually but found that the music lent itself to sex more than any other subject,' said Marvin. 'Really, that was the only reason for tainting it in a sexual way. There had been a couple of other possibilities but I had exhausted them.'

With *Let's Get It On* there had been a half-hearted attempt to synchronize his desires with his sense of what would be spiritually appropriate, but now he appeared resigned to abandoning himself to his passions. As Leon Ware summarizes: 'The message of the album was—make love to everyone you see. That was it, in so many words.'

An important factor in his change was Marvin's consumption of cocaine, which had increased on his 1974 tour and was supplemented with alcohol and marijuana. The conscience that had continued to prick him since childhood was becoming blunted. 'He knew that his only salvation was through God,' says Jan. 'He knew that he should be a good man but it became increasingly difficult for him to separate the good Marvin from the bad Marvin. In his heart of hearts he knew what was right and what was wrong but when you use cocaine you get taken to a place where you don't need to go, and once you feel that it has conquered your heart and your mind and your soul it's as if you give in. You say, "Fuck it. I'm just gonna do what I want to do. However bad it is, however bad it makes my family feel, I'm just gonna go there.' "

His New Age beliefs led him to conclude that he was part of an élite who were evolving towards a higher consciousness and who would escape the eventual destruction that was to overtake mankind. He had plans, he told *Rolling Stone*, to develop a device that, when combined with music, would help people to get to know themselves better. 'He was into biofeedback, visualization, pyramids, vegetarianism and everything else that was going,' says Jan. 'He would walk around with this big brass pyramid on his head. I thought it was the most bizarre thing and he just laughed and said that one day I would understand.'

His increased drug use didn't require him to cut down on his sporting activities. During the fourteen months that he worked on *I Want You* his typical day would begin late in the morning or early in the afternoon with vigorous games of basketball followed by recording from early evening until one or two in the morning. 'We were in and out of the studio at the same time,' remembers Ware. 'We played games in the studio, made music in the studio, made love in the studio, ate in the studio and celebrated our birthdays in the studio. We lived in the studio. It was one of those things where you were doing it and it was doing you at the same time.'

Cocaine was as available as candy to Marvin and he revelled in the temporary bliss that it brought him. 'He would have pieces of the stuff as big as baseballs,' says Gaillard. 'I didn't realize then that Jan was heavily into it until people started saying to me, "Well, you know what your sister's doing, don't you?" Then I realized what was happening. I realized why she was failing to make appointments. Taking cocaine was becoming a full-time job to them.'

At the same time Marvin was beginning to draw an increasing number of disreputable people into his circle of friends, another form of dangerous liaison that fascinated and excited him. He liked being around drug pushers, hookers, gangsters, con-men and people with prison records. 'Marvin would be afraid of people he could trust,' says Gaillard. 'He would lean towards shifty people who might take advantage of him. He would buddy with these types rather than straight-ahead people and I think that this probably had its roots in his childhood where he was abused by his father. My feeling was that he had been abused so much that he wanted to be abused even more. I guess, in a negative sense, it made him feel at home.'

However unconventional his life was becoming, though, it didn't affect his ability as a singer. *I Want You* was a consummate performance, with his voice effortlessly intertwining with the layers of backing vocals to build up a tapestry of sound. As usual, all of the vocals were laid down as he sat at the mixing desk or sprawled on a couch. The casual nature of his approach can be heard at the beginning of 'Feel All My Love Inside', where he can be heard asking Jan to get him a joint and a bottle of wine.

Vocally, he was breaking new ground by building layers of background and counterpointing vocal lines. Joe Schaffner believes that in using this technique he was able to replicate the state of consciousness where thoughts contradict or expand on spoken words. 'It's like we can say something with our lips but in our mind we're thinking something else,' he says. 'Marvin's vocals were like that. He would be saying one thing but what he was actually thinking would often be in the voices in the background.'

The four songs on the album for which Marvin contributed to the lyric—'Feel All My Love Inside', 'Since I Had You', 'Soon I'll Be Loving You Again' and 'After The Dance'—had none of the tenderness of his earlier love songs. Their message was essentially 'I want you because you make me feel good', and there was an added air of impatience. It was as though Marvin couldn't wait to get his trousers off.

Jan was in the studio for much of the recording, flattered to be the object of Marvin's attention but embarrassed by the frankness of his lyrics, that promised her cunnilingus, perversions and thrice-daily sex and told the world how much he enjoyed listening to orgasmic moaning and seeing her walk around naked. It was the age of disco and acts like Donna Summer and Barry White were heating up the dance floor with more and more explicit utterings and orgasmic sounds. Marvin wasn't going to be left behind. His persona throughout *I Want You* was erotically confident, virile, experienced and powerful. He was 'Big Daddy Rucker' and he was going to put his baby 'through some paces'.

'After we met, the emphasis of his work shifted away from the social awareness of *What's Going On* and focused on sex,' says Jan. 'He went from *Let's Get It On* to *I Want You* to 'Sexual Healing' to a song that was originally called 'Sanctified Pussy'. I think that was his way of confronting the feelings he held inside about sex and sin because he knew what was right and wrong. I think there was something at the back of his mind where he thought he would change and he could change people, but in another way he revelled in what he knew to be wrong.'

The period during which *I Want You* was recorded coincided with Anna, who had recently moved from Beverly Hills to 2745 Outpost Drive in Hollywood, filing for divorce after a year of discussion with her lawyers. The case was formally lodged on 26 March 1975 and Anna was asking for $11,000 a month in support for herself and Little Marvin, a $7,500 payment for outstanding house bills—roofing, electronic security—$25,000 in legal fees and $1,000 for her accountant. She told the court that she expected Marvin to argue that he couldn't meet this demand because he had been embezzled by 'certain dishonest business associates' but that this should be investigated. Sure enough, Marvin did claim relative poverty. In a declaration made on 18 June he estimated his monthly income as $20,000, reduced to just over $6,000 when taxes and insurance were deducted. Additionally he claimed that his monthly expenses were $16,850.

Loeb and Loeb hired a music-industry expert, Phil Ames, to investigate his income from the various publishing, performing, producing and recording sources. His findings led them to conclude that Marvin was capable of earning at least a million dollars a year. They pointed out that whereas his personal income might have only been $240,000 a year, Righton Productions had received $1,800,000 in the fiscal year ending 1975, with touring expenses of $600,000. The company, of which Marvin was the sole director, also listed fourteen automobiles among its assets.

However, Marvin was determined not to give anything away. He failed to show up for court appearances on 15 April, 15 May and 20 June, so on 23 June custody of his son was awarded to Anna, and Marvin was ordered to begin paying child support of $500 per month and spousal support of $5,000 per month. The demand was served on him on 24 June.

By 16 August he still hadn't paid a cent, and during a stormy meeting at Anna's new home he told her, 'Baby, there isn't any court that's going to tell me what to do. I'm not going to obey any court order, no matter what they try to do to me. The only thing I'm going to do is take off my hat when I enter the court room. Other than that, I am doing nothing.'

She accused him of depositing $21,000 of royalty cheques made payable to her into his personal account and he finally made a cheque out to her for $6,000, which barely covered half her legal fees and paid nothing towards support.

On 29 August he was again ordered to court for non-payment. This time, when he failed to turn up on 23 September, the court sentenced him to five days in the county jail unless he paid up within the next thirty days. Pushing it to the limit, as always, he finally handed $15,000 to a sheriff's agent on 21 October.

On 16 November in Los Angeles, Jan gave birth to Frankie Christian Gaye, known to family and friends as Bubby. On 28 November Marvin shaved off his beard and all his body hair as a protest against the imprisonment of the boxer Rubin 'Hurricane' Carter, a cause that had also been picked up by Bob Dylan. 'He looked like a sausage,' says Jan. 'I don't know what effect he thought it would have.'

The next night he performed a charity concert at the Cow Palace in San Francisco for the Rev. Cecil Williams and his Glide Memorial Church. He scared promotor Bill Graham by not turning up until the first set, by Quincy Jones, was almost over. Instead of staying in the hotel that had been booked for him the night before, he had chosen to sleep in his camper van.

By now Loeb and Loeb had discovered that he was guaranteed $307,000 for every album that he recorded for Motown, regardless of future sales. He also had over $100,000 waiting for him in royalties from Jobete Publishing. He spent his money recklessly. He had already moved his parents from Washington DC, buying them a large house in the Crenshaw district of Los Angeles, and bought himself and Jan a 5-acre ranch-style home at 23847 Long Valley Road in Hidden Hills, which had a swimming pool, hot tubs, stables for black Arab stallions and a full-size basketball court.

Over the next two years he bought himself more properties and toys. On the advice of Stephen Hill, he bought sea-front real estate between Ochos Rios and Discovery Bay in Jamaica. He also bought a 360-acre ranch in Redding, Upper California, and property in Lake Tahoe, Nevada. Through Righton Productions, he added a 1974 Mercedes Benz 450 SL, a 1974 Chevrolet Malibu station wagon, a 1975 Cadillac convertible and a 1975 Mercedes Benz 450 SL to a car collection that already included a 1955 Mercedes Benz 220 convertible, a 1965 Rolls Royce and a 1966 Jaguar. He also bought a speed-boat and a cabin-cruiser. 'There was plenty of money around then and he started buying up all sorts of cars,' says Mark Gaillard. 'We would drive up to Redding in his brand-new FMC motor-home and play around like little kids. He had tractors, trailers, Big Mac trucks and army trucks. We used to drive around and have a ball. There were lots of parties, lots of fun.'

I Want You was released in March 1976 and sold well, despite some cool reviews. 'The sweet nothings of a drowsy, sweat-streaked lover' was the *New Musical Express*'s rather dismissive comment on what it saw as yet another album of erotic fantasies. A million copies shipped in America alone took it to the top of the R&B charts and to number four in the pop charts. As a single the title track similarly topped the R&B charts and made number fifteen in the pop charts.

In many respects it was a good time for Marvin, but the events that would eventually destroy him were beginning to take shape. He had been failing to pay his taxes and was already $165,000 in debt to the

Internal Revenue Service. As with most things in his life, this was due in part to his ideals—he didn't believe in helping to finance the US military—and in part to his lethargy and irresponsibility. 'He was already having tax troubles when he was living in Detroit,' says Taylor Cox. 'He just didn't fill in any of the forms he was sent. He hated taxes. He felt that they were morally unfair. You can hear it in a song like "Inner City Blues", when he referred to not being able to pay his taxes.'

Despite his hatred of playing live he now needed to tour to plug the holes in his bank account. In ten years his concert fee had jumped from around $5,000 a show to $25,000. He toured America in the summer, with Harold Melvin and the Bluenotes as his support act (the lead singer being a young Theodore 'Teddy' Pendergrass), and arranged for British promoter Jeffrey Kruger to mount his first-ever tour of Britain, which he tried later to postpone, initially by saying that he was under-rehearsed and then by arguing that he didn't want to put additional demand on Britain's dwindling water reserves after the recent severe summer drought. The European tour, which included dates in Paris and Amsterdam, finally got under way on 27 September 1976 at London's Royal Albert Hall. It received only minimal support from Motown, who were by now exasperated by their notoriously difficult artist. 'Stephen Hill felt that word had come down from on high that Marvin was not to be given the red-carpet treatment,' says Kruger. 'Motown only ordered one box at the Albert Hall and wouldn't contribute to the cost of the airport limousine.' Marvin responded by banning some of Motown's key London executives from the backstage area.

At the instigation of Hill and Kruger, the Amsterdam concert was filmed and an additional London show, mounted at the Palladium in Argyll Street, was recorded for possible release as an album, with Kruger getting a production royalty. The TV show, to be made by Dutch television, would be co-distributed by Kruger and Righton Productions.

During a much-delayed interview with *NME* at his hotel in Knightsbridge, Marvin confessed to being stoned and rambled confessionally over a number of topics, including his feelings that *I Want You* was a sub-standard album that he'd given to Motown because they weren't treating him right. 'I had no plans to produce anything on it myself because ninety per cent of the time, when I get mad I get very unproductive,' he told journalist Cliff White. 'They [Motown] keep me mad at them all the time by not treating me properly. I'm like a fine racehorse, but they won't treat me like a racehorse. At least a racehorse gets a rub-down after a race. I don't even get that.'

To disc jockey Paul Gambaccini he again displayed his displeasure with Motown, claiming that he had been manipulated as an artist and that he hadn't received the royalties he deserved for *What's Going On* and *Let's Get It On*. When Gambaccini asked him why Berry had been bad to him, Marvin giggled. 'Never did I suggest that! Where did you get that? Motown did that to me. I'm sure that there is a difference. There must be!' Throughout the interview he implied that he didn't give his best to the company because he wasn't rewarded well. 'Does this suggest that you are waiting to record for another company?' Gambaccini asked. 'No,' Marvin replied. 'It suggests that I am waiting for them to treat me with proper respect.'

While in London he continued to spend money with no regard for his impending financial problems, buying the best cocaine on the market and shopping for exotic antiques, which were then shipped back to America. The tour had been expected to net him £100,000 but by the time it had ended, Marvin had already over-spent. He attended society parties at which he delighted the British upper classes with his easy-going manner and his ability to spin wonderful tales. He even bought himself a shooting jacket and a pair of plus-fours and spent a weekend on a pheasant shoot at the country estate of City property dealer Jack Dellal. Unfortunately, being so stoned, he wasn't able to shoot accurately and didn't bag a single bird.

Marvin and Stephen Hill stayed on at the exclusive Hyatt Carlton Tower Hotel in Cadogan Place, racking up a bill of £6,540, which they assumed that Kruger would take care of. 'It became quite obvious that unless I was prepared to pay the bill they wouldn't be able to leave England without the stigma of legal action,' says Kruger. 'I paid it and Stephen Hill assured me that it wouldn't go unnoticed by Marvin and that it would stand me in good stead for the next tour.'

In March 1977, just as 'Got To Give It Up', his first disco-style single, made it to number one in both the pop and R&B charts, his divorce from Anna became final. For a long time the problem had been getting a settlement from Marvin. Since early 1976 she had been demanding the appointment of a receiver, who would have the power to deduct payments directly from Jobete and Motown. Marvin had now changed lawyers, ditching Harold Gutenberg of Diamond, Tilem, Colden and Emery in favour of Curtis Shaw, recommended by his drummer Bugsy Wilcox. Shaw went straight into action. Marvin's property at Hidden Hills had been seized and offered for sale by auction but he had the sale withdrawn after Marvin made a payment of $15,000 against the mounting arrears. He then devised a plan whereby Anna would be paid $600,000, which would be split between the advance for his next album ($307,000) and the first $293,000 of the profits. In effect, Marvin was going to give her his follow-up album to *I Want You*, although he would retain the publishing rights. He was to pay the requested spousal support until he secured the advance, and would have to make up the difference if the profits didn't reach $293,000 within a two-year period.

It wasn't clear how much Anna really needed the money. In her original declaration she had stated that, 'Other than a very limited amount of capital, and the equity in the family home, I have no funds or sources of income whatsoever.' Her spending habits, though, remained those of a rich woman: $1,500 a month on clothes and $280 a month on beauty products. Marvin, however, claimed that she had undeclared properties, that she owned 3067 West Outer Drive in Detroit and a nearby house at 19315 Appoline. She also had a multi-millionaire brother and a close-knit family who were unlikely to let her starve. That, though, had no bearing on this case: the key issue was not money but the humiliation that Marvin had caused her in living with Jan and allowing her to have his children. 'You can't just walk out of rich folks' lives,' says Elgie Stover, who was still working for Anna. 'Marvin had hurt her pride. She had been known to be his wife. He had left her to live with a girl who was thirty-four years younger than her. She wasn't going to have her pride hurt like that without it costing. She also got hold of Marvin's legacy. Jan didn't get the legacy.'

Curtis Shaw affirms that it was a matter of dignity on Anna's part. Although they had been living separately, she couldn't stand the way that he was openly flaunting his relationship with Jan, and the two children were the final straw. 'Anna just freaked out at that point,' says

Shaw. 'They had been married for about twelve years so it made things a little rough. To tell you the truth, I don't think that Marvin would ever have filed. I don't care if he was living with Jan. He wouldn't have filed for divorce.'

Mischievously, Marvin turned the alimony album into an open letter to his wife, detailing the bliss and subsequent turmoil of their relationship. *Here, My Dear* was a concept album of divorce, probably his most honest and certainly his most confessional recording. He used the bad blood between them to spoil the spirit of the agreement but, being the person he was, he couldn't help creating a work of poignant self-disclosure. 'I sang and sang until I drained myself of everything I'd lived through,' he said. 'That took me three months but then I held back the album for over a year. I was afraid to let it go.'

'He didn't record that album reluctantly,' says Nolan Smith, his musical director at the time. 'It was total creativity. The only difference was that the lyrical content was, shall we say?, vicious. It wasn't a love album. He wasn't expecting any hits.'

'You get his whole life story through his albums,' says his brother Frankie. 'If you want to know about his relationship with Anna, you only have to listen to *Here, My Dear*. Marvin had thought, "I'll give her my next album but it'll be something she won't want to play and it'll be something she won't want the world to hear because I'm gonna tell the truth." If you listen very closely to *Here, My Dear* you'll understand the pain and the love. You'll understand how serious he was and how deep he went. Everything is in that record.'

Over thirteen tracks Marvin unloaded his gripes as well as his tender feelings, and managed to portray himself as a well-intentioned but wounded lover. Knowing of his own unfaithfulness, it must have pained Anna to hear herself accused of lying to God by breaking her marriage vows. She maintained her dignity, though. She wasn't going to get involved in a public slagging match.

The cover showed Marvin as a Roman statue, the city crumbling around him. Inside there was a Monopoly-style board game with a male hand passing a record to a female hand. On his side of the board the man has only his piano and recording equipment. The woman has money, a house, a car and a diamond ring. The word JUDGMENT is emblazoned across the board. 'There was destruction all around him on the cover, and that's how he felt,' says Mark Gaillard. 'He felt that these people were taking everything from him and he wanted to show it. Motown didn't want the album released at first. They didn't want all that negative stuff about the Gordy family out there.'

(When the album was eventually released in December 1978 Anna told *People* magazine that she was contemplating a $5-million–invasion-of-privacy suit. It was never filed and twenty years later she was able to say of the album, 'When I hear it, I love it more and more.')

In September he started another tour of America, this time with Luther Vandross and the Average White Band as his support acts. Dates were handled by different promoters, but in the South disputes arose between some of the leading black promoters, who felt they hadn't been given what they deserved. In Shreveport, Louisiana, one promoter, Alvin Few, was involved in a brutal fight with another, W. G. Garrison. This frightened Marvin. 'It was one of the worst fist fights I have ever seen,' remembers Gerald White. 'I had to be called out to try and sort it out. Alvin was pissed off because Marvin had given W. G. Garrison five dates and he felt that he should have had more.'

On Monday 10 October 1977, Marvin married Jan at a private house outside of New Orleans before a dozen people and a reception was held in a Baton Rouge club owned by W. G. Garrison. Jan had always wanted them to be married because, as an illegitimate child herself, she didn't want to raise her own children in the same way. Yet, despite this legal bonding, the relationship was already coming apart. One of Marvin's latest sexual fantasies had been for Jan to betray him, and he began to encourage her to fancy other men. He not only enjoyed the perversity of thinking about her giving herself to someone else but calculated that he would be stimulated by the resulting emotional turmoil. As his brother-in-law Mark Gaillard had perceptively observed, Marvin appeared to feel more at home in tumultuous surroundings. Tranquillity made him uneasy.

Jan's first affair was with Frankie Beverly, a young black singer whom she had told Marvin about in 1976 after she had seen him performing in San Francisco at the Scene Club and to whom Marvin had given significant help in his career. The couple took off to the Caribbean on a trip financed with Marvin's money. When news of the betrayal got back to Marvin, one of his bodyguards suggested that

Beverly should be punished for what he'd done, but Marvin rounded on him and said that Jesus had taught us that we should forgive our enemies.

Jan didn't need much encouragement to stray. She was becoming increasingly frustrated with Marvin's attempts to control her. He was now approaching his fortieth birthday and she was only twenty-two. He was happy to spend a lot of time at home and turn his back on celebrityhood, while she was ready to party and experience the thrill of public attention. She had given up her chance of further education to be with him and raise his children. As a result, her earning potential had been drastically reduced. 'I had gotten to a point after my son was born where I wanted a life of my own,' she says. 'I wanted to act. I wanted to model. I wanted to be a singer. Marvin, after having been controlled for so many years, was turning the tables by controlling me. It was a constant battle between us as to whether I was going to have a life of my own or whether I was just going to be a part of his life. To be honest I had jealousies. I wanted to do the things that he did. I would look and see the recognition he got and the creative outlets that he had, and I was never able to pursue any of that because I had two babies and a drug problem. I felt I had to leave him in order to maintain some semblance of sanity and some semblance of self. I couldn't stay with him and yet on the other hand I couldn't stay away. He would tell me to get out and I'd be back five days later. Or he'd leave and then be on the phone the next day asking when I was going to join him. The main problem was that I'd grown up with him. I had barely turned seventeen when I met him and then I grew up and he didn't want me to grow up. He wanted me to stay a child. The older I got, the closer I got to becoming a woman and the more I resented him trying to stop me becoming a human being, being a woman and being myself. He was also extremely jealous. That didn't help anything. It didn't matter if it was a man, a woman or a dog. He'd want to know who I was looking at or who I was talking to. It became unbearable.'

There followed a bitter battle of wills, with the couple living together for weeks and then being separated by arguments and violent fallings-out. At times it was only the mutual love of drugs that kept them together and Marvin, in his more moral moments, would mourn the fact that he had corrupted this innocent girl through his own greed and lust. Having resented being manipulated himself he had now become a manipulator.

'Since I had met him at such a young age and he had introduced me to certain things that I had never known before, he felt responsible for my state of mind and quality of life, neither of which were very good because of the drugs, sex and whatever,' says Jan. 'He felt that he was responsible because he'd exposed me to things which I had never known about.'

Following the affair with Beverly, she took up with Teddy Pendergrass, who had left Harold Melvin and the Bluenotes to become a solo singer and was openly competing against Marvin in the 'love man' stakes. What made this affair doubly painful to Marvin was that he had wrongly assumed that Pendergrass was gay. Then Jan started an affair with Rick James, a Motown artist who had spent a lot of time around the studio on Sunset Strip, and annoyed Marvin by referring to him as Uncle Marvin.

James was a hot new act who was thirteen years younger than Marvin and working on a style of music he termed 'funk 'n' roll', which was heavily inspired by George Clinton. With his braided hair and his extrovert stage show with the Stone City Band, he seemed designed to make Marvin feel old and past it. 'Jan knew how much Marvin despised these guys,' says Gerald White. 'They were pulling crowds and Marvin was now on an ego trip. He wanted to be the star of stars. They were the guys who Marvin would talk about at home. He more or less led her to them and then, when he found out that they'd had her, he would go all out to get her back. But she really didn't want to be with nobody but him.'

By 1978, without *Here, My Dear* having been released or even assigned a release date, he was struggling to survive against his encroaching claimants. He had again failed to make any spousal support payments and was $18,000 in arrears in addition to owing Anna's lawyers $25,000. In January the Marvin Gaye Recording Studios were closed down by US marshals because of unpaid franchise taxes. On 28 January he filed for bankruptcy and on 19 April Righton Productions followed suit. Personally Marvin was facing forty-three claims, totalling $6,061,494.10. These included hotel bills, breaches of contract, legal fees, spousal support for Anna, back payments to musicians, studio hire, bank loans and airline tickets. He now owed the IRS $522,314.74 and Stephen Hill, with whom he had fallen out, had put in a bill for $2,171,782, saying that Marvin hadn't been paying him his percentage.

Marvin was furious. He believed that Hill had been misappropriating funds and had distrusted him for some time. During the 1977 tour there had been an incident at a hotel in Beverly Hills after a concert in Los Angeles where Hill claimed that members of Marvin's family had come into his room, held him at gunpoint and stolen all the takings. This was never reported to the police and no one was ever charged. Marvin remained unconvinced by Hill's explanation of events.

Righton Productions had eighteen claimants, totalling $1,113,292.10, and the company's assets, including six cars and real estate in Shasta County and El Dorado County in Northern California, had to be sold. The only glimmer of hope on the horizon was his renegotiated deal with Motown, which guaranteed him $600,000 for each of his next two albums and $1 million per album after that. 'It got to a point where the police would be coming up to Hidden Hills to arrest him,' says Joe Schaffner. 'They couldn't kick the door in. He'd let them in the yard and he'd stand in the window and talk to them. He'd say, "I've got enough food to stay in here for a year, but you can't stay out there for a year." He would laugh at them. He would say, "You're out there, but I'm at home." '

With every move he seemed to upset more people. Promoters were angry when he pulled out of concerts at short notice; Motown was frustrated with the non-commercial album he had handed them; Anna was bitter over the way he had humiliated her; and Jan's stepfather, Earl Hunter, was furious at Marvin's mistreatment of Jan.

'I think that people were really after him by now,' says Mark Gaillard. 'I remember being out at the house in Hidden Hills a couple of times when Marvin would be in big arguments on the phone over business matters, and the next thing there would be people outside the house with guns. I can remember Jan having to tell me to lie low and keep quiet. There was a point when people who were unhappy with Marvin were definitely trying to frighten him. Marvin had his bodyguards out there with him and there would be shooting and all this crazy stuff.'

Anna's lawyer once wrote to the Superior Court of his frustration in being unable to have court orders served on Marvin in person because of the defences around him: 'The respondent lives in a large house in Hidden Hills, California. He has servants and assistants and it is impossible to penetrate the "Palace Guard" surrounding the respondent.'

Unsurprisingly, *Here, My Dear* was not a huge hit when it was released in December 1978, and the two singles from it did badly: 'A Funky Space Reincarnation' made 106 in the pop charts and 'Anger' was unplaced. Reviewers didn't seem to know whether the double album was a huge joke at the expense of Anna Gay and Motown, or a work of genius. Vivien Goldman, writing in *Melody Maker*, decided that while three of the sides ranged 'from good to drab', the fourth side was 'an insult to international record buyers'. Ian Penman, reviewing for *NME*, thought otherwise. It was, he thought, 'almost too much of a good thing' and contained 'a healing hunger and humility, which marks the best of Gaye's 70s work'. The North American tour set up to support it, which he insisted on doing by bus rather than plane, was marred by cancelled and missed concerts. He just didn't seem to care any more.

Because he was now officially a bankrupt, the advance paid for *Here, My Dear* was held by a trustee. Anna was paid $210,000 over the first year but the payments stopped because the album didn't sell. The royalties never exceeded the advance paid to Marvin by Motown. At the same time that he was dealing with renewed efforts by Anna to force him to abide by the contract set up by Curtis Shaw, which required him to revert to monthly payments in the event of low sales, the disputes with Jan came to a head. On 12 May 1979 she moved from Hidden Hills with Nona and Bubby and went to live with her mother by the ocean at Hermosa Beach. On 9 September Marvin came down at midday and took Bubby away from under Barbara Hunter's nose while Jan was in the bathroom. On his way back to his home he phoned the house and, after an abusive conversation with Barbara, said he was going to return for Nona. Fearful of what might develop if she declined, Jan decided that Nona should join him.

Two days later she called to speak to the children but Marvin wouldn't allow her access and threatened her with physical punishment. On 15 September she called again and this time, mainly because he was due to play a concert in Indiana, he relented and told her that she could have both of them 'for good'. She collected them at 3.00 p.m. and Marvin flew out of Los Angeles.

On 20 September Marvin returned to Hermosa Beach at 8.00 a.m., demanding to talk to Jan about their marital difficulties. She walked with him and the two children down to the beach, and when they reached a quiet spot Marvin suggested they get a divorce in Las Vegas but told her that he didn't feel that she deserved any of his money or property. There was an argument during which he twice punched her, knocking her to the ground, shouting, 'We could both die here on the beach.' As she and both the children began to scream, a neighbour who had seen the incident called the police. Marvin continued to be abusive when the police arrived and was hit in the eye during a scuffle with them as they fought to restrain and handcuff him. Jan filed a battery complaint at Hermosa Beach Police Department and immediately started divorce proceedings, on the grounds of irreconcilable differences. Marvin was made the subject of a restraining order and was prohibited from disposing of communal property. They had not yet been married for two years.

'Jan couldn't take any more,' says Mark Gaillard. 'He was physically beating her. I think at one time he broke her ribs on the road and she finally flipped and said, "I gotta get away." She was trapped and trying to get away. I was out there picking up her clothes a few times and driving her to her mom's house. One time he threatened to kill her and we had to go underground for three or four days.'

Throughout all this turmoil Marvin was managing a welterweight boxer named Andy Price, whom he'd met at the Hoover Gym in Los Angeles in 1978 while looking for sparring partners for Tommy Hanna. He even took part in an exhibition with Muhammad Ali at California State University where Ali boxed one round each with Marvin, Sammy Davis Jr, comedian Richard Pryor and *Rocky* actor Burt Young. 'Marvin went into some heavy-duty training for that bout,' remembers Dave Simmons, an old friend from Detroit, who had since moved out to California. 'He was gonna knock Ali out. Everybody else was having fun, but Marvin was deadly serious.'

Between March 1978 and August 1979 Marvin guided Price

through six wins in six fights, then secured him a shot at the world welterweight title against the great Sugar Ray Leonard at Caesar's Palace in Las Vegas on 28 September, just a week and a day after the Hermosa Beach incident. Although Price would only get $50,000 for the fight, his future earnings would be considerable if he won, and Marvin, as manager, would get 30 per cent. Unfortunately Price lost this fight six seconds before the closing bell of the first round, thus ending Marvin's dream of a quick financial fix.

Price knew nothing about music and was unaware of Marvin's growing problems with drugs and money. In fact, he can remember him speaking out against drug-taking and advising Price to invest his money in property and to look after his mother. 'The thing that stands out in my mind is the fact he paid people to do the simplest jobs for him,' says Price. 'For example, he paid a guy to do his shopping for him and if he found that his suit needed cleaning he'd just send this guy out to buy a new one.'

Marvin started to record a new album titled, without any trace of irony, *Love Man* with tracks such as 'I Offer You Nothing But Love' and 'Just Because You're So Pretty'. He was trying to come up with a response to the pretenders to his throne—people like Rick James, Teddy Pendergrass, Frankie Beverly, Peabo Bryson and Michael Henderson. There were even more sexual fantasies, but Motown didn't like what they heard. They weren't interested in Marvin's need for self-exploration. They wanted, and needed, hits. They asked him to go back and improve it.

He desperately needed money as he was accumulating debts faster than he was earning. He began to tour again in America and, in November 1979, flew out for his first tour of Hawaii, where he played to a capacity crowd of 7,000, and Japan, a three-week engagement set up by the Norby Walters Agency. Despite the animosity and the pending divorce case, Jan joined him and they hoped briefly for a reconciliation.

'The concerts went pretty well in Japan,' remembers saxophonist Nolan Smith, 'but Marvin was doing more and more drugs. Oddly enough, he was often at his best when he was high. He would be very happy and generous-minded. I remember that he was so happy with the way we sounded that he offered everyone an immediate raise but then when I went to see him about it when he wasn't high he said, "You must be crazy. I'm not giving those guys a raise!"

After playing Osaka, Nagasaki and Tokyo, the tour was due to pick up again at Long Beach on 31 December, a date that the band were excited about because it meant that they could invite their friends and families to see the show and enjoy a New Year's celebration afterwards. However, when the plane back stopped to refuel in Hawaii, Marvin got off with Jan and the two children and didn't return. Norby Walters's twenty-two-year-old son Richard, who had been assigned to Marvin to ensure that he turned up at concerts, was waiting for him at Los Angeles International Airport. 'The flight came in,' he remembers, 'and Marvin just didn't show up.'

It was a planned escape. Marvin had reasoned that there was nothing worth returning to Los Angeles for except more pain, humiliation and financial ruin. Everything he had built up for himself since 1959 was crumbling away, and he and Jan had fallen out again. They fought so bitterly that he was once close to stabbing her in the chest with a knife. They argued over who should have custody of the children, and she finally left Hawaii with Nona while Bubby stayed on with his father.

Before leaving America Marvin had contracted to return to Europe in January 1980 for a tour organized by Jeffrey Kruger, but as Christmas approached it became clear to Motown and to Curtis Shaw that he wasn't in a fit state to honour the commitment. 'Curtis told me that he had spoken to Marvin on Christmas Eve and that Marvin was in a constant state of depression,' says Kruger. 'Nothing anybody said seemed to take his mind off it and although he'd started to record out there [Hawaii] he simply wasn't up to it. He felt that we should postpone the January tour.'

Kruger was in a quandary. To cancel the tour with only a month to go would be costly, but cheaper than if he had to do it at the last minute. His only chance of salvaging it was to fly out to Maui, the island on which Marvin was now living with his son, to try to change his mind.

On 15 January 1980 Marvin arrived at Kruger's suite at the Maui Sheraton with Bubby at his side. Kruger was shocked at the transformation. Marvin seemed unsteady on his feet and looked emaciated. He told Kruger that he was living in a bread van parked on top of a cliff and was relying on hand-outs from friends to survive. He'd even called Smokey Robinson for financial aid but Smokey didn't want to give him money that he knew would only be spent on more drugs. 'I realized then that it was going to be a long time before he could perform,' says Kruger. 'He told me that he was depressed and pleaded for me not to put pressure on him. He promised that he was going to pull himself out of the rut, give up drugs and start jogging. He said he just needed time and some money and that he thought he'd be ready to tour in March. I advanced him three thousand dollars.'

In February Marvin's mother flew to Maui to help look after Bubby. She had to sell a diamond ring that Marvin had bought her to pay for the rental of a condominium on Kapula Drive in Lahiania. Kruger kept in touch with Mrs Gay, who told him that Marvin's health was improving and that even though the March dates he had suggested wouldn't be possible, there was every possibility of touring in June.

In the meantime Marvin was embracing the outdoor life, considering himself something of a free spirit as he wandered the beaches with his son, searching for shells and exploring extinct volcanoes, but he was troubled by a sense of impending doom. He tried to kill himself by overdosing on cocaine. 'He went overboard,' says a friend in whom he confided later that year. 'He told me that he was trying to commit suicide but that he wanted to do it in such a way that he would die happy.'

Curtis Shaw was visiting him at least every month to keep him abreast of the legal developments in Los Angeles. 'It was a difficult time,' he says. 'Marvin owed the IRS money and I was trying like hell to keep him from being indicted. There was all sorts of behind-the-scenes manoeuvring going on and yet he had no moral or spiritual support from his family. The cow that had supplied the milk had no more milk to give so everyone bailed out. Jan bailed out. His sisters and brother bailed out. His father bailed out.'

On 2 May Kruger returned to Maui and met Marvin at the Intercontinental. This time he was given good news: Marvin was recording at Seawest Recording Studios in Honolulu. The United States Bankruptcy Court had granted the Motown Record Corporation an order to advance funds to him even though he was a debtor because the record was his only means of finding funds. The tracks would be finished by the end of the month and he could tour Europe in June. Keyboard player William Bryant, guitarist Gordon Banks, drummer Bugsy Wilcox and bass player Frank Blair had joined him in the studio and were ready to rehearse for a live show.

By now Marvin had scrapped the idea of the *Love Man* album. He'd already devoted three albums to the joys and miseries of his sexual relationships and he wanted to return to his earlier role as a social prophet. 'I thought—how dumb [to try to assert his authority as a love man],' he later told David Ritz when interviewed for *Essence* magazine. 'What am I doing? There are some serious concerns. For example, man may blow up this planet in our lifetime. That's what the record grew to be.' He was working on songs that reflected his belief that the world was headed for a nuclear showdown, a combination of the apocalyptic warnings he had heard his father preach from the book of Revelation and his own drug-induced visions of personal collapse.

One of Marvin's requests was that the tour climax with a gala concert in front of a member of the British Royal Family. He said he wanted to do this partly to ameliorate the feelings left after the previous cancellations and partly because he wanted to return to America on a high note. Desperate to avoid further delays, Kruger agreed to sort something out. He had mounted a similar charity event in front of the royals for comedian George Burns.

Back in California, Jan was working through the court to try to regain custody of Bubby. A writ of habeas corpus was issued by the Superior Court of California and was to be served on Marvin when he changed planes in Los Angeles on his way from Hawaii to London. But Marvin had other plans: he booked his flight through San Francisco to avoid the lawyers.

Less than a week before the tour was about to start Kruger had a call from Mike Roshkind of Motown Records in Los Angeles, telling him that Marvin wanted a two-day delay on the tour to allow for a final remix of the album. He asked that the cancelled dates be added to the end of the tour and promised that Motown would make up for any financial loss. The opening date, in Liverpool, was quickly rearranged and on 10 June Marvin's musicians arrived in London. The same day, Marvin called Kruger from Maui. 'He said he had a small problem,' says Kruger. 'He had lost his passport and Bubby had never owned one. I told him to get the first plane out of Honolulu and I'd sort the problem out from there on.'

Kruger then had the excruciating job of tracking down Marvin's lost passport and trying to arrange for Bubby to fly without one. He spoke to the head of public relations for Pan Am, who thought it would be impossible for the child to fly, but the head of immigration at the airport in San Francisco agreed to let him through on a temporary passport if his counterpart at London Heathrow would agree. Kruger would have to stand surety for the little boy and make sure he left Britain within twenty-four hours of the tour ending. 'We must have phoned San Francisco airport twenty or thirty times that night,' remembers Kruger. 'Finally, in the early hours of 11 June, Marvin stepped on a plane in San Francisco, where he met up again with his mother. When the plane took off, Pan Am called me. I breathed a sigh of relief and fell asleep at my desk for a couple of hours.'

12

The Road Back

To the hungry soul every bitter thing is sweet.
Proverbs 27:7

Marvin arrived in London on 11 June, gave a brief press conference, then checked into the Britannia Hotel, Grosvenor Square, in the heart of Mayfair, where he rested in preparation for his opening concerts at the Royal Albert Hall in nearby Kensington.

Kruger was keen for Marvin to make a spectacular début, which would erase the bad feelings engendered by the on—off tour, but the tumult of the past week had made him sluggish and he seemed uninspired. Wearing a dark suit, white shirt and knitted hat he was on stage for just under two hours, during which he covered twenty of his hits, including a medley of his songs with Tammi Terrell, which Kruger had suggested he should perform for his British fans. The British music press was disappointed. *Melody Maker* complained about the poor sound. *New Musical Express* ignored this deficiency but criticized Marvin for his diminished power and the 'watered-down Vegas versions' of his songs. 'It seemed remarkable that a man with so much soul in his voice and such obvious sincerity in his latter lyrics has so little

June 1980. On stage at London's Royal Albert Hall at the beginning of what was to be a European exile.

PHOTO: PICTORIAL

Photo taken by the artist Neil Breeden as reference for cover art he had been commissioned to do for 'In Our Lifetime'.

Marvin with his Dutch girlfriend Eugenie Vis and Prince Charles of
Belgium.

PHOTO: BUDDY COMEDY

Marvin on stage at Radio City Music Hall during his final tour of America.

PHOTO: GARY GERSHOFF, RETNA

Marvin's bed shortly after he was shot to death while sitting on the side of the bed closest to the door. He slumped to the floor where he was later cradled by his brother, Frankie.

PHOTO: AUTHOR'S COLLECTION

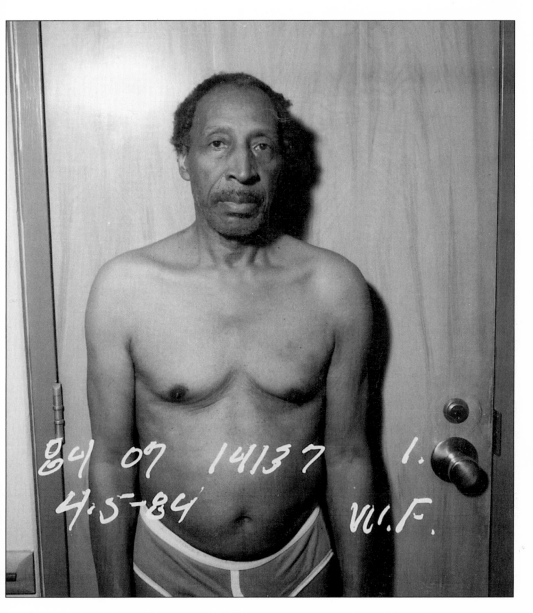

On the day of his son's funeral, Marvin Gaye Senior posed for police photographs to show evidence of the beating he had taken from him. There were noticeable bruises on his back and forearms.

PHOTO: AUTHOR'S COLLECTION

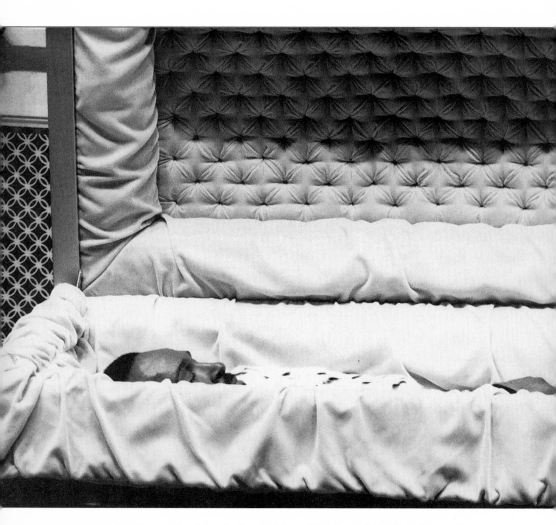

April 5, 1984. Marvin lies in his coffin dressed in the white military uniform he had worn on stage during his final tour.

energy on stage these days,' commented reviewer Adrian Thrills. 'Ain't that peculiar?'

A number of celebrities came to see the show, including Mick Jagger, who'd flown in from Paris, but Marvin was more concerned over who hadn't turned up. Berry Gordy and Mike Roshkind from Motown in Los Angeles had promised to attend but Roshkind was delayed in New York and Berry didn't show. These absences further fuelled his resentment towards Motown. The company cared about him as a generator of revenue, he felt, but not as a person or as a creative artist.

Kruger's priority for the rest of the engagements was to make sure that Marvin turned up for his dates and stayed clean. However, as he soon learned, Marvin was often easier to handle when he was high on cocaine and at his most obstinate when his supply dried up. After a few toots in the morning he would become expansive and make incredible promises. Travelling from Manchester to Edinburgh in Kruger's Lincoln Continental, he sorted his whole life out: he agreed to put on shows in Las Vegas with Lena Horne and set up an overseas corporation in Britain. Kruger went on to set up the shows in Las Vegas but when he mentioned his progress to a sober Marvin he was no longer interested. 'When he was high he was charm personified,' says Kruger. 'He was perfectly rational and you could talk to him and develop his thoughts. When he came down to earth there was a side of him that the public never saw. It was like Jekyll and Hyde. He became a sullen, obstinate man, who had no regard for propriety and no concern for any human kindness that was being shown to him. He knew that his mother was worried sick about his behaviour and that his example in front of his young son was terrible yet he didn't have the strength to listen to the people who were trying to do him good. There was nothing I could do but have my head of security watch him closely. I used every psychological trick in the book to get him to fulfil his commitments and get the tour behind me.'

After eight dates in Britain, the tour went to Geneva, Amsterdam, Rotterdam and Montreux before returning to England for the Royal Gala Performance that he had asked Kruger to set up. It was booked for 8 July at Lakeside Country Club, near Camberley in Surrey, and Princess Margaret, sister to Queen Elizabeth II, was to be the guest of honour. The prospect of mingling with British royalty was so exciting to Marvin's mother and Aunt Toley that they went shopping in Paris to buy appropriate evening wear. They felt that they'd come a long way from the cotton-fields of North Carolina.

Arranged to raise money for the children of the London Docklands Settlement, this charity gala was to be the jewel in the crown of the tour, but turned into a promoter's nightmare and a public-relations disaster for Marvin. The first inkling of trouble came when Kruger arrived at the venue expecting Marvin to be available for a formal introduction to the Princess. Not finding him there, he called his security man, who, after making a couple of phone calls, discovered that Marvin had not even left his room at the hotel. 'I called Marvin and asked him what the problem was and he was incoherent,' says Kruger. 'He told me that he had decided that he wasn't going to come. I told him that the only people he would be letting down would be himself and his family but nothing I said made any difference. I then got his mother to talk to him while I had Peter Prince call Berry Gordy to ask him to try and persuade Marvin. Mike Roshkind and Berry went as far to offer him a cash bonus of fifty thousand dollars if he appeared, but even they couldn't penetrate his drugged head.'

The gala was forced to carry on without Marvin. Eventually he left the hotel and travelled to Camberley, but when he arrived Princess Margaret had already been taken home. Marvin offered no apologies to Kruger. He seemed oblivious to the distress he had caused. 'Hey, tell me,' he asked Kruger, 'why would the Princess want to have this nigger perform in front of her?'

'It was a wild scene,' remembers William Bryant, the keyboard player on the tour. 'I had only been on the road for a couple of years and I found the intrigue very weird. It was like a spy movie.'

The next day the British newspapers were full of the story of the pop star who had 'snubbed' Margaret thus 'sparking fury', but, according to Les Spaine, then head of promotions and marketing for Motown's British operation, the Princess, reputedly a fan of Marvin's music, was relaxed about the whole affair. 'I drew the short straw that night,' says Spaine. 'I was the one who had to go and tell her that Marvin wasn't here. I went up to her and said, "Excuse me, ma'am, I'm afraid Mr Gaye isn't very well. We're trying to sort him out to get him here as soon as possible." She looked straight at me and said, "Do you mean he's out of it?" I thought to myself, She's well sussed! and just smiled back.'

Later Marvin justified his behaviour by saying that Kruger was manipulating him, but it reflected badly on him that revenge took priority over his contractual commitments, the pride of his mother and the needs of the charity. What Marvin considered manipulation—withholding air tickets until the departure day, paying for shows only after they had been completed—Kruger considered the only practical way of ensuring that Marvin carried out his duties. The next day Marvin was due to return to America but, on the spur of the moment, decided not to go. He was going to stay in England, away from the problems that were dogging him in Los Angeles, and he was going to start a new life with Bubby. He even persuaded his mother to stay on with him temporarily to look after the little boy. 'I was here and I decided to stay,' he explained later to a British journalist. 'I felt an extra measure of energy and peace of mind here. Also, it is more expedient for me to be on this side of the ocean [so that] my legal people can deal with my financial and personal problems in America and I can be free of the responsibility.'

Marvin had always had a special appreciation of England, its social customs and manners. He had a particular affection for the English upper class with its cut-glass accent and attention to etiquette. He claimed that it brought out the aristocrat in him. He also liked the fact that he could walk the streets of London without being hassled. Celebrity wasn't as important here as it was in Los Angeles.

He stayed in a four-storey house in Bedford Gardens, Kensington, which was soon littered with the sleeping bodies of other musicians from his band, who still hadn't returned to America. Even his mother was reduced to sleeping on the floor. Within a few days of settling here he was joined by Eugenie Vis, a twenty-four-year-old Dutch girl he had met after the Amsterdam concert. She was to be his first live-in lover since breaking up with Jan and the on-off relationship lasted throughout his European exile. Eugenie was, in her own words, a naïve country girl who didn't know what she was letting herself in for. She'd had one long-term boyfriend, had never taken drugs and hadn't heard of Marvin Gaye until the night she was taken to the concert by her friend Mehta Joanknicht, who had backstage passes. There she met bass player Frank Blair, who arranged to see her the next evening for a meal.

'They had a dance floor in the bar at the Hilton,' says Blair. 'She got kind of drunk and we went back to my room and made love. Marvin saw me with her the next day and he told me that he really liked her. I felt sorry for him because he was so lonely. So I checked her out and said that I'd introduce him to her and that if he liked her I would move on. That's how they got together.'

She had a call at her apartment from Marvin's valet, Felice Joe James, informing her that Marvin wanted her to come to the hotel straight away. 'I thought I would go and experience whatever was going to happen,' she says. 'I took a cab to the hotel and met Marvin in his suite. I knew that by going there it would be about sex but I thought, OK, let me experience it. When we finally made love I was shocked because it was without any feelings of warmth. I started to cry and because of this Marvin couldn't make love any more but, in fact, this turned out to be the point where we really began to make contact. Because sex was out of the way we started to talk through the night and that was when he invited me to come to London and stay with him.'

He wrote her a prose poem on notepaper from the Britannia Hotel in which he described the experience as having taken him 'from an angry ocean of confusion to a place of divine grace'. He said that, above all, he needed understanding and love: 'Who will quench my bottomless thirst for passion and love? For there is more to please . . . at least, for now.'

When Eugenie arrived in London she was disturbed to find that Marvin was already sleeping with another woman. He didn't seem to find this unusual and thought that both women could stay with him in the apartment. It was a repeat of his own father's behaviour in front of his mother and contained an echo of the humiliation to which he had been subjected in his childhood. 'It was weird,' says Eugenie. 'The woman couldn't stand it. She wanted to know why I was staying there and Marvin just told her, "Well, if you can't stand it then just go." So she went, and I stayed.'

It was the beginning of a bizarre relationship governed by Marvin's appetites, in which Eugenie was treated as little more than a slave girl, who could look after children, cook, shop and provide sex. Because she was inexperienced and eager to please, she allowed herself to be abused to a point where her identity was almost lost. Sometimes she felt like an observer of this relationship, where a woman was allowing herself to be stripped of all self-respect to satisfy a man.

Like his father, Marvin was misogynistic. The function of women, he believed, was to serve and obey men. They had to know their place. In 1972 he had shocked Ben Fong-Torres of *Rolling Stone* by telling him that women should be 'made to feel inferior to men'. He was now living a life of pure indulgence. He would sleep through the morning and take his first line of cocaine early in the afternoon, snorting it through a straw. Often he would stay in bed all day, receiving guests at his bedside, in another repeat of his father's behaviour. At night he would go out, leaving Eugenie at home. He wasn't proud enough of her to want to introduce her to his glamorous social world where he mingled with restaurateurs, pop stars, socialites and club-owners. His sexual kicks consisted of fantasies of domination and Eugenie was placid enough to comply. She didn't challenge him when he returned home with other sexual playthings, who would be entertained for a couple of hours in the bedroom before being sent on their way. The cocaine they were both taking created an unreal world where the normal rules of respect and decorum no longer applied. 'When Marvin wasn't using coke he made love from the heart and he was affectionate,' says Eugenie. 'When he was using coke it was a kind of power play and he liked me to be submissive. Coke increases your appetite and makes sex more instinctive. With Marvin it was a vicious cycle. I think that sex was Marvin's way of getting close to women without getting hurt. He felt that he was the master. He was a very sensitive guy who had wounds that weren't healing. He escaped from his problems in drugs, and drugs made his attraction to sex even greater.'

Cocaine, at fifty pounds a gram, was an expensive pastime in the Britain of 1980. He was not only taking two or three lines a day himself but was expected to keep a bowl on the table for the use of his friends. Old friends from Motown would pass through London and would take their share of powder away with them.

His only source of income was a thousand pounds a week, an allowance being sent through by Berry Gordy but, to maintain his lifestyle, he knew that this would have to be supplemented with earnings. He had moved apartments, first to a place shared with Felice Joe James and bass player Frank Blair in Kilburn, North London, and then to his own apartment at Rutland Gate, Knightsbridge, in a serviced building with a doorman. When his mother returned home on 10 July he had the additional cost of hiring a nanny, Patsy Taylor, to look after Bubby. 'He was always trying to get more money out of Motown International when he was in London,' remembers Karen Spreadbury, the company's press officer at the time. 'He would try to get fresh advances and the time came when there just wasn't any more money left and we had to say, "That's it." '

The most important piece of unfinished business was the album he'd worked on in Hawaii, now provisionally titled *In Our Lifetime?*. He had brought the tapes to England with him and, to ensure its speedy completion, Berry Gordy conferred with James Fisher of Motown UK, who booked Marvin into Odyssey Recording Studios at 26 Castlereagh Street in London's West End. Gordy then dispatched two of his employees, who went under the pseudonyms of 'Mr Smith' and 'Mr Jones', to meet Odyssey's owner, Wayne Bickerton. 'These two gentlemen in pinstriped suits arrived one evening and made their way up to my office,' says Bickerton. 'They said they wanted to talk to me about Mr Gordy and the album that Marvin Gaye was doing. They wanted me to ensure that the project was finished and that the master tapes were delivered to Motown. I had to tell them that, as a recording studio, we were just a facility and that getting a certain number of tracks done on time was not our responsibility. That was something for them to sort out. They went down to the studios and set their plan up. A lot of people left the control room. The next day they flew back to America.'

What happened over the next few weeks is uncertain because at least three people believe that they personally delivered the master tapes to Motown and yet, according to Marvin, the album that was finally released, in January 1981, was not the version he had approved in London. The most likely explanation is that copies of the tapes were covertly made by Motown during the London sessions and were already in Los Angeles ready for manufacturing as he did what he thought were the final mixes.

What we know is that Marvin went into Odyssey in the summer of

1980 and began reconstructing the Honolulu tapes. Bickerton estimates that he was in Studio Two for between six weeks and two
months, during which various musicians flew in from LA to record
overdubs. The problem, he feels, was that Marvin just didn't know
when to finish. 'He would start off with a concept for a track but
would then lose his way,' he says. 'I think he lacked a sense of discipline and the presence of someone he respected who could tell him
when he was doing something wrong. I think it was a big mistake for
him to produce the album himself.'

After these sessions Bickerton took the tapes to Los Angeles and
handed them to Lee Young, Motown's vice-president of A & R. The
Odyssey Studios tapes in Motown's vaults today are dated 3 September
1980, but are not the tapes used for the final mix. 'I got paid on the spot
for all the outstanding studio bills,' says Bickerton. 'I don't know
whether Marvin knew that the tapes had gone. I think that A&R deci-
sions were now being made for him.'

Having finished at Odyssey Marvin then went on to Air London
Studios in Oxford Street, where he continued recording with Frank
Blair. 'Effectively, Frank took over the project,' says engineer Jon
Walls. 'Marvin was there for the first week and then I never saw him
again. After he left, the whole project was surrounded in secrecy. We
moved out of Studio One and started doing mixes in Studio Two. It was
really silly. The album had taken him two years to record and then we
suddenly had something like four days to finish all the mixes.'

Les Spaine says he took these remixed tapes to Peter Prince, who
sent them to Motown in Los Angeles in the company's weekly pouch.
Marvin, who by now was in hiding somewhere in London, was begin-
ning to suspect that Blair and Felice Joe James had been hired by Berry
Gordy to spy on him and to get the tapes out as soon as possible. Jon
Walls remembers Blair leaving with tape boxes after the secret remixes.

'Berry Gordy and Lee Young gave us some orders,' admits Blair.
'They told us what we were to do with the tapes. Marvin later argued
with me about that and I had to tell him, "Man. Our balls were on the
line!" This is a deep story. Our balls were on the line and we tried to get
in touch with Marvin but we couldn't find him any place. We didn't
even know if he was alive. We just did everything that Berry Gordy
and Lee Young told us to do.'

Blair wasn't the only person searching for Marvin. Although he was calling Jan from Europe he never let her know his precise location. Her attorney, Stanley Bowman, had sent a copy of a summons to Hidden Hills and, as required by law, had it printed in the Los Angeles *Daily Journal* over five consecutive Tuesdays through August and September.

> You have been sued [read the Summons (Marriage) for Case Number D005734, re the marriage of Petitioner Janis E. Gaye and Respondent Marvin P. Gaye, Jr]. The court may decide against you without your being heard unless you respond within 30 days . . . If you fail to file a written response within such time, your default may be entered and the court may enter a judgment containing injunctive or other orders concerning division of property, spousal support, attorney's fees, costs and such other relief as may be granted by the court, which could result in the garnishment of wages, taking of money or property, or other relief.

On 8 October Marvin took delivery of art work that he had personally commissioned from a young British illustrator named Neil Breeden. Motown had already printed up 450,000 sleeves for the *Love Man* album it thought it was getting complete with neon lettering and a dazzling colour photo of Marvin in a silk suit. Besides having changed the title, Marvin hated the image of himself as a romantic star. For his revised version of the recording he wanted an illustration that reflected the battle between good and evil and had supplied Breeden with a crude sketch of an angelic version of himself facing a demonic version of himself over a chessboard. Scrawled in the margins were the opposing virtues and vices that he felt were at stake—love, faith, pleasure and courage versus hate, despair, pain and fear. He also wanted a back-cover illustration of himself and Bubby enclosed in bubbles and floating through the atmosphere, but there wasn't enough time to complete it. Marvin was pleased with Breeden's execution of his idea and offered him any vice he wanted. 'I was carted off into the bathroom with Marvin, two of his friends and Marvin's Colombian drug dealer, where there was a pyramid of cocaine,' he says. 'I'd never seen so much. My mouth just dropped. Marvin then proceeded to show me how to snort it through a McDonald's straw.'

When the album was released Marvin was furious and complained bitterly in a series of interviews designed to promote it. He was angry with Berry Gordy, he was angry with Motown and he was angry with Frank Blair. He complained that one track, 'Far Cry', had a guide vocal that he had improvised at the microphone and that the title on the cover, *In Our Lifetime*, was missing the vital question mark and therefore altered the meaning of his concept. 'I can't really claim this piece as my work or my production,' he told *Melody Maker*, adding that it was only three-quarters finished. 'In fact, I disavow this publicly as being my work.' Then, asked if he would ever record again for Motown, he announced that he wouldn't. 'I can't imagine how I'll ever record another album with Motown unless a miracle happens,' he said. 'I feel that if I can find another record company that's more interested in me as a complete entity—producer, artist, arranger, musician—and who recognizes those qualities in me, and who feels that these qualities are essentially good, and that I should be respected, and that one should be treated as special if one is special, then that is the company I'll sign for.'

In Our Lifetime was undoubtedly a flawed album, caught somewhere between the erotic funk of *I Want You* and the apocalyptic warnings of *What's Going On* but not as good as either. Lyrically it was as unfocused as it was musically. Marvin seemed to have lost the precision of expression he had enjoyed in the early seventies and a track like 'Love Me Now Or Love Me Later', which he considered pivotal to the project, was packed full of unmemorable words.

He was becoming increasingly obsessed with ideas of a battle between good and evil, something that had stimulated his imagination as a child when he heard the stories of trumpets, dragons and the beast with ten horns and seven heads that his father told. In a significant departure from the Christian understanding of this spiritual showdown, he was now no longer convinced that good would triumph. Evil seemed equally powerful. Humanity had no choice in how it was affected by this rivalry. It was a throwback to a dualistic philosophy of the third century known as Manichaeism, after its founder Mani, which combined Persian, Christian and Buddhist ideas and, like gnosticism, saw the body as the locus of evil, and the soul, or spirit, as pure. This could push someone either in the direction of monasticism, an attempt to deny the flesh to give the spirit greater control, or in the direction of antinomianism, which proclaimed that it didn't matter what you did with the body because the spirit was independent.

Marvin showed both tendencies. He would go through periods of abstinence, when he would become intolerant of anyone else taking drugs or living promiscuously. 'The problem,' he told Chris Salewicz of *NME* in 1981, 'is this stupid flesh that envelops our spirit, that we cannot seem to control, and there are stupid pleasures and material interests and all kinds of things to stop us evolving towards infinity. . . '

Frank Blair can remember a time when someone lined up their cocaine on the cover of Marvin's Bible and Marvin went berserk, kicking the table over and shouting, 'Get that shit off the Bible.' He saw no apparent inconsistency in reading the Bible one minute and snorting cocaine the next, but he thought it was sacrilegious to bring the two together. At other times he was contemptuous of the idea that a spiritual person had to exercise restraint. Church, he would argue, had never left his heart. 'I don't think that being religious means that you can't have sex,' he had asserted to *Rolling Stone* in 1974 when questioned about his promiscuity. 'I think it's ridiculous to say that you can't be a priest and also screw.'

When asked for the source of his visions of earthly destruction he would cite the French prophet Nostradamus, Carlos Castaneda and the book of Revelation, but his fears offered more of an insight into his own troubled psyche than they did into the future of mankind. The reality was that Marvin was facing his own apocalypse, and the forces of good and evil were competing for his soul. What he now appeared to concede was that the good within him might ultimately face defeat.

'Through his music he could deal with things, but as a private individual it was difficult for him to deal with his evil side,' says Jan Gaye. 'I remember that once during a heated argument he said to me, "You know, Jan, there is no God. If there is a God, I am God." I looked at him and said, 'What are you talking about?' He said, "There is a good God and a bad God." I asked him how there could be such a thing as a bad God and he said, "Well, I can't really explain it to you but it's something that tears me apart." '

When it got round that he was living in London he was invited to prestigious parties and receptions where he met the city's glitterati along with the shadowy figures who acted as their drivers, security guards, fixers and debt collectors. These social opposites reflected the very light and darkness that fascinated and threatened to engulf him. At Maunkberrys, a fashionable nightclub in Jermyn Street, he met a black Englishman who called himself Cool Black, a karate black belt who worked on the door. In passing, Marvin mentioned some money he was owed in England, and that week Cool Black went to collect it. Marvin was so grateful that he offered him a job and Cool Black briefly became his personal bodyguard, business manager and valet.

'I would go to collect his coke because if they arrested anyone we didn't want it to be Marvin because that would make the headlines,' says Cool Black. 'I could pick it up knowing that the stuff would be clean, knowing that no one was taking surveillance photographs. I knew the right people to buy from and if you know the right people you know how high up the ladder you're getting. They knew the Colombians and they would tell me what was good. I would always take some of it first to try it because an artist can't take anything impure into his body.'

While Cool Black acted as a trusted go-between, Marvin's primary drug dealer was also allowed into the inner circle. He specialized in high-quality cocaine, and he was one of the few dealers who would supply him on credit.

With his more sophisticated London friends Marvin kept the more sinister side of his life concealed. To Chantal d'Orthez, a twenty-four-year-old champagne heiress once described by the *Daily Express* as 'one of our saucier society beauties', he was the epitome of elegance. She met him at a private dinner given by Liz Brewer, a notable society hostess and fixer who thought that Marvin had 'tremendous style' and involved him in her celebrity circuit. 'He always dressed beautifully,' remembers Chantal. 'He was a very refined man who wore beautiful hand-made shoes and was very aware of his looks and presence. He was very elegant. There was nothing trashy about him.'

They ate together and went to clubs but never had an affair. It was a strange meeting of opposites: the black boy raised in the housing projects of Washington DC and the white girl whose father was a French count and her mother the actress Moira Lister. With her he was always the perfect gentleman and he never introduced her to any of his seedy friends or took her back to his apartment. 'His life was very divided,' she says. 'He had one side of his life and he said categorically to me, "I don't want you to know about the other side of my life." So that was it. It was something he didn't want me exposed to. It could have been that he was ashamed of it. I left it at that. I respected that he wanted it that way.'

His most unusual friend of the time was Lady Edith Foxwell, sixty-three-year-old granddaughter of the Ninth Earl of Cavan, who had a noted attraction to young black men. She had once been married to Ivan Foxwell, producer of such films as *The Colditz Story* and *The Quiller Memorandum*, but since divorcing had made her reputation as London's 'Queen of the Night' and was currently the co-owner of the revamped Embassy Club in New Bond Street. She introduced him to her circle of friends, including Viscount Linley, Princess Margaret's son, and had him to stay at her huge, rambling country home in Wiltshire, where he would walk in the fields at weekends and visit the local pub, the Carpenter's Arms. 'The first time he came down he was due to arrive in time for lunch but didn't turn up until 9.00 p.m. at night,' recalls Lady Edith. 'I remember he had his son with him, and a nice English girl who looked after him. He lived minute by minute. He was very vague about everything that was happening in his life. It was as though he was just drifting.'

John Benson, an English musician whom Marvin had met at the Embassy club, was with him the night of 8 December 1980. Marvin was on the phone to America as news began to break of John Lennon's murder. Whoever he was talking to relayed news of the events as they came through on television. 'When he hung up he started talking about his own death,' says Benson. 'He said, "If I was shot, it would probably be the best thing that could happen to my career. Everyone could be paid off and all my bills would be settled." He then talked to me for about half an hour about his death.'

His final London move was to a luxury apartment on Park West Place, close to Marble Arch, loaned to him by Oiu Aboderin, a Nigerian chief whose company, Lagos International, owned the humorous magazine *Punch*. Aboderin interested Marvin in the idea of touring in West Africa, and even went as far as checking possible venues and setting up appointments for vaccinations. For centuries black Americans had been encouraged to forget where they came from. Marvin was of the first generation actively to embrace its African heritage. In 1968 James Brown had had a million-seller with 'Say It Loud—I'm Black and I'm Proud', which caught the mood of the desegregated era. In the seventies he became one of the first black American soul stars to perform in Africa. 'Marvin wanted to do a world tour that went to Brazil and Australia and Africa,' says Cool Black. 'Africa was going to be the big finale. He was going to get out of the plane in Africa and kiss the ground of Africa, the land where his ancestors came from. That was part of his comeback plan.'

'He used to talk a great deal about Africa and slavery,' says Lady Edith Foxwell. 'He would tell me that the blacks were such great singers because they had learned to communicate to each other through songs and that they had good physiques because the slave masters selected the finest men and women to have children together.' He also told friends that he believed that he was descended from African princes and that was why he had such an aristocratic bearing.

But before any comebacks could be considered Marvin knew that he had to clean up. He also knew that he had to make the final break with Motown. 'They think I'm through,' he said. 'They think that I can't be productive any more. If Berry doesn't let me go, I'll retire. I know I can't record for them again.'

The feeling was probably mutual. His albums had been selling progressively less and *In Our Lifetime*, despite the anticipation, was a relative commercial flop. One of the main problems was that he was no longer coming up with tracks that would make obvious singles. Neither of the two tracks taken from *In Our Lifetime* even made the Top 100.

As 1982 began, he reached a new low point. Having failed to respond to the summons issued by the County Clerk in Los Angeles, he was ordered to appear for trial on 26 January. Again he ignored the summons, and Judge Carl Pearlston granted an interlocutory judgment of dissolution, which required Marvin to make monthly payments to Jan and the children commencing 1 February. She was also awarded custody. Having realized that he now had to do something or risk losing everything, Marvin instructed Curtis Shaw to file a divorce petition on his behalf, requesting that the default judgment of 26 January be set aside. He was hoping that by making himself the petitioner he might get a better settlement. Eventually the two petitions were consolidated.

At this point his fortunes changed. For several months he had been courted by Freddy Cousaert, a forty-two-year-old Belgian promoter and club owner, who wanted Marvin to come to Ostend and use it as a base to relaunch his career. In September 1980, Cousaert had been told by Count Suckle, owner of the Q Club in Praed Street, Paddington, that Marvin was due to make a guest appearance that Christmas. 'I couldn't believe it,' says Cousaert. 'I couldn't believe that this hero of mine, this living legend, could be living in London and playing at such a small venue. Suckle told me that a guy called Teddy was managing Marvin and so I got in touch and suggested that I could set up a European tour for him, playing big centres like Amsterdam, Brussels, Frankfurt and Paris.'

The following month he met Marvin at the apartment in Rutland Gate and discussed the possibility of touring. Marvin seemed interested and asked him to mail him details of venue capacities and merchandising plans. This attention to detail struck Cousaert as odd because Marvin's whole life seemed in disarray—the apartment was overrun with hangers-on, there was no food or drink in the fridge, drugs were in abundance and Marvin was distressed over a phone call from Jan. However, after Cousaert returned to Ostend and mailed back the details, Marvin phoned up and requested another meeting. At this second meeting he seemed agitated and walked out half-way through, leaving Cousaert to deal with his 'manager', Teddy, who clearly knew nothing about management. Disconcertingly, while he was out he phoned in to ask Teddy if Cousaert was still there.

That evening, Cousaert left to attend the premiere of *Freedom Road*, a movie about slavery starring Kris Kristofferson, and Marvin turned up for the party afterwards. Cousaert was staggered to find him given a huge reception by the crowd at the party and it seemed to be at this point that things clicked. 'We could be a team,' Marvin told him. 'We could do well together.'

By November 1980 the two were discussing specific tour plans, and Cousaert mailed Marvin an advance although he was worried that Marvin just wouldn't get himself together. It was then that he suggested Marvin come and stay with him in Ostend and bring Eugenie and

Bubby. He knew Marvin liked wind and rain because he had recently taken himself to Brighton on the south coast of England to get away from the city and to watch the waves roll in.

On 15 February 1981 Cousaert came to London and drove Marvin and Eugenie down to Dover, where they took a Sealink ferry to Ostend. Eugenie was so stoned that she had no recollection of the journey but Marvin was together enough to accept an invitation to go up on the bridge and have drinks with the captain.

'Freddy was a nightclubby type of person,' remembers Karen Spreadbury, 'but he was also a very shrewd businessman. He had Marvin in his pocket. Marvin had to move from London anyway because he'd outstayed his welcome in so many places and Motown UK could no longer support him. Along came Freddy, who not only promised him more work but helped him to get a new record company.'

Ostend, a cold, windswept town on the Belgian coast, was unlike any place that Marvin had ever lived. It wasn't fashionable, the only black people around were members of a visiting American basketball team, and there was no drug scene to speak of. Cousaert fixed them up with an apartment on the fifth floor of 77 Rue Promenade, overlooking the sea.

'He saw it as an opportunity to go into exile,' says his guitarist Gordon Banks. 'It forced him to clean up because there are heavy penalties for drug offences in Belgium. In England there were so many people who knew him but in Belgium not only did they not know him but many of them people didn't even speak his language. It was the perfect place to escape to.'

Almost immediately Marvin began to change. He stopped taking cocaine and began jogging, cycling and punching the heavy bag in a local boxing gymnasium. His sexual interests changed from the role-playing fantasies that he had been into during the London period to a more gentle and loving approach. 'It became different,' says Eugenie. 'It became more of a spiritual way of making love rather than the ordinary way of having sex. He was reading books on Tantric sex and it was the way of consciously feeling each other's energy. He would talk to me about how you could heighten your pleasure through different ways of breathing. He thought sex could be a healing thing.'

13

Resurrection

As cold waters to a thirsty soul, so is good news from a far
country.   Proverbs 25:25

Just as Marvin had moved to England to escape the problems of
America, he had come to Belgium to leave behind the temptations of
England. As debts accumulated and the patience of those who had
tried to help him was wearing thin, he knew that it was time to pack
his bags and start over again—again. 'It was a good time to leave
because things were getting worse and worse for him in London,' says
Eugenie. 'Money was difficult. There were all kinds of problems building up. Like Marvin had done before when things got difficult, he just
moved. In Ostend he was able to pull himself together.'

Cousaert, who spoke excellent English, was not only an astute businessman used to promoting black American musicians in Europe but a
sincere fan of Marvin's music since the day in 1965 when he had
bought a copy of 'Ain't That Peculiar' from Harlequin Records in Soho's
Berwick Street. After meeting him it became Cousaert's dream to
rebuild the life of this hero whose career was at its lowest point for
twenty years.

Marvin responded well to the attention. Like his previous mentors, Harvey Fuqua and Berry Gordy, Cousaert combined his caring with toughness. Like them, too, he was a physically strong man with a love of sport, boxing in particular. Marvin and Eugenie became absorbed into Cousaert's family, eating meals with him, his wife Lilliane and their two young daughters in their *pension* on the sea-front and talking with them late into the night. 'I became both his closest friend and a kind of a brother,' says Cousaert. 'We did everything together. We jogged together, we cycled together and we even wore one another's clothes because we were the same size.' Marvin echoed the sentiment: 'Ostend became my orphanage,' he admitted, during a candid moment. 'After all, I was virtually an orphan.'

Although Ostend, with its population of 80,000, was not a throbbing metropolis like Detroit or Los Angeles it had other rewards to offer. Marvin visited churches, art galleries and museums, and learned European history from Cousaert, who was also an experienced tour guide and spoke six languages. He felt invigorated by the freshness of the breeze blowing in over the North Sea and by the relative tranquillity of the streets. The brooding grey skies of winter synchronized with his own melancholy moods. In Europe he felt connected to the history of art and detached from show-business. When describing his work during this period he would constantly stress the difference between art and commerce and draw comparisons between what he was doing and what artists such as Rembrandt and Picasso had done on canvas. He began to feel respect and appreciation.

'He found peace in Ostend,' says Eugenie. 'There weren't people coming into his home all the time as there had been in London. It was quiet. Marvin had a piano and he just started to write music again.'

He and Eugenie even socialized like a normal couple, playing darts at a nearby pub, buying their bread from a small bakery and making friends with local people like Donald and Margaret Pylyser, who had none of the power complexes and jealousies that characterized the music scene in Los Angeles. 'I didn't know shit about Marvin when I first met him,' says Pylyser, a composer and musician, influenced at the time by African music and bands such as Talking Heads, who wrote three songs with Marvin during his stay. 'I didn't know about his divorce and I didn't know about his problems with drugs. He didn't talk about the difficulties he was having. He would just talk about life. He came over as a very normal person.'

After he had spent time relaxing and detoxifying his system, Marvin was ready to contemplate his comeback. The most urgent matter was to settle his debts, and with this in mind Cousaert began to plan a summer tour of Europe that would make him £56,000. Then came the vexed issue of his relationship with Motown. If, as he had threatened, he was never going to record with the company again, how could he get out of a contract that still had nine years to run? Would Motown be willing to release him or would they punish him for his past demeanours by making him stay? Cousaert thought that Motown was the best label for him to be on, but Marvin was determined to leave.

As he mulled over these possibilities his future was already falling into place. Following his disgruntled interviews in the British press after the release of *In Our Lifetime*, word was out that Marvin could be open to offers. Elektra/Asylum offered to fly him and Cousaert to New York on Concorde. Arista was ready to come to Ostend. Larkin Arnold, senior vice president of CBS Records and then one of the highest-placed black men in the recording industry, had been tipped off by Curtis Shaw. 'Curtis told me that potentially he could be available,' remembers Arnold, 'so I told him to hook us up. I needed to get over to Belgium to see him for myself because the only thing that concerned me was his mental state. I'd heard about him disrespecting Princess Margaret, the drugs and the whole situation. Much to my surprise I found him in fairly good spirits and in good health. He was jogging on the beach and keeping fit. I felt that he had the capacity to do something new. I don't think true genius ever dies. You can cloud it up, you can submerge it in a lot of problems and tensions, but if God has blessed you it hardly ever really goes away. Especially in the field of music.'

The fact that Arnold was black and that he'd proved himself more powerful than Berry Gordy by luring Michael Jackson to CBS in 1975 appealed to Marvin. He thought Arnold would understand his frustration with the white-dominated record industry.

Negotiations with CBS continued as spring turned into summer, with Arnold meeting Marvin in Ostend and Brussels, fine-tuning a workable contract, listening to Marvin's new songs and suggesting music from the current *Billboard* charts such as Kool and the Gang that might inspire him. They sat together and reviewed his past albums, picking out the strengths and weaknesses, plotting a way forward that would combine the necessary commercialism with artistic integrity.

When it finally came, the break with Motown wasn't as traumatic as everyone had feared. Aware that nothing good was going to come from Marvin if he was held to a contract with which he was unhappy, the company agreed to let him go for a payment of $1.5 million. It was a cool, business-like end to a tumultuous relationship of both blood and money that had dominated his entire adulthood.

The relationship between Berry and Marvin was deep and complex. Berry viewed his wayward artist as a rather recalcitrant child. Marvin viewed his boss and former brother-in-law as an overbearing father. But, in the final analysis, both men loved and respected each other. 'Deep down in my guts I admire the man immensely,' said Marvin of Berry in 1983. 'He'll be remembered a damn sight longer than any Motown artist.'

Still eight months away from signing the final draft of his contract with CBS, Marvin embarked on his A Heavy Love Affair tour—during which he expressed his disgust with Motown by refusing to sing 'A Heavy Love Affair', his latest single on the label. It opened on 13 July 1981 at the Hippodrome in Bristol, England, and then played three nights at the Apollo in London, where the reviewers applauded rapturously what they saw as displaying a fresh optimism. 'An easy natural perfection,' commented *New Musical Express*. 'The voice is rich, dark, soulful; the music a smooth selection of dream songs.' *Melody Maker* called it 'riveting', 'a pure revelation' and said that Marvin was 'assured and confident'. 'He exuded confidence and strength, intuitively knowing when to hold back or burst forward,' said reviewer Paolo Hewitt. 'Tackling his material with such a positive attitude, his performance was soul itself, stunning in its execution and hypnotic in variety.'

The tour finished on 4 July in Ostend, with a show at the Casino, televised live for Belgian TV. Immediately afterwards he went into studios at the seventeenth-century Château d'Hierouville forty kilometres north of Paris to produce a French band in a straightforward money-making exercise he had contracted to do while in London. The project turned into a fiasco. After a week at the château, which had top-class cuisine and accommodation, and even its own vineyard, he and the band were all so stoned that the tapes were accidentally erased and the project lost.

Meetings with Larkin Arnold followed in Paris, where Marvin stayed two nights at the elegant Hôtel George V off the Champs-Elysées. Jan flew in with Nona to try to reach an agreement over the children. She then followed him to Ostend, where she and Nona stayed at the apartment while Eugenie was ordered to move to a local hotel. Ever optimistic, Marvin harboured the fantasy of resurrecting their marriage, inspired in part by the happy Cousaert household, but the betrayals of the past were insurmountable. The episode ended in more fights, and Jan left in September for America with Bubby and Nona. 'Marvin and I broke up and got back together so many times,' she says. 'There were many times when Eugenie would be on her way out and I'd be on my way in. There was a lot of drama. I think Marvin was embarrassed about Eugenie and she was kind of swept under the carpet. In a way I felt sorry for her. She was used. She walked him through a real tough time and I applaud her for that.'

The time spent apart during Jan's visit and the clarity of thinking made possible by six drug-free months caused Eugenie to reassess her position as the mistress of Marvin Gaye. Despite all the fights and accusations between him and Jan she realized that a strong bond remained. His wife's lengthy phone calls from America still had the power to devastate him. Once he had even cancelled a concert because he felt so emotional after talking to her. However far away she was, she was always under his skin. On a piece of hotel notepaper after one such phone call he had written, 'The greater the love, the greater the pain.' 'I began to ask myself what I was doing living in Belgium,' says Eugenie. 'I knew that I needed to do something with my life so I decided to study in Amsterdam during the week and return to Ostend for the weekends. Marvin didn't want me to go, but it was good for him because he found himself alone and he started to write again.'

Eugenie linked up with Deon Estus, the American bass player who had been on the Heavy Love Affair tour and who was still in Europe, hoping for more work with Marvin. The two of them had a brief affair in London. After returning to Ostend, Eugenie discovered that she was pregnant. When Marvin was told what had happened he was furious and paid for her to have an abortion. Estus, who never even knew about the pregnancy, was not invited again to work with Marvin.

Cousaert began to exert pressure on Marvin to come up with new songs. Marvin wanted to make an autumn tour of Britain because he knew he could make quick money that way but Cousaert, on the advice of Larkin Arnold, discouraged him because he knew that CBS wouldn't get their album on time. As always, Marvin resented being told what to do: 'You're not my father, Freddy,' he told him. 'I left my father when I was sixteen.' Yet he took the advice, and knuckled down to some composing.

By the autumn of 1981 a handful of songs had emerged, and he worked on them in the home studio he had set up in his apartment with £25,000 worth of equipment purchased for him by CBS in Brussels. His cohorts were keyboard player Odell Brown, who had stayed in Belgium since the last tour, and guitarist Gordon Banks, now his brother-in-law through marriage to Sweetsie, who flew back to help him. Within three months Marvin was ready to start recording and Cousaert booked him into a little-known four-track studio in Ohaine, a village just outside Brussels, where he laid down four tracks. Producing the sessions himself, he used Banks and local musician Danny Bosaert on guitars, Brown on keyboards and Donnie Hagen on drums.

At this point the project had no shape or direction. Marvin would spend hours lying on a couch, writing snatches of lyrics on pieces of paper. Discarded titles included 'Obsessive Observer,' 'Bad Cut' and 'This Is The Only Place We've Got.' As with *In Our Lifetime*, the themes were either maudlin ruminations on his romantic life or visions of the end of the world, as the fragments of lyrics left with Eugenie Vis show.

Larkin Arnold tried to get him to lighten up by encouraging him to listen to contemporary pop and steering him away from attempting another significant concept album. His last two recordings had missed the mark, Arnold told him, because they were too personal and tried to say too much. 'His biggest problem,' says Arnold, 'was that he had become suffocated by *What's Going On*. The challenge of trying to match that album had stifled his regular creativity. He was working on songs about nuclear disarmament and it just wasn't falling together. I would say, "Marvin. Don't try and match *What's Going On* because you dealt with everything that had to be dealt with on that album. You dealt with racism, sexism, war, poverty and the environment. You touched on all the major topics of the day. What more can you say?" I told him that rather than stop recording because he didn't have another epic he should go ahead and record anyway because people just wanted to hear his voice, regardless of what the topic was.'

He liked to compose by recording himself singing along to cassettes of rhythm track. He would start with a title or a couple of prepared lines and work with nothing more than a Roland synthesizer and the drum machine given to him by Stevie Wonder when they met in London. The music would suggest words, which in turn would suggest subjects. It was a musical approximation of the speaking in tongues that he had witnessed in childhood. The first songs to hit the mark had been 'Midnight Lady' and 'Rockin' After Midnight'—with a riff from Danny Bosaert—sex and dance songs, which seemed to fulfil Arnold's requirement for a commercial album. 'As an artist you want to record songs you feel strongly about,' said Marvin. 'But, in my case, I don't think commercially. As a record man, Larkin Arnold thinks commercially and since he and CBS have been so marvellous to me, I decided to give them artistic control.'

'It was natural for him to want to make something commercial,' says Eugenie, 'but I think that at that time he was going in a more noncommercial direction and now he found himself pushed back by CBS. Things to do with sex were, of course, very good if you wanted to make a commercial album.'

His brother Frankie thinks that what happened in Belgium set the course for his final days, taking him away from his true calling as a songwriter with a social conscience and an awareness of the spiritual realm, and turning him into a black sex god. 'It was always a struggle for Marvin between the truths of his upbringing and the world out there,' says Frankie. 'The force behind the industry said to him, "Marvin. You cannot sing religious songs. You've got to sing sexy songs because that's where the money is. That's what the people expect from you." He was torn.'

Arnold denies that this was so. 'This was basically the album he came up with,' he says. 'After having dealt with the issues of the world the thing he told me was that there would always be problems until the relationships between men and women were resolved. A lot of the things that people do wrong and don't do right are because of frustrations in their relationships.'

'Sexual Healing' was recorded during the December sessions as a funky instrumental. Odell Brown wrote it while he was staying at the Cousaerts'. He was so sure that he had a hit on his hands that he asked for Larkin Arnold to be present when he handed over the tape to Marvin: he didn't want his tune ripped off and credited to Marvin alone. Marvin struggled to find a lyric to match the rhythms of the music. Brown encouraged him to sit on the breakwater down on the beach and grab some images from the lashing waves and the overcast sky. Using this as a stimulus, Marvin painstakingly put together lines that spoke of a storm raging inside him and the waves that threatened to engulf him.

It was left incomplete until March 1982, when the American writer David Ritz turned up in Ostend uninvited, ostensibly to research a story on Marvin for *Rolling Stone*. One night Marvin showed Ritz some of the sado-masochistic magazines he had been collecting, in particular some violent cartoon strips where women were being penetrated by various objects. Taken aback, Ritz suggested to Marvin that he was in need of some 'sexual healing'. Marvin was immediately taken with the phrase and suggested using it as the title of the album. Ritz had used it to mean that Marvin required healing from his sexual dysfunctionalism but Marvin saw it as meaning that sex itself contained healing powers. After Ritz had left for America, Marvin worked the phrase into Brown's song.

Despite his profligacy, Marvin still felt that he was sexually repressed. Pornography and prostitutes for him, he felt, were ways of acknowledging the fantasies he had been taught to be ashamed of. Eugenie once spoke to a prostitute that Marvin had just spent time with, who told her that he hadn't penetrated her. He had just wanted to talk and fantasize. 'Too many of us have pent-up sexual energies that are never released,' he explained to the *Los Angeles Times* later that year. 'That screws a lot of people up. What they need is to live out their fantasies. Their sex lives are sick and they need sexual healing. Everybody would be happier and less crazy if they could do what they wanted to sexually.' It was a persistent Marvin Gaye theme. Ten years earlier he had told Tim Cahill of *Rolling Stone* that he was 'a fantasy person' and complained that society 'makes people creep and crawl, and accentuates perversity. I suppose it makes it more fun for the pervert, though. Who wants to be perverse if everybody says "OK. Go ahead. We don't care"?'

Marvin's fantasies revolved around voyeurism and domination, perhaps because emotional involvement and sexual inadequacy were among his greatest fears. He had problems with impotence and premature ejaculation, which made voyeurism an attractive option, and his worries about being manly enough were alleviated if the woman agreed to a submissive role.

Eugenie felt that his primary sexual need was to feel in complete control. 'He liked to be the master,' she says. 'He also liked to experiment. Once he had a whip and he played with it. Another time he asked me to sleep with some other women because he wanted to see that, but he never hurt me or let himself get out of control.'

Obsessively hygienic, he would take frequent showers and would clean the toilet at least twice a day. The dirtiest sexual act, for him, was kissing because he felt it was too intimate. 'He would do it,' says Eugenie, 'but it was a very touchy area for him.'

In the spring of 1982 Marvin had to take temporary leave of Belgium, because he didn't have a resident's visa, and decided to come to England. On a previous visit to London in the middle of February he had made contact with his old friend John Benson, who was DJ at Legends. While hanging out at the club he met Maryam 'Mimi' Talebpour, an Iranian divorcée who had fled with her family to England following the overthrow of the Shah of Iran in 1979. They had been attracted to each other and he planned to spend his time out of Belgium with her at her country home near Woking in Surrey. 'We used to call her the Persian Princess,' says Benson, who introduced the couple. 'She wasn't a young girl. At the time she was in her mid-thirties. She wasn't a raving beauty either but she was a woman of substance and she was a woman who satisfied Marvin aesthetically and spiritually.'

The affair was also unusual in that Marvin allowed it to run concurrently with his relationship with Eugenie, neither woman realizing the significance of the other. He told Mimi that Eugenie was no more than someone who 'looks after me and does the cooking and cleaning' and that he had been celibate for the past three years, which he later repeated to the *Los Angeles Times*. He did not let Eugenie know that Mimi was anything more than a friend.

In the country Marvin spent his time writing while Mimi gardened and cooked. Together they would take long walks across the fields and discuss their view of nature and religion. During this time, according to Mimi, he proposed to her. She declined, not because she didn't love him, she says, but because she sensed the enormity of the problems surrounding him. There would be phone calls from Jan and from Eugenie, even though he denied having given them the number. Then there were the crazy friends in London who were supplying him with cocaine. 'I didn't think that things were right,' she says. 'If I want another half I want my other half to be my other half. I didn't want all these women calling up. It was just like a stupid movie. I had gone beyond that. I had other goals in my life.'

One of his fantasies was to have all his favourite women living in the same house or at least near to each other. He told Eugenie that he wanted to buy Jan a house in Brussels while they lived together outside Ostend. With Mimi he planned a similarly ideal situation in Jamaica, where he was going to develop his land outside of Ochos Rios. 'He would draw maps,' says Mimi. 'He would say, "When we get married we'll go here and we'll build a house here." The last time he did a drawing he drew a house and said, "That's the part of the house where the children will stay with their mom." I said, "Wait a minute! Where I come from, people don't bring their past wives along.' "

When it finally came time to leave, Mimi's housekeeper drove Marvin to the local station, where he caught a train to London and made his way back to Belgium by ferry. 'She later told me that Marvin started crying while he was in her car,' says Mimi. 'He told her that he didn't want to leave me and my house but he had to go because he had to sort things out in Ostend. Marvin wasn't the sort of man to look you right in the eyes and tell you that he loved you, but he was romantic in his heart and in his soul.'

Once back in Ostend, it was time to complete the second half of the album, as he was already up against the original deadline set by CBS when he signed the contract in March. To prevent a repeat of the *Love Man/In Our Lifetime* débâcle Larkin Arnold arranged for Harvey

Fuqua to go to Ohaine to oversee the final recording sessions. Arnold's main concern was that he didn't want the release date of Marvin's album to conflict with that of Michael Jackson's *Thriller*, scheduled for December, which he was also responsible for overseeing.

Within four days of Arnold's invitation Fuqua was on a plane to Belgium with his girlfriend Marilyn Freeman. Marvin welcomed the reunion with his old mentor but Cousaert felt threatened because it naturally diminished his role. Fuqua, for his part, didn't much care for Cousaert. 'We sort of kept him out,' he says. 'It was distracting to have a manager standing around.'

Through a company (AAEAA) set up for him by Cousaert and a French accountant, Marvin was able to buy a twenty-one-room house in the village of Moere and move in with Eugenie, who excitedly bought new furnishings. It was here that Fuqua and Freeman stayed while the album was finished. With his unique gift at shaping harmonies and melodies, Fuqua began to polish off the project. 'I used the tracks that had already been laid down and we cut some more after I arrived,' he says. 'We did the album piecemeal. Marvin had been a little lazy about it but we finally got it done.'

There were new influences in the second half of the album, prompted by Marvin's exposure to African music in Paris, where he'd met musicians from Algeria, and by the dance music and reggae he'd heard in London. 'Joy' was a tribute to his early church background and 'Third World Girl' was written after a seance he took part in with Eugenie and some Belgian friends in Ostend. 'We made contact with Bob Marley,' says Eugenie. 'There was a message from him for Marvin which was that he should write a reggae song. It was as a direct result of this that he went away and wrote "Third World Girl."'

Just as the album took its final shape, Interpol turned up at Cousaert's home looking for Marvin, who, they claimed, had been around when a Guyanese drug dealer had been shot in Copenhagen. 'If Marvin had said that he was in Copenhagen but had never seen the guy, they would have left him alone,' says Cousaert. 'But Marvin told them that he had never been there, which he hadn't. The truth was that his brother Frankie had been there, but not with any bad intentions. This dealer was also a promoter and he was using Frankie to try to get Marvin to Copenhagen. He had already been to Belgium and I'd told him to leave.'

Cousaert eventually cleared the matter up with Belgium's Minister of Justice, who supplied Marvin with a hot-line number to call if he had further problems with the police. There was no need for him to leave the country again but Marvin claimed that he wanted to go in order to stay on the safe side of the Belgian authorities. What Cousaert suspected was that Marvin was using the incident as an excuse to break free of his control, and that Harvey Fuqua was weaning him away because he sensed that Marvin's career was entering an upturn.

His suspicion that Marvin was restless and ready to leave proved well grounded. Fuqua took him off to Munich, where Bobby Stern, an American musician living in Germany, was brought in to overdub tenor sax on two tracks and harmonica on another at Arco Studios. Here they were joined by Eugenie and Marilyn Freeman, who had announced that she was Marvin's new manager, even though she had no show-business experience and had previously worked as a school administrator.

'Marvin liked Freddy,' says Eugenie, 'but at the same time he felt that he was into business and that he was overpowering. One of the things he talked about was how Freddy was like a jealous wife. He meant it well but his ego took over.'

From Munich Fuqua returned to Los Angeles to mix the album at Devonshire Studios while Marvin and Eugenie headed for Paris, where they stayed at the Sheraton and then at an apartment, owned by an African musician, in Montparnasse close to La Coupole. While they were there, Jan arrived back with Bubby and Nona, and Eugenie had to return to Amsterdam.

'I followed Marvin all over the place,' says Jan. 'These were attempts to mend things and we'd go through a couple of weeks of everything being great, and inevitably an ex-girlfriend or an ex-boyfriend would come into play and we'd break up. But then we would always get back together, despite the Eugenies and the Teddy Pender-grasses. We always thought of each other as soul-mates.

'It was humiliating for Eugenie, I'm sure. I know I had my share of humiliation with her because he had her in my face and I greatly resented it. So he removed her and I stayed, and then he and I got into a fight and the next thing I knew was that I was on my way out and she was on her way in. We passed each other in the hallway several times.'

With the CBS advance supposedly safe in a Swiss bank, Marvin decided to go to Geneva and see if he could draw on it but, after handing his passport to a cashier, discovered that he was not yet a recognized signatory to the account. According to Cousaert, this was because, in Ostend, Marvin had refused to sign French documents until they were translated for him and this had left Cousaert and his French accountant as the only signatories.

When refused access Marvin went berserk and demanded that Cousaert come to Geneva to sort it out. When Cousaert came a physical fight ensued. Marvin genuinely thought he had been cheated, that Cousaert had been feathering his own nest with Marvin's earnings. It was all he needed to push him firmly on the side of Fuqua and Marilyn Freeman, both of whom were as suspicious of Cousaert as he was of them.

'Things were already tense between Freddy and Marvin when we left Belgium,' says Eugenie. 'Now Marvin thought that he understood why Freddy spent so much time on his account books. Marilyn Freeman and Harvey Fuqua came to Geneva with money to help him out and then they all came up to Holland.'

When he arrived he called his assistant Kitty Sears in Los Angeles and asked her to contact Don Joe Medlevine of Marquee Entertainment to see if he would tour him in America when the album came out. Medlevine, a well-connected Jewish promoter who ran the Circle Star Theatre in San Carlos, California, and counted Frank Sinatra and Wayne Newton among his clients, was interested and agreed to sort out Marvin's most immediate problem—the debt to the IRS, which would prevent him from working and could even result in his arrest on landing. Marvin couldn't have forgotten that, three months before he left America in 1979, Medlevine had paid him $75,000 for two nights at the Circle Star.

'I made the arrangements with the IRS,' says Leonard Bloom, who had just purchased Marquee Entertainment from Medlevine but was still using Medlevine's contacts and expertise. 'He had a huge tax liability at that time. If I hadn't have done that he couldn't have performed.' The debt wasn't cancelled but arrangements were made for regular instalments to be paid directly from his record royalties and tour receipts.

Marvin left Europe in late September 1982 after a final television show in Holland because he'd just heard that his mother was to go into hospital for a kidney operation. He told Jan to tell Cousaert that he would return to Europe in two weeks' time, saying, 'I don't think I could live in America again.' During his last evening with Eugenie, in a Rotterdam hotel, Marvin brought back another woman to play with. Eugenie, who up to now had meekly tolerated his indiscretions, broke down. 'I realized that things were never going to work out the way I wanted and so I took a huge sniff of cocaine and I had to go to a doctor because I felt like jumping out of the window,' she recalls. 'It had been strange that night because Harvey had been asking me if I wanted to marry Marvin and we had discussed the possibility of me coming over later. Harvey had said that when someone like Marvin returns to America it was important that he make a good entrance and, of course, it wouldn't have been good at that time for him to have been seen with a white girlfriend.

'I went back to the house in Moere and cleared out all of Marvin's things, including the instruments that he had got from CBS, and then I went back to Amsterdam to cool down. We spoke to each other on the phone after that but with more time on my own I had a chance to think over what had become of my life. He later sent me an airline ticket to come and join him but I sent it back.'

Marvin flew back to Los Angeles from Rotterdam with Fuqua, Freeman, Jan, Bubby and Nona. Although he despised America for its obsession with glamour he was also drawn to it because of the huge rewards and the possibility it held out of recognition from the recording industry. His stubbornness made him an artist who felt at home in Europe but his insecurity made him a star that fed on the glitz of America.

His return home couldn't have been timed more perfectly. 'Sexual Healing', his first single in eighteen months, was heading to the top of the charts, as was *Midnight Love*, which would eventually sell over two million copies, making it his best-selling album since *Let's Get It On.* CBS threw a big party for him at a club on Sunset Strip, where he was awarded gold discs for both records. After snorting cocaine in the men's room Marvin joined Larkin Arnold on stage to address the guests, who included both Anna and Jan. 'Someone asked me yesterday about my belief in God and this sex business,' he started. 'I'll answer now as I did then, that perhaps in the past my consciousness was not all it should have been. But during the recording of this record I felt very close to my Maker and I see this as a means towards the end of serving him.' He then sang an a capella version of the Lord's Prayer, which moved everyone in the room.

He stayed with Marilyn Freeman in her Brentwood apartment. On 15 November the final judgment was passed on his second marriage. Jan was to have custody of the children, with Marvin granted 'reasonable' visitation rights. He also had to pay $2,000 a month for the children, $2,500 a month to Jan and a $2,500 attorney's bill.

A week later he went to Palm Springs to meet up with Don Joe Medlevine, who was staying at the home of Frank Sinatra's mother. Marvin took his own mother with him to help her recuperate after her operation and rented a house for them both. Inexplicably, during his wife's time of need, Marvin's father had returned to Washington DC for an extended visit during which he sold the house on Varnum Avenue and all its contents. Polly Solomon remembers that during this stay he paid several visits to the House of God dressed in a burgundy suit that seemed a little 'fly' for the church members. He played the piano for them and sang some gospel songs but he was clearly no longer a part of what was going on. 'Once you are gone from the Church for a long time there is a difference,' says Polly. 'You lose connections. He no longer had the fire, the spark, the enthusiasm. We hoped that he would come back. We loved him and tried to show that all was forgiven. We put our arms out to him but it didn't last.'

14

Climax

The wicked flee when no man pursueth: but the righteous
are bold as a lion.   Proverbs 28:1

Nineteen eighty-three should have been one of the best years of
Marvin's career. *Midnight Love*, despite its superficiality, had ini-
tiated a remarkable come-back for a man believed to be a commercial has-been. Following his two divorces, he was back on friendly
terms with both his ex-wives, had a luxurious rented home in Bel Air
and the potential to settle his huge debts. Don Joe Medlevine had
bought him a silver-grey Clenet and a navy blue BMW to replace the
fleet of cars he had been forced to sell off.

Instead it was a year of tragic decline, during which all his weaknesses, anxieties and insecurities conspired to destroy him. It was as
though he was destined to live out the words of 'Flyin' High (In The
Friendly Sky)', the song he'd written with Elgie Stover in Detroit for
What's Going On, where he'd spoken of being so stupid-minded that he
was constantly drawn to the place where danger waited for him. Con-
tributing to his problems was cocaine, which he was now freebasing.

'He had always done a lot of cocaine but no one can handle freebasing,' says trumpet player Nolan Smith. 'I guess Marvin thought that he had been taking cocaine for so long that he could do it, but he couldn't. It took him out. That's what messed up Marvin.'

The most immediately obvious effect of the drug was that he became increasingly suspicious of everyone, especially his closest friends. He argued with Harvey Fuqua and Larkin Arnold, sacked Marilyn Freeman and was convinced that Jan had hired a gunman to kill him. He even accused Kitty Sears, his faithful personal assistant, of conspiring against him. 'He just started to do too much of the stuff,' says Mark Gaillard. 'He was on the stuff all the time and after a while he was completely out there. It got to the point where he was hallucinating. He would imagine that everyone was trying to do something to him. He was afraid of his own friends.' The drug that had once bathed him in a sweet glow of confidence was now controlling and humiliating him. The fears and pangs of conscience it had once anaesthetized were now immune to its powers and he felt himself being taken over by all that was worst in his nature. 'He became a person who really hated himself,' says Joe Schaffner. 'it was as if he had been injected with something and it was now starting to grow in him. As it grew, it got worse. It was like a cancer.'

Asked if he was a happy man, Marvin had admitted to British journalist Gavin Martin that he wasn't. 'I'm sad because I'm schizophrenic, torn between many passions, desires and lovers,' he said. 'I'm sad because I know the bottom line, I know what is going to happen to this world. It saddens me that I have to condescend in order to be heard.'

Jan witnessed him alternating between two opposing visions of himself. At times he would see himself in an almost saintly role, as though he had been sent to earth on a mission. Then he would change and would wallow in his baseness, blaming the drugs for all his excesses. This came over in interviews from this period. He told New York music writer Nelson George that he had a mission, 'to tell the world and people about the upcoming holocaust and to find all those of higher consciousness who can be saved'. To another journalist he joked about stripping on his forthcoming tour or maybe even having sex on stage. 'That would be a hell of an act!'

'Coke was his excuse for revelling in all the evils of life,' says Jan. 'Then he would repent and go into his preaching mode. He would tell everyone working for him who was doing drugs that they were wrong. Then he would get weak again as most addicts do. There would be times when he would go to God. He would be on his knees praying. Once, when we were freebasing together, he broke his pipe by putting his Bible on top of it and standing on the Bible. That was his symbolic way of saying, "God, please remove this evil from my life." Then, two or three days later, we had bought another pipe and were sitting around stoned.'

In January 1983 his father returned from his sojourn in Washington DC and the two men faced each other for the first time since 1979. Things hadn't improved. Marvin was disgusted that his father hadn't been around in his mother's time of need and that he hadn't shared with her the proceeds on the sale of the Washington home. His father disapproved of his son's latest sexy music. When he established himself back at Gramercy Place, the relaxed and jovial atmosphere that had prevailed for the last six months suddenly changed.

'From the day I met Marvin until the day he died Marvin's father was jealous of him,' says Jan. 'You could feel it in the air. You could cut it with a knife. It was the fact that Marvin had always had women after him, the fact that Marvin was one of the most classically chiselled handsome men whereas he was a mutant version of Marvin. It was the fact that Marvin could sing and be paid for it. The fact that Marvin could circulate with the élite.'

The most painful thing, for Marvin's father, must have been the realization that the son whom he had chastised had not only survived the humiliations but had gone on to supersede him in every area of life. It was Marvin, and not he, who had the huge congregations and whose opinions on spiritual matters were discussed in the media. It was Marvin whose money had provided the family with a home. 'It's supposed to be the daddy who is the president of the family,' says Ed Townsend. 'It created conflicts when Marvin became the president and started to earn more than his daddy and everybody ran to Marvin instead of to his daddy. People tend to obey those who support them, those who put the bread on the table.'

Although he was aware of his elevated position in the family, Marvin didn't appear to resent his father. There were things he disliked about him—in particular his treatment of his mother—but his overriding desire for the whole of his life had been to win his father's love and to feel that he had been a success in his eyes. 'Marvin wanted his father's approval but, more than that, he wanted to show him that he was better, that he was more attractive and more talented,' says Jan. 'Marvin was all the things that his father would never be and it was because of all the bad treatment he received as a child—the beatings, the demeaning comments, the "you'll never be anythings", the "so whats" and the "you're not all that goods". The reality of it was that Marvin was all that, and more.'

Marvin's deterioration was a secret known only to his family, friends and business associates. To the watching world he was a storming success. He was chosen to sing the national anthem at the opening of the NBA All-Star game at the Forum in Inglewood on 13 February 1983 and just over a week later, at the Shrine Auditorium, he picked up two Grammys (his first) for the Best Male Vocal and Best Instrumental Performance in the R&B section. Although he was now dating Faith Thomas, an insurance consultant from San Francisco, he took Anna as his special guest. Ironically, the award was given to him by his old love rival Rick James. According to his valet Odell George—known to everyone in the business as Gorgeous George—he was so proud of the achievement that he kept his tuxedo on for the next two days.

Marvin III, as Little Marvin was now known, by now seventeen and keen to get to know the father who had been absent for so long, attended the NBA event with Marvin, who chose it as the moment to reveal to the boy his true parentage. They were in the dressing room along with his bodyguard Gerald White and four other people when he blurted it out. 'He just said, "Son, there's something I need to tell you. I want to be truthful with you. I'm your father, but Anna is not your mother,' " says Gerald. 'The kid just broke down in hysterics and ran out of the room. I went down the hall and brought him back. Later I told Marvin that he should never have done it.'

Since returning from Europe Marvin had been avoiding making concrete plans for his tour with Marquee Entertainment, but financially he knew it was something he had to do. CBS had been pushing him because the album was now four months old and they were worried about a tour taking place when it had gone cold. The fact that he was with Marquee Entertainment was a controversial one for the black promoters who had been let down by Marvin in the past. Not surprisingly, they felt that they should benefit from his come-back. Alvin Few of Atlanta, in particular, expected that Marvin would compensate him for past mistakes. In the end, only two black promoters were allowed to buy dates on the Midnight Love tour of America—Al Hayman of Los Angeles and W. G. Garrison of Baton Rouge.

Don Joe Medlevine, who was then seventy-three, became very close to Marvin, showering him with gifts and offering him advice. 'Marvin never had the love from his father that he so desperately wanted,' says Kitty Sears. 'That's why he went with Don Joe. That's why he clung to him. That's why he always called him Dad, because Don Joe respected Marvin and he treated him like a son.'

The tour became an expensive one, lasting over four months and using twenty-five musicians, plus backing vocalists. During each two-and-a-half-hour show there were costume changes and back-projection sequences of Marvin singing with Tammi Terrell. Sponsorship deals with Chrysler and Budweiser were planned but eventually there wasn't enough time to negotiate them properly. In the month before rehearsals Marvin checked into a San Francisco hotel and sent Gorgeous George out to buy him a tape deck and copies of all his albums. 'He told me he couldn't remember all the lyrics,' says George, 'so every morning of every day I would put Marvin's stuff on the ghetto-blaster and let him relearn them.'

The tour was dogged by problems right from the start. On 13 April, Marvin was summonsed to appear in court on 7 July because of his failure to maintain his payments to Jan. By the time the tour got under way, the *Midnight Love* album was history. Larkin Arnold's attention was taken up with another CBS project—Michael Jackson's *Thriller*, destined to be one of the biggest-selling albums of all time. Marvin's current single, 'Joy', hadn't even made a chart entry. Michael Jackson's singles 'Beat It' and 'Billie Jean' had made it to number one. The inadequate preparation time had resulted in sluggish ticket sales.

'The tour started too late,' says Joe Schaffner. 'It was too long after he'd won the Grammy and the album itself really wasn't strong enough to support a whole tour. He just didn't have the product to support the event.'

Yet it wasn't the economics of the tour that bothered Marvin once he hit the road but the politics. Threats were made, which filtered back to Marvin and made him fear for his life. He imagined a hired assassin shooting him as he performed, and became convinced that he was being supplied with cocaine cut with a poison. His two bodyguards, Andre and Gerald White, were flown in from Tampa, Florida, to head up a security team.

The Whites, who had a combined weight of over seven hundred pounds and were known as the Bruise Brothers to those on the tour who didn't care for them, worked well together. Andre, who stood six foot five, tended to reason with Marvin while Gerald bullied him and told him not to be so damn silly. Both of them terrified potential interlopers. One unfortunate cocaine dealer who found his way to Marvin's hotel suite was made by Andre to consume his own merchandise on the spot. He lost consciousness and had to be taken to hospital.

The two most important tasks for the brothers were to remove Marvin's fears of being attacked and to keep him clean. This latter task was made virtually impossible because the drugs were eventually being supplied to him by his own relatives and friends of his relatives. 'By being head of security I could control everything,' says Gerald, 'but I couldn't control his own family. They would get cocaine to him.'

When the tour hit Radio City Music Hall in New York there was backstage confrontation with the controversial activist and preacher Al Sharpton, and the White brothers were called in to sort it out. 'Sharpton's group felt that black promoters weren't getting what they deserved,' says Andre. 'I had to explain that we had gotten the money for these dates and we were going to play them. They got a little . . . I guess you could say "disappointed", and started threatening. I had to let them know that we had ways of sorting that out.'

'There were some very ugly scenes in New York,' remembers Kitty Sears. 'Andre and Gerald were waving guns and telling everyone to get out the way. Don Joe just invited Al Sharpton back to the Waldorf Astoria. Al had some non-profit organization and so Don Joe says, "Why don't I give you a donation?" We didn't hear from Al after that.'

Andre White was becoming concerned at Marvin's cocaine consumption. One night in New York he found him in his bedroom, his head hung over a bowl, with blood pouring out of his nose because of damaged membranes. Another time Marvin dismantled the phone next to his bed because he said there were voices speaking to him from it.

When they reached Baltimore, Andre made an arrangement with the civil-rights leader Dick Gregory, now a leading nutritional expert, to collect Marvin and have him detoxified on a farm in Massachusetts during a short break between dates. But, as with so many important engagements in his life, he blew it out, stubbornly refusing to leave his hotel room, although Gregory had interrupted his work schedule to help him. As the tour progressed he became more and more paranoid, convinced that there was a killer lurking in the wings. He had his brother Frankie join the tour and his old friend from Los Angeles, Dave Simmons, who had to stand at the side of the stage watching for potential assassins. His sister Sweetsie had to bring him his water on stage to prevent anyone poisoning him. He even had a Baptist preacher, Dave Futch, to offer him spiritual consolation and lead a prayer time before each show.

In Merillville, Indiana, he was confronted by members of El Rukns, the notorious Chicago street gang whose leader, Jeff Fort, was jailed four years later for conspiring to commit explosions in America on behalf of the Libyans. El Rukns had connections both with the Black Muslim movement and with organized crime. They challenged Marvin over his use of a white promoter for the tour. 'They thought Marvin was doing wrong,' says Gerald. 'Andre and I had to come in to tell them that Marvin didn't control everything and that Don Joe had done a deal with the IRS to get him back into the US.' In Detroit Marvin was convinced that Jan's stepfather, Earl Hunter, had ordered a Mafia hit because of the way he had treated Jan. When he played the Joe Louis Arena he had his security team doubled and also alerted the local police department, who sent along an extra seventy-five officers. In his mind all those people that he had ever sinned against in the past were lining up and calling for his execution—the burned drug-dealers, the cheated husbands, the angry fathers, the spurned promoters, the frustrated record companies, the underpaid musicians, the unpaid lawyers, the IRS, the FBI, the Mafia.

'He was getting in worse shape physically every night and it became harder and harder to carry on,' says Dave Simmons. 'Then there were these constant stories that someone was trying to kill him. It was like a mad B movie. He would stay in his room all the time, take the elevator up to different floors and leave by back stairways. Whenever we came back at night we'd have to drive round the hotel several times before going in.'

The paranoia reached a peak after a concert on 15 July at the Meadowlands Arena in East Rutherford, New Jersey, when Eric Sharp, a monitor engineer who'd recently been sacked from the tour, was found hanging from the shower rail in his motel room. He died in Andre White's arms after being cut down. It was almost certainly a suicide brought on by a romantic rejection but for Marvin it was a warning shot from the enemy he knew was out there waiting. 'That was meant for me,' he told Gorgeous George.

'I tried furiously to revive the boy,' remembers Andre. 'His eyes were rolling. I don't think he was conscious. Marvin was so drugged that he thought he could bring him back from the dead if we prayed for him. That's when I had to pull him back because I knew that if he started laying his hands on the body it would create suspicions with the police.'

Unbelievably, Jan came along for part of the tour, apparently unable to pull herself away from the impending destruction despite having just forced Marvin to pay part of his back alimony under threat of a July court appearance. It was as though each needed to feed off the other's weaknesses and insecurities, as though a part of them craved the pain and abuse. They began sharing drugs together again.

'He would bring men and their women back to the hotel,' says Gerald White. 'There would be five or six people in the bed at the same time and Marvin would be watching them. It was like he wasn't ashamed of it. What kind of man do you know who would do that sort of thing if he wasn't a freak?'

One day Jan collapsed with severe palpitations because of the drugs she was taking. In a hotel room in Fort Lauderdale, Florida, she began arguing with Marvin about a member of the band that he was accusing her of fancying.

'Marvin was sitting there cleaning his nose out because it was so wrecked with cocaine,' says Jan. 'In the middle of this argument he took the pot of hot water he was using and threw it over me. Gerald White then physically picked me up and put me outside the hotel. I had no airline ticket, no money, no nothing. I never saw Marvin alive again.'

Marvin claimed that he felt so sick after the incident that the next two dates, in Tallahassee and Memphis, were cancelled while he checked into a private hospital in Sunrise, Florida, suffering from 'exhaustion and dehydration'.

The tour drew to a close in California during August, at the Universal Amphitheater, and Marvin retreated to his parents' home on Gramercy Place, still fearing that he was being stalked. He took an upstairs room between the bedrooms of his mother and father. Just as his father stayed in his room and drank vodka, Marvin stayed in his room and snorted cocaine. Frankie Gaye and his wife Irene stayed in the guest-house.

Marvin never specified who he thought wanted to take his life. Some of his friends, like Dave Simmons, who would come over to try to get him to play basketball and forget all his problems, thought it was purely the effect of the drugs working on his wounded personality. Others thought that he might have good reason to worry—that he'd defaulted on payments to drug-dealers, that he'd upset people in the record industry, that he'd cheated with men's wives and girlfriends. 'It wasn't a delusion,' argues Gordon Banks, who'd played guitar on the final tour. 'Marvin had left Motown and had signed with CBS. There were management companies after him. People wanted to make money out of him and when he said no to them, they got mad. Everything had to go through Don Joe and that upset a lot of people.'

Whatever the reality of the threat, the idea of someone lurking in the shadows ready to execute judgement on him was also a projection of his inner turmoil. He had knowingly wronged people and, according to his metaphysics, there was a price to pay. How could he, sinner that he was, expect to escape the destruction that awaited the impenitent?

There seemed no way out. The normal means of dulling life's fears—drugs, alcohol, sex, fame, wealth—had only served to deepen his sense of doom. The more he tried to escape from the enclosing darkness the further he found himself pulled in. He began to talk of suicide again although, when in a more peaceful mood, he would say that suicide was an unforgivable sin. 'He felt that everyone was using him,' says Andre White. 'He felt that a lot of people loved him only for what he could do for them or for what they could get out of him. During the tour he had told me that he didn't feel people loved him for what he was and that his mother was the only person who really loved him. He always longed for the love of his father but he never got it.'

On 13 August Jan, who by now was caring for the children out of her welfare payments, called him to talk about his continued failure to keep up his payments. He reacted angrily, threatening to punish her physically and telling her that he planned to donate all his property to charity so that she would never get any of it. On 23 August he was summonsed to appear in court on 19 September because he now owed $9,900 in child support, $30,000 in spousal support and $2,500 in attorney's fees. He didn't show up. He was summonsed again for a court appearance on 19 December. Again he didn't show.

His mother, still a devout Christian, would read the Bible to him in an attempt to revive his spirit. She got together with Shelton West, minister of the local House of God congregation, and prayed and fasted for her son for three days and three nights. 'We prayed that he would be healed of that suicidal mind,' says West. 'He felt condemned because he had diverted from God. He would even tell us never to do what he did, never to go the way he had gone.'

In February 1984 the police came to interview him after a girlfriend, Carole Pinon Cummings, complained that Marvin had physically assaulted her on 28 January, slapping her around and knocking her down a flight of stairs. No charge was brought against him.

The same month Deborah Derrick, a twenty-four-year-old English girl whom he'd met in London through Cool Black, came back into his life. She had married an American personal-fitness trainer, William Derrick, whom Marvin also knew from his London period, and the couple had moved to Los Angeles, where the relationship had broken up in 1982. She and Marvin began sleeping together—she claimed later that she became pregnant during this time but had a miscarriage. 'He just about killed her,' says William Derrick, who had fallen out with Marvin over the affair. 'He would take women and convince them that he loved them. When he had done that he would make them prove to him that they loved him. When he finished with Deborah he threw her out of his house naked.'

Leonard Bloom says that it was during this period that he was contacted by a teenage girl who claimed that she was Marvin's daughter from a brief liaison in the sixties. Jan had also heard rumours of her existence. Her name was Michelle and she was from Chattanooga, Tennessee. 'I asked her some questions—where she was born and when, who her mother was—and then I spoke to Marvin,' Bloom says. 'He remembered the incident but said that he had never met the child. I asked him if he was absolutely sure so he told me the details and they coincided with everything the girl had said. So I got back on the phone and told her to come on over. We paid for the tickets and she visited with him. It wasn't a money thing. She wanted to see her father, and that was it.'

Marvin didn't seem to want any of his women to go. No matter who he was currently involved with, he seemed compelled to seek reassurance from his past loves. He would speak to Mimi's mother, who was now living in Los Angeles, telling her how much he cared for her daughter, and then he would call Eugenie in Amsterdam and urge her to join him in America. He would spend hours on the phone talking to Jan, asking her who she was going with, and had taken to visiting Anna, hoping beyond hope to resurrect his first marriage.

'The last time he called me was in March nineteen eighty-four,' says Eugenie. 'He must have been really into drugs because the only thing he was really interested in was knowing who I'd had sex with. That was an indication of what sort of state he was in. I told him that I was a wreck and he said, "Well, I'm also a wreck. Let's be two wrecks together."

Kitty Sears and Gorgeous George both felt that he was being drawn back to Anna. 'His love with Anna was a different type of love,' says Kitty. 'When he was with Jan he was still talking to Anna. In the end he was going back to her. He was going home. That's where he belonged. He had peace there.'

Without doubt Anna had exercised the most stabilizing influence on his life. Although she had a fiery temper and a penchant for an expensive lifestyle, she never encouraged his weirdness. 'If it hadn't been for Anna, things may not have turned out the way they did for him,' admits Jan. 'She was his wife, girlfriend, mother, best friend, confidante and manager. She did it all. I tip my hat to her for that.'

Relations with his father worsened as the months of inactivity dragged on. They hadn't lived together in the same house since 1957, and the old resentments had not only been undiminished but had been joined by new ones. The father believed he was being usurped by his son and, as far as he was concerned, that went against the natural order of things. Didn't even the Scriptures say that the father should be the head of the house? He suspected his wife of having affairs simply because she was warm and affectionate towards Marvin's friends, and also because for the past ten years he had been progressively drinking more and more after a lifetime of teetotalism. (The House of God's anthem proudly asserts, 'We don't drink no wine/We don't eat no swine . . . ') Over the past five years his family had regarded his drinking as a problem.

'Marvin Senior was jealous because Marvin was the resource through which the family lived,' says Shelton West. 'That made him somewhat humiliated and because of his humiliation he would start accusing his son of taking over the family. He felt that his son was running everything and humiliating him by showing him up to be an insufficient provider. This kept them arguing back and forth and there came a period when they were doing this and Marvin knew that he could anger his father. He knew exactly what to say and he knew when to say it. I remember once or twice Marvin Senior showed me this gun that he kept under his pillow and sometimes I even became afraid to go over there because he would be so upset at Marvin and he'd say, "I'm gonna kill him. I'm gonna kill him." I would try to talk him down but he was a hard person to calm. He always felt more secure in his way of thinking than most people. It was that pride that made him feel superior and made him feel he was a great teacher. If you disagreed with him he'd tell you that you didn't know what you were saying, that you were just a child.'

The arguments and the threats made life worse for Marvin. It was as if nothing in his life had changed. On the verge of his forty-fifth birthday, he was still single, unfulfilled and suffering under his intolerant father. He spent his days sitting around in his bathrobe worrying that someone could shoot him from a vehicle going down the nearby Santa Monica Freeway. He bought surveillance equipment that would enable him to detect unusual sounds outside the house. One night he threw a gun out of the window at a shape that he thought he could see moving around. Another time he assured Kitty Sears that there was a shadowy figure in the bushes.

On 8 March he suddenly dumped Curtis Shaw, his lawyer since 1976, and hired Howard Rasch. The court was now stepping up its action to get money out of Marvin and had issued subpoenas to representatives of CBS Records, Marquee Enterprises and ASCAP (the company that collected Marvin's mechanical royalties) to appear on 29 March in Los Angeles. It wanted to determine what his real earnings were likely to be through record sales, concert performances, airplay and songwriting. On the day that this was due to happen, Dave Simmons met with Frankie and the two of them decided that the only way to rescue Marvin from himself was to take him forcibly to an addiction unit where he could clean himself up. Marqueee Entertainment had purchased a property for him in Florida where he could be rehabilitated afterwards and where he had the use of a studio to record his next album. Two days later Simmons and Frankie met up again and agreed that they would do this on the Sunday, 1 April. It was not to happen.

'On the Sunday I got up and began getting dressed,' remembers Simmons. 'I lived about ten minutes away from Gramercy Place. I was getting ready to leave when the phone rang. It was Irene, Frankie's wife, and she was saying, "Frankie needs you. Get over right away. Father has just shot Marvin.' "

It was 12:20 p.m. Marvin had been lying on his bed dressed in a maroon bathrobe talking to his mother when his father appeared in the doorway. He had wanted to discuss a misplaced insurance policy with her and was shouting at her to help him find it. This particular argument had started the previous evening. Marvin invited him in to talk about it but he said he'd rather wait and walked back to his room and sat down at his desk. Marvin got up and followed him and a fight broke out between the two men. 'You can't talk to my mother that way,' he allegedly said. The father would later claim that he was pulled off his chair and then punched and kicked by Marvin while on the ground. Police photographs taken four days later showed severe bruising to his back and forearms.

In his statement to the police the father said that Marvin then left the room but came back soon after shouting, 'Motherfucker! You want some more?' before punching and kicking him again. Marvin returned to his room and sat back down on the bed.

The father then appeared in the doorway with the .38 calibre hand gun which Marvin had asked Gerald White to provide him with. He took aim and shot Marvin in the right chest, slightly above the nipple. The bullet perforated his lung, heart, diaphragm, liver, stomach and left kidney. As Marvin slid off the bed and slumped forward in a sitting position his father moved closer and fired another bullet at point blank range which went into his left shoulder and exited from his back.

Frankie, who was watching the movie *Shane* on the TV in the guest apartment, heard the shots but dismissed them as the sounds of a car backfiring outside in the street. Then came the screams of his mother. He ran barefoot into the house and up one of the two staircases to where Marvin's body lay slumped beside his bed. He desperately tried to resuscitate him with the skills he learned in Vietnam while his wife Irene phoned the emergency services. In spite of the quick arrival of the paramedics, valuable time was lost while Irene sought to retrieve the gun from Mr Gay. She confronted him, but he seemed confused and couldn't say where it was. She eventually found it beneath his pillow and threw it out on the front lawn. Reassured that it was now safe to go in, the paramedics found Marvin was still alive but only able to groan as Frankie cradled his head and tried to comfort him. He left the house on a stretcher and was taken to the California Hospital at 1414 South Hope Street, where they worked for five minutes in the emergency room to restore his heart beat before declaring him dead at 1:01 p.m.

The father, who had given himself up and was found by police sitting on the front steps of the house, was initially arrested and taken to the Wilshire Division police station for unlawful shooting because it wasn't known whether Marvin would survive. It was only when news of the death came from the hospital that the case was assigned to the homicide division. As soon as the gravity of the incident became known it was featured on the local news bulletins and Gramercy Place began to fill with gawking onlookers. Even the detectives sent in to investigate the scene of the crime and interview Mrs Gay as the only eye witness to the crime had to fight their way through the crowds.

'It was kind of crazy because word of the shooting spread so quickly,' says Woodrow Parks, the first homicide detective on the scene, who arrived with his partner Jim McCahn. 'There must have been over a hundred people standing around the house even though only an hour had passed. We had to park almost half a block away because of the traffic jam. There were journalists all over the place and most of the TV channels had already got wind of it.'

The initial news reports suggested that the assailant might be a man riding a red motorcycle, the last person seen leaving the house that morning. This was William Derrick, who had visited Marvin as an act of reconciliation now that the affair with Deborah was over. When he arrived the disagreements between Marvin and his father had already started and so he left quite quickly.

'I left because I didn't want to be a part of the arguing,' says Derrick. 'Before I got home, the father had shot him. When I got back my room-mate, who'd heard the news, thought that I had done it. Then Debbie called up and asked me why I had done it. Everybody thought I had done it because of what he'd done to my wife.'

Detectives Parks and McCahn were the first to inform Mr Gay that his son was dead and that he was being charged with homicide. He took the news matter-of-factly, and they weren't sure whether this was because he was deranged or because he didn't care. 'What shocked me,' says McCahn, 'was that he seemed more concerned about what was going to happen to him than the fact that his son was dead.'

Astonishingly, a week later, he gave an interview to a journalist from the Los Angeles *Herald Examiner*. During it he complained that none of his family had visited him in his cell at the Los Angeles County Men's Jail and that he was cold without his bathrobe. Asked about the shooting, he admitted that he had done it but said that it had been done in self-defence and that he had thought the gun was loaded only with pellets. 'I pulled the trigger,' he said. 'The first one didn't seem to bother him. He put his hand up to his face, like he'd been hit with a BB [ball bearing]. And then I fired again. I was backing towards my room. I was going to go in there and lock the door. This time I heard him say,

"Oh," and I saw him going down. I do know that I did fire the gun. I was just trying to keep him back off me. I want the world to know it wasn't presumptuous on my part.' Asked if he had ever loved Marvin, he at first hesitated and then said, 'Let's say that I didn't dislike him.'

Dr Ronald Markman, the psychiatrist who examined him to see if he was competent to stand trial, didn't believe it was the fear of violence that prompted him to shoot but the humiliation of having been assaulted. 'I've examined over three thousand killers in my career and I believe that people kill basically because they're humiliated,' he argues. 'It's not a question of whether you're a pacifist, a minister or a rabbi. It's a question of whether you are capable of being humiliated and whether you are able to deal with that humiliation short of the need to destroy.

'That day Marvin had humiliated his dad by knocking him down. So you have a forty-five-year-old man hitting a seventy-year-old man. He was knocked to the ground. He got up without a word but he went and got a gun and returned to kill him.'

Yet the reasons behind this particular murder were even more complicated. Why would the peace-loving Marvin suddenly attack the man whose respect he had always yearned for over such a petty incident? Why had he never done it before?

The answer, according to the phone call he had had with Andre White just two weeks before, must be that he had deliberately decided to end his own life. His father had always told him that he had brought him into his world and, if Marvin should ever lay a hand on him, he would take him out. 'It's an old saying among black families,' says Reese Palmer. 'You don't fight your parents. If you're really trying to die—that's the way to go. It's like the Bible says, "Honour thy father and mother that thy days may be long." When you don't do that, Satan steps in and then comes the execution. I think Marvin must have asked his father to kill him because I understand that he had given him the gun. Why would he give his father a gun?'

It was a view later shared by Marvin's mother. 'She told me that Marvin intentionally infuriated his father,' says Shelton West. 'She said, "That made me know that he wanted his daddy to kill him." To me his father didn't kill him. Marvin committed suicide.'

His funeral took place four days later at the Hall of Liberty Chapel in the Forest Lawn Memorial Park, by which time between eight thousand and ten thousand fans had filed past his open casket at the nearby Chapel of the Hills. Marvin was dressed in the military uniform that he had worn on stage during his last tour and which Marvin III had chosen for him when he visited the funeral home. Marvin's tour band, directed by McKinley Jackson, played the overture. Everything was paid for by Marquee Entertainment.

Almost all the major players from his life were among the five hundred mourners in the chapel: Berry, Anna and Marvin III, Jan, Nona and Bubby, Frankie and Irene, Harvey Fuqua and Larkin Arnold, Norman Whitfield and Eddie Holland. Bishop Rawlings, from the House of God in Lexington, Kentucky, preached the sermon; Smokey Robinson read the twenty-third psalm; Stevie Wonder sang a specially written song 'Lighting Up The Candle'; and Dick Gregory gave the eulogy. 'It was probably the most difficult thing I've ever had to do,' says Gregory. 'What do you say when you're in the middle of a situation where the son has been killed by the father? What do you say? What can you say? I just reverted to the Martin Luther King spirit of non-violence and non-hatred. I said that if we can forgive white folks for slavery, there comes a time when we have to share that same love for black folks who've committed wrong.

'I asked everyone to close their eyes and make believe that Marvin's father was sitting on the front row and make believe that they were hugging and embracing. I said that we can heal this because the God who produced the father is the same God who produced the son, and he would dare anyone to be happy about one of his children and resent the other.'

After the funeral Alberta Gay turned to Gerald White and said, 'That's one gun I wish you had never given to my son.' Marvin's body was cremated and the ashes were taken by Anna, Bubby, Nona and Marvin III aboard a yacht, from which they were scattered in the Pacific Ocean. A small proportion of the ashes were held back, and Anna still keeps them in her home.

Dr Markman's psychiatric examination of Mr Gay led to the discovery of a tumour on his pituitary gland, which was removed in an operation on 17 May. Markman argued that the tumour could have affected his ability to deal with his feelings of frustration and anger. 'In a way, it

did for him what he could not do for himself. It freed his emotions from
the tightly bound control he forced upon himself all his life,' he says.
'Tragically, wrapped up in that rigid bundle of emotions was a deadly
rage that focused on his son.'

The next month it was determined that he was competent to stand
trial. State of California prosecutor Dona Bracke wanted him to be
charged with first-degree murder but, after plea-bargaining, this was
reduced to voluntary manslaughter. The justification for the reduced
charge was the fact of Marvin's physical provocation, Mr Gay's age, the
possible effect of the tumour on his mental perception and the finding
that the victim was, in the words of defence lawyer Michael Schiff,
'under the influence of PCP or having some PCP in his system at that
time'. (The autopsy report had detected PCP—known on the street as
angel dust—and cocaine in his blood.)

'I think that it was a fair charge,' says Woodrow Parks. 'It wasn't
first-degree murder or even second-degree murder. Everything he said
made sense and was truthful.'

On 20 September Mr Gay entered a plea of no contest, and at 10.20
a.m. on 2 November he stood before Judge Gordon Ringer at Los Angeles Supreme Court to await his sentence. The question before Ringer
was not his guilt but the severity of the sentence. It was within his
power to hand out a jail sentence of up to thirteen years for voluntary
manslaughter and use of a gun. Deputy District Attorney Dona Bracke,
representing the State of California, still rejected the claims of self-
defence ('He didn't have to get a gun and shoot his son') but at the same
time didn't think prison would serve any useful purpose either for
society or for Gay himself.

Defence counsel Arnold Gold suggested that probation would be
the fairest sentence because, 'in our opinion the victim was the aggres-
sor and the provoker. He inflicted a severe beating to the defendant
contemporaneous with the shooting. We have pictures of the defendant by the booking officers to confirm that beating and the severity of
that beating.'

Michael Schiff added that the tumour could well have made Mr Gay
feel that danger was imminent and that he had acted 'in self-defence
and in self-preservation'. He pointed out that Gay was an old man with

various physical ailments who was no threat to the community. 'It was an isolated event.'

'This is one of those terribly tragic cases in which a young life was snuffed out,' said Judge Ringer, in his summing-up. 'But, under the circumstances, it seems to be agreed by everybody, including the very able and experienced investigating officers in this case, that the young man who died tragically provoked this incident, and it was all his fault. You are to go, Mr Gay.'

Mr Gay requested to be able to address the court and in a barely audible whisper he said, 'If I could bring him back, I would. I was afraid of him. I thought I was going to get hurt. I didn't know what was going to happen. If I could bring him back again, I would. I really was afraid at the time. I'm real sorry for everything that happened.' Then, trembling, he was led away.

Ringer sentenced Marvin Pentz Gay Sr to a six-year suspended sentence and five years' probation. The terms of the probation, modified on 18 November, were that Gay should not 'drink any alcoholic beverage and stay out of places where they are the chief item of sale', 'own, use or possess any dangerous or deadly weapons, remain living at the Inglewood Retirement Home and not move out'. At the insistence of the prosecution he also had to agree to receive psychiatric counselling.

Mr and Mrs Gay never lived together again. She filed for a dissolution of the marriage on 15 June on the grounds that he had murdered her son, and died of cancer three years later. After his five-year probation period at the Inglewood Retirement Home, Mr Gay moved to a home in Long Beach, where he lived until his death in October 1998.

Anna continues to live in the house on Outpost Drive, and Jan lives in an apartment in Redondo Beach with Bubby and Nona and Nona's baby son Nolan. Frankie and Irene live in an apartment in Santa Monica with their young son and two daughters. Eugenie Vis lives alone in Amsterdam and designs costumes. Harvey Fuqua lives in Las Vegas and continues to perform and produce. Berry Gordy sold Motown Records to MCA in 1988 for $61 million.

Everyone who was involved with Marvin was deeply affected by the loss. Coming as it did on 1 April, many at first thought a sick joke was being played on them. Yet few in the end were surprised. 'To me it was inevitable that he go the way that he did,' says Jan. 'I don't necessarily mean violently, but young and without a reason. It was senseless but almost unavoidable considering his mental and emotional state at the time. I could never imagine him living to be an old man. It wasn't something that was meant to happen to him. He was drawn to danger. He was drawn to . . . not evil, but the dark side of life. The dark side of life and the dark side of the mind really fascinated him. There was stuff that I can't even talk about that just went so deep, so dark and so bizarre. That was the driving force with him for many years. It wasn't evil, just dark. That's the only word I can think of. Forbidden, dangerous, scary, off-the-wall ways of thinking and behaving.'

Clarence Paul, who maintained his friendship with Marvin through the Los Angeles years, met up with him in the week before his death and found him in a terrified state. In the months before his own death he told Elaine Jesmer that Marvin was into a 'weird sexual thing' during his final months and that it was something so bizarre that he could never tell anyone about it. He also felt that his fears of being assassinated were somehow connected with this. 'It was a really bad thing, whatever it was,' says Jesmer. 'Clarence told me that it really scared him, and not much scared Clarence.'

'In the end, there was no place left for him to go,' says Jan. 'I think it was like being in a wagon going downhill with no brakes. How do you stop it? You either jump out or you let it go and hope for the best. I think he was hoping for the best.'

'I knew two Marvin Gayes,' says Andre White. 'They were totally different. I knew a loving, kind, sweet, ingenuous person, and I knew a person who was mischievous and who would do harm but only to himself. The harm he did even stretched out to having himself killed. He took out a contract on himself.'

Epilogue

A good man leaveth an inheritance to his children's children:
and the wealth of the sinner is laid up for the just.

Proverbs 13:22

Just over a year after his death the first posthumous Marvin Gaye album was released. *Dream Of A Lifetime* was made up of doctored jam sessions and unreleased material licensed from Motown and put together by Harvey Fuqua and Larkin Arnold. Funky 1980s tracks were awkwardly positioned alongside orchestral works from the early 1970s and a lot of the vocals were clearly work-outs rather than final takes. For an artist who was so diligent in his pursuit of vocal perfection, it was an embarrassing memorial. But in other ways *Dream Of A Lifetime* was an accurate inventory of the baffling contradictions that haunted Marvin right up to his death—his declarations of submission to Jesus and his bondage to desire, his tender romanticism and his brutal lust, his brown-eyed funk and his blue-eyed balladry, his traditional values and his Bohemian streak, his soft-spoken humility and his bawling pride. 'This was my tribute to Marvin,' says Larkin Arnold. 'This was my picture of him. He had all these conflicts in him and they came out on that album. All the different sides of him were shown.'

The crucial issue when assessing Marvin's character is whether these were conflicts, as Arnold suggests and David Ritz concludes in his biography *Divided Soul*, or whether they were contradictions. It is a conflict if you are firmly committed to travelling along the straight and narrow but occasionally find yourself stumbling. It is a contradiction to try to walk the narrow path and the broad road at the same time. Temptation is a conflict. Hypocrisy is a contradiction.

In fairness to Marvin, the most controversial songs on the album may not have been intended for release. Musicians who worked with him indicate that he often joked around improvising dirty ditties just to make his friends laugh and loosen up the atmosphere. Nevertheless, 'Masochistic Beauty', '(Them Niggers Are) Savage In The Sack' and 'Sanctified Lady', the three tracks that earned the album its warning sticker, contain significant insights into his psyche. Driven by deep-rooted attitudes towards women and God, they were not merely mean-ingless rhymes. William Bryant, the keyboard player on 'Sanctified Lady', confesses that he was alarmed by the change in direction. 'I didn't say anything at the time,' he admits, 'but I felt that he was edging a little too far into the dark side of his nature. It bugged me a lot.'

The earlier recordings on the album such as 'It's Madness' and 'Symphony' were full of pining love and appropriately bathed in lush orchestration. The later tracks, in absolute contrast, were sheer animal lust. This wasn't someone simply rejoicing in healthy sensuality. This was someone who, as rock critic Robert Christgau observed, 'found himself despising women for doing the kinky things he forced them to do'.

The most brutal of the songs was 'Masochistic Baby', a song that prefigured the outrageous misogyny of late 1980s rap. His women are demeaned by being referred to as slags or freaks. His pleasure is in their utter humiliation. He barks the instructions, and those he thinks are nothing more than little bitches perform for him. Songs like this could be dismissed as bawdiness or smut if they didn't so accurately parallel his attitude in real life. He had always been misogynistic ('I'm an old-fashioned chauvinist,' 1973) but was increasingly drawn to sadism and deliberate degradation. In one of his last interviews he told a journalist that he had recently tied a girl to a chair because, 'You see, it bores me to always do the same thing to women.'

'Sanctified Lady', the album's opening cut, was widely known to have been titled 'Sanctified Pussy', the offending word drowned, for the most part, in the final mix. This song highlights his central conflict, or contradiction. Although flippantly delivered and containing more 'language which may offend some people', it purported to be a plea for a spiritual woman who also enjoyed sex. 'Most people don't understand that song,' says Arnold. 'What Marvin was basically saying was that he wanted a nice, cultured, God-fearing, religious woman.' The idea had been suggested by a comment made to him by his masseur, Perry Fuller, a deeply religious man with a warm sense of humour who had one day listened to all of Marvin's grievances about women and then told him what he thought he really needed.

'Perry had said, "Hey, what you need is some sanctified pussy," and Marvin kept that phrase in his mind,' says the song's co-writer, Gordon Banks. 'He meant that Marvin wanted a woman who knew right from wrong so that she was sanctified, but that he also wanted a woman who would put out for him.' This could have meant that Marvin was seeking an honest reconciliation of his spiritual and sexual desires, but equally well it could have meant that he wanted someone who tolerated what he often referred to as his freakish pleasures along with his religious talk, just as his mother had tolerated the cross-dressing and prophesying of his father.

Although 'Sanctified Lady' was specifically about sex and religion, always a preoccupation with Marvin, it was a microscosm of the wider division in his life: that between his selfish appetites and his high ideals. As an idealist he believed in love, peace, reconciliation, harmony and the Christian life. This became his public image after the success of *What's Going On*. Yet as a man who was driven by wild instincts, his private life was marred by discord, debauchery, self-indulgence and unfaithfulness.

Marvin had the ability to switch from sinner to saint as though he was channel-surfing. The third track on side one of *Dream Of A Lifetime* was 'Masochistic Beauty'. The third track on side two was 'Life's Opera', which closes with a moving version of the Lord's Prayer and the invitation to get closer to God. *Midnight Love* opened with 'Sexual

Healing' and closed with a dedication to, among others, our Heavenly Father, Jesus. On his final tour he would sometimes pray in one room with a preacher and leave to score drugs in another. Elgie Stover tells amusing stories of Marvin speeding to the airport at 100 m.p.h. 'with a joint in one hand and a prayer in his mouth'.

'He was a torn person,' says Andre White. 'He was a very religious person but he was torn between God and the Devil. We would pray together for help. I would tell him that he couldn't have a Bible in one hand and a joint in the other. But Marvin had interpretations of the Bible that only he could have.'

It could be that he was a sincere Christian so damaged by his upbringing that he was never able to live a consistent Christian life. On the other hand, it could be that he was a pagan who superstitiously clung to certain elements of Christianity and was burdened with a residual guilt as a result of his exposure to the Ten Commandments as a child.

Marvin was undoubtedly attracted to the person of Jesus Christ. When he spoke or sang of Jesus there was genuine reverence. There was also respect and appreciation for the Bible and for the Church, even though his interpretations of Christian doctrine became more and more heretical during the 1970s and 1980s. Yet it's hard to turn up evidence that would show he was anything more than an appreciator of the figure of Jesus. There seemed to be no sustained and heartfelt attempt to become a disciple of this teacher. There was no regular church attendance, no evangelism, no sacrifice, no genuine repentance and no spiritual growth. 'He would sometimes feel remorse,' says Shelton West. 'Periodically he would come down and his conscience would bother him. Then the condemnation would cause him to go back up and attempt to escape his conscience.'

Marvin was taught in the House of God that the acid test of Christian faith was not what you said but the evidence of the Holy Spirit in your life. The text cited was Galatians 5: 19–23: 'The acts of the sinful nature are obvious: sexual immorality, impurity and debauchery; idolatry and witchcraft; hatred, discord, jealousy, fits of rage, selfish ambition, dissensions, factions and envy; drunkenness, orgies and the like. I warn you, as I did before, that those who live like this will not inherit the kingdom of God. But the fruit of the Spirit is love, joy, peace, patience, kindness, goodness, faithfulness, gentleness and self-control. Against such things there is no law.' As it was something that Marvin held to be true, it is instructive to measure his life against this checklist.

Did Marvin love? He loved his mother and his children, but always found it difficult to tell his women that he loved them. 'He would tell me that he cared for me,' says Eugenie. 'He would say, "You can be anything you want with me," or "We can be together always," everything but "I love you." I had to hear from other people that he missed me.'

He believed in love as a principle. The essential message of *What's Going On* could be reduced to 'love God and love your neighbour'. It could be significant in this context that the only concerts he performed during his long lay-off were for charities. In January 1975, despite having had an operation on his foot, he honoured a commitment to play a ninety-minute benefit concert in Toronto for retired football players.

Did Marvin have joy? He always talked about having experienced real joy as a child at church in Washington. This became a reference point for him. Significantly, he would always dedicate his song 'Joy' to his father when he performed it in concert on his last tour. 'My father used to preach,' he said, when he introduced it in Indianapolis, 'and this song is about my daddy.' He always believed that he had lost contact with this original source of joy, and talked about trying to regain it through prayer and meditation. He was careful to distinguish between temporal chemical highs and spiritual joy.

He could be very convivial and enjoyed telling stories and jokes. He particularly enjoyed mimicry and loved to call friends using a phoney British accent. 'He could tell jokes better than he could sing,' says songwriter Dickie Cooper. 'I got a bigger kick out of his stories than I got from his singing. He could have been a great comedian. Whenever I think about him I think about him with a smile.'

Yet there was a deep underlying sadness that came from his pain. 'He was very talented but I always thought that he had a very sad personality,' says Lady Edith Foxwell. 'He was basically a sad person. Maybe he wasn't that way when he was younger but life dealt him some terrible blows.'

As his life progressed the sadness turned into despair. There was loss of motivation, suicide attempts and almost permanent anxiety. He was unhappy with those around him and most of all he was unhappy with himself.

Was Marvin peaceful? Because of his cool attitude he appeared to be a man of peace but he enjoyed stirring up dissension. This wasn't usually physical—although he became violent with Jan and his father in later years—but involved provocation. He once told the *Los Angeles Times* that 'Weirdness and craziness are great things. I got hip to that a long time ago. It's helped me out of some tough situations.' William Derrick, who met Marvin in 1980, believes that towards the end of his life he was manipulating situations in the secret hope that he would be punished by his enemies. 'He would deliberately try to enrage people,' he says. 'I believe that he must have wanted to die the way that he did.'

He never had inner peace. He was too full of fear. He was frightened of performing, frightened of flying, frightened of spiders, frightened of scorpions and frightened of sleep. 'Fear is a horrible thing that we're faced with,' he once said. 'But to overcome and conquer all fear is very dangerous as well as beautiful. It can cause your death because you become reckless. It takes a very wise man to conquer those things and then to exist.'

Was Marvin patient? Not really. He had a low boredom threshold, which led to constant restlessness. The exceptions were his work, over which he was painstaking, and the sports in which he wanted to prove himself. He was often unable to devote his full attention to business matters or media interviews. In London he conducted several press interviews while still in bed and spoke to a *Los Angeles Times* journalist in 1973 while watching a football game on television. Les Spaine, Motown's head of promotions while Marvin was in London in 1980, remembers having a meeting with him at his apartment. 'I was having this conversation with him,' says Spaine, 'and I said, "I can't believe this." He said, "Why?" I said, "Well. You're sitting on the toilet with the door closed talking to me on the other side." I said, "This is bullshit." Other times he would go into the studio and he would be fine and productive. When the guy was firing, he was a sight to watch.'

His laziness was legendary. He could spend literally days in bed, loved to hang around in a bathrobe and was happy to stay at home doing nothing. One of his earliest problems was being motivated to write, record or perform. It took a strong woman like Anna to get him off his backside. He admitted that he had a love for what he called 'loafing'.

Was Marvin kind? He could be extremely sweet and generous. He bought his father a Cadillac in 1968, a house in the 1970s and once gave him $500,000 at the end of a tour. 'He gave people a lot of gifts,' says Joe Schaffner. 'I remember a jeweller came by his home in Detroit and Elgie Stover was standing by looking at the watches and rings and Marvin said that he could have whatever ring he wanted and a watch to match. He did that a lot. He would buy thirty-year-old Scotch by the case even though he wasn't really a drinker, just so that he would have something there when people came by.'

Was Marvin good? Jan, more willing than most to describe his 'evil' side, summarizes him as 'a wonderful, funny, talented, creative, incredible human being'. Typical of the responses of those who worked with him is that of Sylvester Potts from the Contours, who says, 'Marvin was well liked by everybody. He had a pleasant atmosphere about him. He was very easy to get along with. I still miss him.'

Was Marvin faithful? No. This was probably his single greatest weakness. He broke recording contracts, marriage contracts and contracts to appear in concert, despite his declaration, given in a 1982 interview, that 'I know how to be loyal. When I give my promise, I keep to it.' He was perpetually late for appointments, he missed flights and kept interviewees waiting, sometimes for hours. One of his most frustrating habits was to make promises one day then claim to have forgotten them by the next. Shortly before he died he told Bobby Womack that he would sing on his new album, and his brother Frankie that he would record songs that he and a friend had written. Both promises were forgotten.

His missed concerts became legendary. Nolan Smith remembers one date at a jazz festival in Denver when Marvin missed the flight out from Los Angeles because he was watching a basketball championship on television. 'He didn't think it would be a problem,' says Smith. 'He thought he'd just take the next flight. Then the game went overtime, so he missed the second flight. His only option then was to charter a flight. By this time the rest of the band was in Denver. Marvin got to the airport, saw the Lear jet, thought it was too small and he decided he wasn't going to do it. By this time we were already on stage. When we learned that Marvin wasn't going to be coming, they whisked us off stage and a riot ensued. I understand that a lot of damage was done to the stadium.'

On his 1980 tour of Britain he was booked to fly to Scotland to do a television special with a full orchestra. Les Spaine took him to Heathrow Airport, where Marvin went in one door of a toilet, out of another and took a cab back to the Britannia Hotel. (The story is often told that he climbed out of a window but, for obvious reasons, airport rest rooms do not have windows.) 'We went back to the hotel and he was sitting there having breakfast,' says Spaine. 'When I arrived it was as though nothing had happened. It was, "Hey, Les. How are you, man? Have some coffee." I then had an argument with him in which I told him that if he didn't want to do something he just had to tell us. The disarming thing was that he was always so polite. He was a very likable character.'

Was Marvin gentle? Almost everyone who knew him well comments on his graciousness and, particularly, his love of children. 'Marvin had a lot of feminine characteristics,' says Eugenie Vis. 'He had a soft side, a yin side. I think he often played the macho role, but naturally he wasn't macho.'

Cool Black remembers that his favourite form of greeting with his male friends was always a hug. 'When Marvin embraced you with a full hug he released his whole self as a human being,' he says. 'He used to say that a hug is better than a handshake because you could tell more about someone when you hugged them than you could from a handshake. He was a very deep man.'

Was Marvin self-controlled? No. Especially not when drugs took over—and almost half his life was spent on one drug or another. 'It was like total abandon,' says Jan Gaye, of the years she spent with him. 'It was, like, "I'm on coke and that's my excuse for doing this. I'm taking prescription drugs, I'm drinking," and along with all these things go the other evils of life, which entail prostitution, abusing people physically, mentally and emotionally, or whatever. Then he would stay sober for six months before he got weak again, as most addicts do unless they have some kind of a programme or some kind of a higher power. A big part of his life was just the fact that he was an addict. He had an addictive personality and, in my opinion, had his father not killed him he would be dead now anyway. It was unfortunate because when he wanted to be strong, when he was not surrendering to the drugs, it was almost as if he was a saint. That was something he revelled in in a positive way.'

Shortly before his final tour Gavin Martin, of *NME*, asked Marvin whether he thought he was a Christian. Marvin mulled the question over. 'Do I do the things Christ did?' he asked himself. 'I'd come up pretty bad on that score. I'd make a fair score, but I wouldn't be too high. I still consider myself a Christian because I believe in and love Jesus Christ. I'm not a fully evolved Christian at this point, but we're working on it.'

Shortly after the final tour he made contact with Shelton West from the House of God in Los Angeles and told him that he desperately needed to get out of the city to clean up and pull himself together. 'He said to me, "Shelton, there have been many times when I've wanted to come to church but every time I wake up and tell myself that I'm going today, then I'll allow something to get in the way. When I get back I want you to drag me to church even if you have to tie a rope around me. I've got to reconnect. I've got to reorganize my priorities." I made him that promise. So there was the condemnation, there was the inner turmoil, there were the financial problems and there were the problems with his wives. These things were on his mind all the time along with his desire to remain successful in the singing business.'

'He wanted to be a messenger,' says the Reverend Cecil Williams of Glide Memorial Church in San Francisco, who met him in the early 1970s and stayed in contact. 'He wanted to be like a preacher. But it had always been a struggle for him to be better than he really was and to do some of the things that he articulated in his music. He was always looking for perfection and yet when he tried to achieve it he found that he was imperfect, and what he wanted to happen and what he did were sometimes in conflict. So the messenger found it difficult to be the messenger who did what was in his message.'

His problems all stemmed from the rejection he felt from his father. Deeply sensitive, the lack of love and support created an internal pain that never left him. His life was spent attempting to find ways of dulling that pain. When stardom and money failed to help, he tried drugs and sexual adventure. It's significant that his drug of choice, cocaine, is a confidence-booster which is part-anaesthetic and part-stimulant. 'He was a very sensitive guy who didn't heal his wounds but took them with him,' says Eugenie. 'He was someone who escaped in drugs and this made his attraction to sex even greater than it would have been normally. At the same time, he was a very spiritual man who tried to express this in his songs and his life, although I have to say that this came through more in his words than in his deeds. Marvin used to blame his father for things that he himself had a hard time dealing with. He wasn't able to see the faults in his father and then correct them in himself.'

Marvin's inconsistencies didn't detract from his art. In fact, they contributed to its power and intensity. He made music as an alternative reality to which he could escape from his own pain and from the world he was so convinced was doomed. Feeling rejected and lonely, he created masterpieces of love. Living among a chaos of his own making he built exquisitely organized harmonies. Losing the faith he felt he'd once had, he sang songs of praise to God. Feeling vulnerable and weak, he declared that we can rock the world's foundation.

Marvin always had music around him. Uriel Jones, who toured with him in 1962, remembers that even that far back he was continually toying with a portable keyboard, lost in music. Eugenie argues that he was often able to say things in his music that he didn't feel confident enough to say in person. 'That's why he used to say, "I live for my music,' " she says. 'He was so sensitive and yet so hurt that he couldn't express himself. He couldn't become healthy. Through his music he found he could be open.'

'Music is my escape,' he told Dennis Hunt of the *Los Angeles Times* in 1973. 'It's a total part of my life. I find peace in music. I hate to let my music go. I'd rather have it all to myself. If I had my way I would keep all my music in my room and not let any of it go.'

Fortunately he did let it go, and his legacy has proved enduring. In the 1960s he not only influenced fellow Motown artists such as Smokey Robinson, the Originals and Stevie Wonder, but white rock acts like the Beatles and the Rolling Stones, both of whom covered songs originally recorded by Marvin. In the 1970s his imprint was obvious in the style of singers such as Michael Jackson, Al Green, Teddy Pendergrass and Frankie Beverly. *What's Going On* broke new ground for social/political albums just as *Let's Get It On* extended the possibilities for explicitly sexual love songs. Although Prince cites James Brown, Little Richard, George Clinton and Jimi Hendrix as his progenitors, it was Marvin who trail-blazed the particular form of sexio-religious funk with which he forged his identity.

Rap artists of the 1980s benefited not only from his sexual commentary and his political frankness but from the fact that he was one of the first black artists to hold out for artistic autonomy, to produce, write and sing his own material. 'Marvin Gaye saw the social value of putting his personal suffering into his music,' says Ice Cube.

White rock acts of the 1980s and 1990s, such as George Michael and Simply Red, have obviously been indebted to his vocal style. Bono cites the spiritual concerns of Marvin's songs as having been a source of consolation when U2 were criticized for not being rock 'n' roll enough in their sometimes overt talk of God.

All of Marvin's albums remain on release—an achievement in itself—and the frequent repackaging and compilations ensure that his music is available to new generations. He remains one of the few recording artists to have created a classic single ('I Heard It Through The Grapevine') and a classic album (*What's Going On*). Both of these records are still frequently ranked highly in 'best of' polls. A 1988 *Rolling Stone* poll of rock critics saw 'I Heard It Through The Grapevine' ranked at number eight. A similar poll in Britain's *Mojo* magazine put 'Grapevine' at five and the single of 'What's Going On' at ten. Critic Dave Marsh's personal ranking of the 1001 best rock and pop singles ever in his book *The Heart of Rock and Soul* put 'Grapevine' in the top position.

When the music channel VH-1 polled 600 international musicians in 1998 to compile a list of 100 all-time favourite pop artists, Marvin came fourteenth. The only black artists ranked above him were Jimi Hendrix, James Brown, Stevie Wonder and Ray Charles.

His legacy as a husband, father, lover and businessman has been less impressive. He left behind a trail of broken hearts, personal debts and unfinished business. He died still owing Anna $293,000 under the terms of the *Here, My Dear* contract. Because he left no will and had not cleared his back tax, his estate, which was only recently wound up, did not benefit his children. The flow of royalties has only served to pay the IRS.

His sudden death blew his family apart. Although he was twice divorced, his former wives were devastated. Neither has married since and nor has Eugenie Vis, who has been through therapy to understand the effect of those two years on her life. The story is much the same with each of them. How could they ever find someone who would match Marvin? He may have treated them shabbily, but they loved him nevertheless.

His children were devastated too. Marvin III was seventeen when he died, just the age when he needed his father most. Some friends blame the murder for the erratic lifestyle he has since led, culminating in a 1993 conviction for cocaine-possession, and for his inability to knuckle down to a profitable occupation. Like his father, he has also been pursued by state and federal tax authorities over unpaid demands.

Like Marvin III, Bubby and Nona still live with their mother. None of the Gaye children has ever taken a nine-to-five job, although Nona has made her name as a singer and as a model. Bubby likes cartooning, Little Marvin still entertains the idea of becoming a singer like his father. Jan may write a book about her life with Marvin.

Nona Gaye summed up the feeling of the survivors when she said, 'When you shoot somebody, that's not the only person that you're killing. I can speak from personal experience. I'm not dead inside, but a big part of me is gone because my father is dead—and not just because he's dead, but because he was murdered.'

Where Are They Now?

LARKIN ARNOLD, 58, is an entertainment attorney in Beverly Hills, representing recording artists and producers.

NICKOLAS ASHFORD, 57, continues to write and perform with Valerie Simpson, 52. They both appear as celebrity DJs on KISS FM (New York) five afternoons a week and own a restaurant, the Sugar Bar, at 254 W 72nd Street.

GORDON BANKS, 45, lives in Virginia and plays in a band called Midnight Love. He has the master tape of 'Masochistic Beauty', recorded at his home, which he is planning to sell.

CHUCK BARKSDALE, 65, lives in Chicago and still performs with the Dells.

PRENTISS BARNES, 74, left the Moonglows in 1959. Ten years later he lost an arm when a train hit his car on a crossing in San Antonio, Texas. He lives in Jackson, Mississippi. He was inducted into the R&B Hall of Fame in 1995 as a member of the Moonglows.

RENALDO 'OBIE' BENSON, 57, still performs with the Four Tops. He has homes in Las Vegas and Detroit.

FRANKIE BEVERLY, 53, lives in the Bay Area and performs and records with Maze.

WAYNE BICKERTON, 59, left his position as chairman of the Performing Rights Society in London to become chairman of SESAC, an American performing rights society based in England. He was recently awarded an honorary doctorate by Liverpool University.

THOMAS 'BEANS' BOWLES became chairman of the Greystone Jazz Museum, a member of the Jazz Alliance of Michigan and leader of the Greystone Jazz Orchestra. He died in 2000 at the age of 74.

JOHNNY BRISTOL is producing himself on a spiritual album and a secular album. He performs in concert.

BILLIE-JEAN BROWN studied law after leaving Motown in 1979, and is now an attorney for the City of Los Angeles.

AL CLEVELAND died in 1997.

BUDDY COMEDY worked as a teacher and a cab driver before assisting his brother in a Washington DC photography studio. He died of throat cancer in 1997 at the age of 58. He left behind a wife, two children and four grandchildren.

MICAH COOPER, 64, left the automobile industry to start his own business making back-lit awnings. He now makes oak easels.

HANK COSBY, 71, still writes and produces in Detroit.

FREDDY COUSAERT died in 1998 at the age of 60 after being knocked from his bicycle in Belgium.

BILLY DAVIS, 68, has been writing and producing commercials since 1970, his main account being Coca-Cola. In 1971 he co-wrote 'I'd Like To Teach The World To Sing' for the New Seekers. Billy Davis Enterprises is based in New York.

LOUVAIN DEMPS works as a professional nanny in Atlanta, Georgia. In 1992 she recorded a solo album, *Better Times*, for Ian Levine's Nightmare Records. She also preaches and sings gospel music.

DEBORAH DERRICK left Los Angeles immediately after Marvin's death and came to London. She died in Hong Kong in 1992. She was 30.

LAMONT DOZIER, 59, has his own studio in Los Angeles where he still produces records. His last solo album was *Inside Seduction*.

ESTHER GORDY EDWARDS runs the Motown Historical Museum in Detroit.

FUNK BROTHERS: WILLIAM 'BENNY' BENJAMIN (drums) died of a stroke in 1968; JAMES JAMERSON (bass) died of cirrhosis of the liver in 1983; EARL VAN DYKE (keyboards) died of cancer in 1991; JACK ASHFORD (percussion) lives in Atlanta; ROBERT WHITE (guitar) died in 1995; JOE MESSINI (guitar) owns several car washes and now plays harmonica; EDDIE WILLS (guitar) lives in Mississippi; JOHN GRIFFIN (keyboards) lives in Grand Rapids; RICHARD 'PISTOL' ALLEN (drums) still plays gigs around Detroit.

URIEL JONES (drums) is 66 and plays a weekly Detroit gig with Bobby Cooke and Friends; JOHN TRUDELL (trumpet) contracts musicians for the Fox Theater Orchestra in Detroit; and JACK BROKENSHA (percussion) lives in Detroit and still plays regularly.

HARVEY FUQUA, 71, lives in Las Vegas and Los Angeles. He still performs with a version of the Moonglows, which was formed in 1995, produces albums and is a technical director for Smokey Robinson.

MARK GAILLARD, 51, is a general contractor and musician. He performs and records with Mark Gaillard and the National Blues Band.

SLIM GAILLARD died in London in 1991. He was 80.

MARVIN GAY I died in Long Beach, California, in October 1998 after developing pneumonia. He was 84.

JEAN GAY (now Houston), 63, lives in New York and works in insurance.

FRANKIE GAY, 58, lives in Santa Monica, California, with his wife Irene and their children April, Frank and Fiona. He writes and occasionally records. He wrote the soundtrack to the movie *Penitentiary* and re-recorded 'It Takes Two' with Kim Weston for Channel 2 News in Chicago. Irene works in a bank.

ANNA GORDY GAYE, 78, still lives in the Hollywood home she once shared with Marvin.

JAN GAYE, 44, lives in Redondo Beach, California. She has never remarried.

MARVIN GAYE III, 35, lives with his mother, Anna, and pursues a musical career. He is the father of Marvin Gaye IV, who was born in 1996.

NONA GAYE, 26, has recorded an album, *Love For The Future*, duetted with Prince on 'Love Sign' (a track on *1-800-NEW-FUNK*), and has modelled Versace in Paris. She has a two-year-old son called Nolan.

ZEOLA 'SWEETSIE' GAYE (now Woodard), 54, became a Jehovah's Witness after Marvin Gaye's death. She is three times divorced and lives in Los Angeles, where she works for an accounting firm. Her husband Gary died suddenly in 1998.

ODELL GEORGE ('Gorgeous George'), 59, works as a tailor in Atlanta, Georgia, and as a valet to the Isley Brothers.

BERRY GORDY, 70, sold Motown Records to MCA in 1988 for $61 million. In 1997 he sold 50 per cent of the publishing companies Jobete Music and Stone Diamond Corporation to EMI for £82.5 million. He is quoted as saying that he now wants to concentrate on his first love, which has always been songwriting.

DENISE GORDY, 51, has appeared in the films *Reform School Girls* (1986), *My Man Adam* (1986) and *Toy Soldiers* (1991) as well as in an episode of *Charlie's Angels* (1976). Her daughter, Bianca Lawson, was a leading actress in the 13-part comedy TV series *Goode Behaviour* and played the part of Megan Jones in the second season of *Saved By the Bell*.

POPS GORDY died in 1978 at the age of 90.

STEPHEN HILL retired in Jamaica, where he died in 1996 at the age of 76.

IVY HUNTER, 61, is still writing and recording. He has recently built himself a 24-track studio and is planning to record a solo album.

JEFFREY KRUGER, 66, continues to run the Kruger Organization in Hove, England.

BOBBY LESTER reformed the Moonglows in 1978, but died of a heart attack in 1980. He was 50.

DON JOE MEDLEVINE died of throat cancer in 1993. He was 84.

BILL MURRY, 68, is semi-retired but works as a character actor in movies and television commercials. He is planning to write a book about his show-business experiences.

JAMES NOLAN, 66, works in a Department of Correction in Kentucky.

JAMES NYX died in 1998 at the age of 83.

REESE PALMER, 61, is manager of a car-parking facility in Washington DC, and since 1988 has performed with the Orioles. He lives in Landover, Maryland, with his wife Barbara.

CLARENCE PAUL died in May 1995. He was 67.

MAXINE POWELL still teaches her classes on confidence and presentation in Detroit.

MARTHA REEVES, 59, lives in Detroit and continues to perform.

PAUL RISER, 57, was responsible for the string and horn arrangements on R. Kelly's International hit single 'I Wish I Could Fly'. He is currently preparing an album of Motown hits to be recorded with symphony orchestra.

SMOKEY ROBINSON, 60, lives in Beverly Hills, California, and still records and performs regularly. His solo album *Double Good Everything* came out in 1991. *The Best Of Smokey Robinson & The Miracles* was released by Motown in 1995, and *Smokey Robinson: The Ultimate Collection* in 1997.

T-BOY ROSS was murdered in June 1996, along with his wife Patricia. Their bodies were found three weeks later in a derelict house in Detroit. He was 47.

KITTY SEARS runs Tomorrow Entertainment, a television and film production company, in Sherman Oaks, California.

JOE SCHAFFNER, 59, lives in Detroit, where he is a hardware department manager for a Home Depot store.

KATHY ANDERSON SCHAFFNER, 56, stopped performing in 1969 with the break-up of the Marvelettes. She now works for a cable company in Detroit.

DAVE SIMMONS, 61, lives in Los Angeles and is the State of California's Resource Developer for developmentally disabled children.

CHESTER SIMMONS died of a heart-attack in 1988.

WILLIAM 'MICKEY' STEVENSON, 58, lives in Los Angeles and has written the musicals *The Gospel Truth*, *Sing Sister Sing* and *Chocolate City*. He is currently writing a musical with Smokey Robinson.

ELGIE STOVER, 61, is a partner in a barbecue restaurant on Hilton Head Island, South Carolina.

MARYAM 'MIMI' TALEBPOUR, 54, married in 1984 and lives with her musician husband and their daughter in West London.

ED TOWNSEND, 70, lives in Los Angeles and runs a production company in Hollywood.

DAVID VAN DE PITTE, 59, works as an orchestral conductor and arranger, and performs in concert with String Quartet Number One.

EUGENIE VIS, 43, lives in Holland and works as a costume maker. She has never married.

LEON WARE, 60, has recorded eight solo albums, the most recent of which is *Taste Of Love*. He has his own label, Kitchen Records, and lives with his wife Carol in Marina Del Rey.

KIM WESTON, 60, is still performing and now lives in Southern Israel.

ANDRE WHITE, 55, is part owner of a grocery-store chain in Atlanta, Georgia, and publisher of the Afro-American newspaper the *Georgia Sentinel*.

GERALD WHITE, 54, owns and runs a restaurant in Florida. He served nine years and seven months in prison for conspiracy to traffic cocaine. He was released in September 1997.

NORMAN WHITFIELD lives in Los Angeles and is planning to write an album for the Four Tops.

STEVIE WONDER, 49, recorded the albums *Jungle Fever* in 1991 and *Conversation Peace* in 1995.

Acknowledgments

I have tried to list the main resources used in my research. I ended up doing around 160 interviews with 130 people, travelling to Amsterdam, Detroit, Lexington, Las Vegas, Los Angeles and Washington DC, and doing a lot of reading in various libraries. The British Library and the National Sound Archive in London were particularly useful.

I should make special mention of David Ritz's excellent book *Divided Soul: The Life of Marvin Gaye*, which was a landmark popular-music biography when it came out in 1985, and to which I was indebted in so many ways.

I haven't mentioned every single newspaper or magazine article because space wouldn't permit but I have tried to mention the main articles in which Marvin was interviewed. For the same reason, I haven't mentioned every book.

BOOKS

Bianco, David, *Heatwave: The Motown Fact Book* (Perian Press, Ann Arbor, 1988)

Boyd Jr, Carl and Hazel Mason Boyd, *A History of Mount Sterling Kentucky 179–1918* (self-published, 1984)

Christgau, Robert, *Christgau's Record Guide: The '80s* (Da Capo Press, New York)

Clark, Elmer T., *The Small Sects of America* (Abington Press, New York, 1949)

Coleman Jr, J. Winston, *Slavery Times in Kentucky* (University of North Carolina, Chapel Hill, 1940)

Davis, Sharon, *I Heard It Through The Grapevine* (reprinted Mainstream, Edinburgh, 1991)

Des Barres, Pamela, *Rock Bottom: Dark Moments in Music Babylon* (Little, Brown, London 1996)

DuPree, Sherry Sherrod, *The African-American Holiness Pentecostal Movement: An Annotated Bibliography* (Garland Publishing, New York, 1996)

George, Nelson, *Where Did Our Love Go?* (St Martin's Press, New York, 1985)

George, Nelson, *Buppies, B-Boys, Baps and Bohos: Notes on Post-Soul Black Culture* (HarperCollins, New York, 1992)

Gillett, Charlie, *The Sound of the City* (Souvenir Press, London, 1971)

Gordy, Berry, *To Be Loved* (Warner Books, New York, 1994; Headline Books, London, 1994)

Guralnick, Peter, *Sweet Soul Music* (Virgin Books, London, 1986)

House of God Convention Report (1942)

Jesmer, Glaine, *Number One with a Bullet* (Farrar, Straus and Giroux, New York, 1974)

Landau, Jon, *It's Too Late to Stop Now* (Straight Arrow, San Francisco, 1972)

Licks, Dr, *Standing in the Shadows of Motown: The Life and Music of James Jamerson* (Dr Licks Publishing, Wynnewood, 1989)

Love, Preston, *A Thousand Honey Creeks Later* (Wesleyan, New England, 1997)

Markman, Dr Ronald, *Alone With the Devil* (Piatkus, New York, 1990)

Marsh, Dave, *The Heart of Rock and Soul* (New American Library, New York, 1989: Penguin, London, 1989)

Miller, Jim (ed.), *The Rolling Stone History of Rock 'n' Roll* (Random House, New York, 1981; Picador, London 1981)

Morse, David, *Motown* (Studio Vista, London 1971)

Reeves, Martha, *Dancing In The Street* (Hyperion, New York, 1994)

Ritz, David, *Divided Soul* (McGraw Hill, New York, 1985; Michael Joseph, London, 1985)

Robinson, Smokey, *Inside My Life* (McGraw-Hill, New York, 1989; Headline, London, 1989)

Sanders, Cheryl J., *Saints in Exile: The Holiness Pentecostal Experience in African Religion and Culture* (Oxford University Press, New York, 1996)

Singleton, Raynoma Gordy, *Berry, Me, and Motown* (Contemporary Books, Chicago, 1990)

Spencer, Jon Michael (ed.), *The Theology of American Popular Music* (Duke University Press, Durham, North Carolina, 1989)

Taraborell, Randy, *Call Her Miss Ross* (Birch Lane Press, New York, 1989)

Turner, Tony, *Deliver Us From Temptation* (Thunder's Mouth Press, New York, 1992)

Tyler, Andrew, *Street Drugs* (Hodder & Stoughton, London, 1995)

West, Cornel, *Prophetic Fragments* (Eerdman's, New York, 1988)

White, Adam, and Fred Bronson, *The Billboard Book of Number One Rhythm 'n' Blues Hits* (Billboard Books, New York, 1993)

Wolff, Daniel, *You Send Me: The Life and Times of Sam Cooke* (Quill, New York, 1996)

NOTES

Prologue

Interviews with George Hewley, Lady S. P. Rawlings, Shelton West, Gerald White. Andre White supplied me with a transcript of his March 1984 conversation with Marvin Gaye. Alice Adamczyz of the Schomburg Library in New York was helpful in collecting American newspaper cuttings.

Articles

'Marvin Gaye Is Back and Looking Up', Robert Palmer, *New York Times*, 18 May 1983

1. The Ordinary World

Interviews with Geraldine Adams, Frank Boulding, Buddy Comedy, John Astor Cooper, Micah Cooper, Clifton Gay, Howard Gay, Jan Gaye, Sheryan Harris, Gloria Herring, Sylvia Inman, Rev William P. Johnson, Julia Mabson, Reese Palmer, Lady Rawlings, Barbara Solomon, Polly Solomon, Shelton West. I visited the House of God in Lexington, Kentucky, and was shown around the city by Larry Johnson and Sheryan Harris. The late Buddy Comedy gave me a special tour of Marvin's childhood haunts in Washington DC and also supplied me with previously unpublished photographs. Ann V. Todd researched the family tree for me in Lexington, using the facilities of Lexington Public Library and the Kentucky State Archives. She did an outstanding job.

Articles

'50 Is Magic Number for Bishop', Rick Balley, *Lexington Herald-Leader*, 6 July 1985
'Marvin Gaye's Ky. Relatives Still Mourn Death', Philip Campbell, *Lexington Herald-Leader*, 3 April 1994

2. The Call to Adventure

Interviews with Geraldine Adams, Prentiss Barnes, Eddie Belton, Wardell Belton, Buddy Comedy, Bo Diddley, Harvey Fuqua, Peter Graves, Jackie Magyari, William B. Mayes, James Nolan, Reese Palmer, Max Pitts. Information about the various air bases was available on different Internet sites. Details of Marvin's military service were obtained from the National Personnel Records Center in St Louis, Missouri. Rene Arsenault of Sony Music's Legacy label gave me information concerning the dates of the first recording session by the Marquees.

Articles

'Blue Velvet: The Ultimate Collection', sleeve notes by Peter Grendysa, Words On Music Ltd for Chess/MCA, 1993

3. Meeting the Mentor

Interviews with Billy Davis, Harvey Fuqua, Bill Murry, James Nolan, Reese Palmer. Anna Gordy declined a full interview but was kind enough to tell me about her first meeting with Marvin. I used the resources of the Detroit Public Library to research back issues of the *Detroit Free Press, Jet* and *Essence*. D. J. Resnick of the KD Writers Service in Beaumont, Texas, generously researched the story of the Moonglows' drug bust in Beaumont.

Articles

'2 From Music Troupe Held In Narcotics Case', Dennis Connell, *Beaumont Enterprise*, 12 September 1959

'Moonglows, Recording Stars, Jailed In Texas', *Jet*, 1 October 1959

4. Crossing the Threshold

Interviews with Thomas 'Beans' Bowles, Janie Bradford, Billy Davis, Lamont Dozier, Harvey Fuqua, Uriel Jones, Bill Murry, Bobby Rogers, Jimmy Ruffin, Kathy Anderson Schaffner, William 'Mickey' Stevenson, Polly Solomon, Paul Tarnopol. I visited Detroit and was taken to the Motown Historical Museum and the Motown exhibit at the Henry Ford Museum by the Detroit Convention and Visitors Bureau. Christopher Alexander was the docent who answered my questions at the Motown Historical Museum.

Articles

'Anna, Tri-Phi, Harvey and Check-Mate', Nick Brown, *Record Collector*

5. Tests and Trials

Interviews with Thomas 'Beans' Bowles, Micah Cooper, Lamont Dozier, Abdul Fakir, Dave Godin, Uriel Jones, Bill Murry, Sylvia Moy, Maxine Powell, Peter Prince, Joe Schaffner, Kathy Anderson Schaffner, Kim Weston.

Articles

'Fayette Man Dies After Fight With Another Eddyville Inmate', *Lexington Herald*, 1 June 1963

'Gaye In For TV, Radio', *Melody Maker*, 21 November 1964

'Marvin Gaye: Blind Date', *Melody Maker*, 28 November 1964

'One Killed, One Wounded in Shoot-Out at Restaurant', *Lexington Herald-Leader*, 10 November 1979

'Obituary; George William Gay', *Lexington Herald-Leader*, 23 September 1982

6. Allies

Interviews with Billie-Jean Brown, Louvain Demps, Denise Gordy, Ivy Hunter, Sylvester Potts, Maxine Powell, Bobby Rogers, Joe Schaffner, Elgie Stover, Barrett Strong, Kim Weston, Gerald White. The John. T. Lynch company of Long Beach, California, helped obtain certain birth and criminal records for me.

Articles

'Top Tunes', Ronnie Oberman, *Washington Evening Star*, 27 November 1965

7. Enemies

Interviews with Hank Cosby, Ben Fong-Torres, Ivy Hunter, Ray Moore, Bill Murry, Paul Riser, Joe Schaffner, Kathy Anderson Schaffner, Bill Selden V, Elgie Stover. Bill Baran of Detroit was invaluable in providing me with contacts for this period. Elliott Irving of WFLO Radio put me in touch with the organizers of the Farmville concert.

Articles

'Remembering Tammi Terrell', Marie Leighton, *Smokey Robinson & the Miracles Official Fan Club Newsletter*, vol. 2, No. 4

'The 100 Best Singles of the Last 25 Years', *Rolling Stone*, 8 September 1988

8. The Inner Cave

Interviews with Lem Barney, Billie-Jean Brown, Hank Cosby, Taylor Cox, Tommy Hanna, Joe Schaffner, Dr Robert Sims, C. P. Spencer, Elgie Stover, Dr James Wardell. Bill Miley filled me in on Tommy Hanna's boxing record.

9. The Supreme Ordeal

Interviews with Billie-Jean Brown, Louvain Demps, James Nyx, David Van De Pitte, Joe Schaffner, Elgie Stover, John Trudell, Dr James Wardell. The Performing Rights Society in London were able to give me a printout of all songs written or co-written by Marvin.

Articles

'Lexington Marine Is Killed In Vietnam', *Lexington Herald*, 17 November 1968

'What's Going On' (review), Vince Aletti, *Rolling Stone*, 5 August 1971

'In Memory of Marvin Gaye', Cornel West, *Christianity and Crisis*, 1 June 1984

'His World Was Just A Great Big Union', Adam White, *The Times*, 25 March 1994

10. Reward

Interviews with Buddy Comedy, Dickie Cooper, Louvain Demps, Ben Fong-Torres, Jan Gaye, Elaine Jesmer, Bill Murry, David Van De Pitte, Joe Schaffner, Elgie Stover, Ed Townsend. I visited Los Angeles three times in the course of writing the book and on the first visit was entertained by Frankie Gaye and his wife, Irene. Ben Fong-Torres kindly sent me a tape of part of his *Rolling Stone* interview with Marvin. Ed Townsend invited me and my family to his home in the San Fernando Valley. Bono put me in touch with Jan Gaye in the first place. Leigh Blake and Earle Sebastian were helpful with contacts.

Articles

'All But Super Fly Fall Down', Vincent Canby, *New York Times*, 12 November 1972

'A Visit With Marvin Gaye', Ben Fong-Torres, *Rolling Stone*, 27 April 1972

'The Spirit, the Flesh and Marvin Gaye', Tim Cahill, *Rolling Stone*, 11 April 1974

11. The Central-Crisis

Interviews with Taylor Cox, Mark Gaillard, Frankie Gaye, Jan Gaye, Jeffrey Kruger, Andy 'The Hawk' Price, Sammy Sanders, Joe Schaffner, Kitty Sears, Nolan Smith, Elgie Stover, Norby Walters, Richard Walters, Leon Ware. Jeffrey Kruger was enormously helpful in not only consenting to an interview but in giving me copies of all his Marvin Gaye material from his as yet unpublished autobiography. Documents pertaining to Marvin's bankruptcy were obtained from the United States Bankruptcy Court in Woodland Hills, California (thanks to Josie Womack). Documents pertaining to the divorce between Marvin Gaye and Anna Gaye were obtained from the Superior Court of California, Los Angeles (thanks to Boyce Suson).

Articles

'Earthly Fights and Mystic Flights', Cliff White, *New Musical Express*, 9 October 1976

'Gaye Files 2 Bankruptcy Pleas', John Sippel, *Billboard*, 7 October 1978

'Why Marvin Gaye Sang Goodbye To His Marriage', Bart Mills, *Daily Mail*, 13 June 1979

12. The Road Back

Interviews with Gordon Banks, Wayne Bickerton, Cool Black, Frank Blair, Neil Breeden, William Bryant, Gloria Byart, Freddy Cousaert, Lady Edith Foxwell, Jan Gaye, Christine Isted, Jeffrey Kruger, Chantal d'Orthez, Peter Prince, Les Spaine, Karen Spreadbury (a.k.a. Sharon Davis), Eugenie Vis, Jon Walls. Amy Herot supplied me with information from the original master tape boxes for the *In Our Lifetime* sessions. James Marsh, producer of the BBC *Arena* documentary *Trouble Man* (1994), was extremely helpful in giving me contacts for this period in Marvin's career. I used the libraries of the Press Association and Companies House in London. Robert Doornenbal did some excellent detective work for me in Amsterdam. Documents pertaining to the divorce between Marvin Gaye and Jan Gaye were obtained from the Superior Court of California, Los Angeles. I am most grateful to Caryl (Caz) Phillips, who spoke to me for a *New Yorker* piece he was writing on Marvin's Belgian exile and then shared his research notes with me.

Articles

'Gaye Liberties', Adrian Thrills, *New Musical Express*, 21 June 1980

'Gaye Eulogy', Pete Wingfield, *Melody Maker*, 21 June 1980

'Pop Star Snubs Margaret', *Daily Mirror*, 10 July 1980

'The New Age Metaphysics of Marvin Gaye', Chris Salewicz, *New Musical Express*, 28 February 1981

13. Resurrection

Interviews with Larkin Arnold, Gordon Banks, John Benson, Wayne Bickerton, Freddy Cousaert, Marilyn Freeman, Harvey Fuqua, Jan Gaye, Austin Okwesa, Kitty Sears, Les Spaine, Maryan Talebpour, Eugenie Vis. Jan Gaye was especially helpful throughout the book, answering many questions on the phone until we eventually met in Redondo Beach in the summer of 1997. She also supplied me with many other contacts. Eugenie Vis invited me to her home in Holland and kindly answered any question I cared to put to her, as well as giving me copies of various tapes, documents and photographs.

Articles

'Star In The Remaking', Mick Brown, *Guardian*, 21 February 1981

'Glad To Be Gaye', Paolo Hewitt, *New Musical Express*, 27 June 1981

'Marvin Gaye Tells What's Been Goin' On', Dennis Hunt, *Los Angeles Times*, 28 November 1982.

'The Consuming Passions of Marvin Gaye', Patrick Zerbib, *The Face*, April 1983

'What's Going On With Marvin Gaye?', David Ritz, *Essence*, January 1983

'Sad To Be Gaye', Gavin Martin, *New Musical Express*, 28 October 1989

'How Tamla's Lost Soul Gave Life One Last Spin', Richard Brooks, *The Observer*, 6 March 1994

14. Climax

Interviews with Gordon Banks, Leonard Bloom, Dona Bracke, Mark Gaillard, Frankie Gaye, Jan Gaye, Odell George, Dick Gregory, George Hewley, Detective James McCann, Dr Ronald Markman, Detective Woodrow Parks, Joe Schaffner, Michael Schiff, Kitty Sears, Dave Simmons, Nolan Smith, Maryan Talebpour, Ed Townsend, Eugenie Vis, Shelton West, Andre White, Gerald White. Besides various detailed newspaper reports of Marvin's death, many of which were given to me by Karen Spreadbury (a.k.a. Sharon Davis), I also consulted the records held by the Superior Court of California in Los Angeles and the Coroner's Department of the County of Los Angeles.

Articles

'Acquaintances of Singer's Father Shocked', Merelene Davis, *Lexington Herald-Leader*, 30 April 1984

'Marvin Gaye Shot, Killed; Father Held', Jamie Alison Cohen, *Los Angeles Herald Examiner*, 2 April 1984

'Singer Marvin Gaye Shot To Death', Susan Kirvin, *Daily News*, 2 April 1984

'DA To File Murder Charge Against Marvin Gaye Sr', Miles Beller, *Los Angeles Herald Examiner*, 4 April 1984

'I Didn't Mean To Do It', Patricia Klein and Mitchell Fink, *Los Angeles Herald Examiner*, 4 April 1984

'Tribute to a Trouble Man', Paolo Hewitt and Gavin Martin, *New Musical Express*, 7 April 1984

'Marvin Gaye', Colin Irwin, *Melody Maker*, 7 April 1984

'Marvin Gaye: His Tragic Death and Troubled Life', *Jet*, 30 April 1984

'Trouble Man', Michael Goldberg, *Rolling Stone*, 10 May 1984

'A Voice Set Free', David Ritz, *Rolling Stone*, 10 May 1984

'Marvin Gaye's White Live-In Mate Suffers Miscarriage', *Jet*, 25 June 1984

'Marvin Gaye; What's Going On With His Family Five Years later', Aldore Collier, *Jet*, 15 May 1989

'What Was Going On, Marvin?' Mick Brown, *Daily Telegraph*, 24 March 1994

15. Epilogue

Interviews with Larkin Arnold, Gordon Banks, Cool Black, William Bryant, Dickie Cooper, Lady Edith Foxwell, Perry Fuller, Jan Gaye, Bob Killbourn, Sylvester Potts, Joe Schaffner, Nolan Smith, Les Spaine, Elgie Stover, Eugenie Vis, Shelton West, Andre White, Reverend Cecil Williams. Records of Los Angeles County Superior Criminal Court and Los Angeles County Municipal Criminal Court.

Articles

'Marvin Gaye Interview', Dennis Hunt, *Los Angeles Times*, 23 September 1973

'The Consuming Passions of Marvin Gaye', Patrick Zerbib, *The Face*, January 1983

'Inner City Blues', Motown Record Company (Internet)

Discography

This list combines British and American singles. If the release dates varied greatly between Britain and America I have indicated this in brackets. If a single was released in one territory only I have indicated this, too, in brackets. Highest chart positions in the relevant territory are also included.

SINGLES

Date	Title
May 1961	Let Your Conscience Be Your Guide/Never Let You Go (US only)
January 1962	Mr. Sandman/I'm Yours, You're Mine (US only)
May 1962	Soldier's Plea/Taking My Time (US only)
July 1962	Stubborn Kind Of Fellow/It Hurt Me Too 46 US
December 1962	Hitch Hike/Hello There Angel (US only) 30 US
April 1963	Pride And Joy/One Of These Days 10 US
September 1963	Can I Get A Witness/I'm Crazy 'Bout My Baby 22 US
February 1964	You're A Wonderful One/When I'm Alone I Cry 15 US
April 1964	Once Upon A Time/What's The Matter With You Baby (with Mary Wells) 17 US/50 UK
May 1964	Try It Baby/If My Heart Could Sing 15 US
September 1964	Baby Don't You Do It/Walk On The Wild Side (US only) 27 US

October 1964	What Good Am I Without You/I Want You 'Round (with Kim Weston) 61 US
November 1964	How Sweet It Is (To Be Loved By You)/Forever 6 US/49 UK
February 1965	I'll Be Doggone/You've Been A Long Time Coming 8 US
June 1965	Pretty Little Baby/Now That You've Won Me 25 US
September 1965	Ain't That Peculiar/She's Got To Be Real 8 US
January 1966	One More Heartache/When I Had Your Love 29 US
May 1966	Take This Heart Of Mine/Need Your Lovin' (Want You Back) 44 US
July 1966	Little Darling (I Need You)/Hey Diddle Diddle 47 US/20 UK
December 1966	It Takes Two/It's Got To Be A Miracle (with Kim Weston) 14 US/16 UK
April 1967	Ain't No Mountain High Enough/Give A Little Love (with Tammi Terrell) 19 US
June 1967	Your Unchanging Love/I'll Take Care Of You 33 US
August 1967	Your Precious Love/Hold Me, Oh My Darling (with Tammi Terrell) 5 US
November 1967	If I Could Build My Whole World Around You/If This World Were Mine (with Tammi Terrell) 10 US/41 UK
December 1967	You/Change What You Can 34 US
March 1968	Ain't Nothing Like The Real Thing/Little Ole Boy, Little Ole Girl (with Tammi Terrell) 8 US/34 UK
July 1968	You're All I Need To Get By/Two Can Have A Party (with (with Tammi Terrell) 7 US/19 UK
August 1968	Chained/At Last (I Found A Love) 32 US
September 1968	Keep On Lovin' Me Honey/You Ain't Livin' Till You're Lovin' (with Tammi Terrell) (US only) 24 US
September 1968	His Eye is On The Sparrow/Just A Closer Walk With Thee (US only)
October 1968	I Heard It Through The Grapevine/You're What's Happening (In The World Today) 1 US/1 UK
January 1969	Good Lovin' Ain't Easy To Come By/Satisfied Feelin' (with Tammi Terrell) 30 US/26 UK
January 1969	You Ain't Livin' Til You're Lovin'/Oh How I'd Miss You (with Tammi Terrell) (UK only) 21 UK
April 1969	Too Busy Thinking About My Baby/Wherever I Lay My Hat (That's My Home) 4 US/5 UK
August 1969	That's The Way Love Is/Gonna Keep On Tryin' Til I Win Your Love 7 US
November 1969	What You Gave Me/How You Gonna Keep It (After You Get Get It) (with Tammi Terrell) (US only) 39 US

December 1969	How Can I Forget?/Gonna Give Her All The Love I Got (US only) 41 US
March 1970	The Onion Song/California Soul (with Tammi Terrell) 50 US/9 UK
April 1970	Abraham Martin and John/How Can I Forget? (UK only) 9 UK
May 1970	The End Of Our Road/Me And My Lonely Room (US only) 40 US
January 1971	What's Going On/God Is Love 2 US
June 1971	(February 1972 in UK) Mercy Mercy Me (The Ecology)/ Sad Tomorrows 4 US
September 1971	(May 1972 in UK) Inner City Blues (Make Me Wanna Holler)/Wholy Holy 9 US
November 1971	Save The Children/Little Darling I Need You (UK only) 41 UK
April 1972	You're The Man (Part 1)/You're The Man (Part 2) (US only) 50 US
December 1972	(March 1973 UK) Trouble Man/Don't Mess With Mr. T 7 US
June 1973	Let's Get It On/I Wish It Would Rain 1 US/1 UK
September 1973	You're A Special Part Of Me/I'm Falling in Love With You (with Diana Ross)
October 1973	Come Get To This/Distant Lover 21 US
January 1974	You Sure Love to Ball/Just to Keep you Satisfied (US only) 50 US
January 1974	(October 1974 in UK) My Mistake (Was To Love You)/Include Me In Your Life (with Diana Ross) 19 US
March 1974	You Are Everything/Include Me In Your Life (with Diana Ross) (UK only)
June 1974	Stop, Look, Listen/Love Twins (with Diana Ross) (UK only)
June 1974	(July 1975 in UK) Don't Knock My Love/Just Say, Just Say (with Diana Ross) 46 US
September 1974	Distant Lover/Trouble Man (live) (US only) 28 US
November 1974	I Heard It Through The Grapevine/Chained (UK only)
April 1976	I Want You/(vocal)/I Want You (instrumental) 15 US
July 1976	After The Dance/Feel All My Love Inside 74 US
September 1976	You Are Everything (with Diana Ross)/The Onion Song (with Tammi Terrell) (UK only)
March 1977	Got To Give It Up (Part 1)/Got To Give It Up (Part 2) 1 US/7 UK
January 1979	A Funky Space Reincarnation (Part 1)/A Funky Space Reincarnation (Part 2) 106 US
September 1979	Ego Tripping Out/Ego Tripping Out (instrumental)
February 1981	Praise/Funk Me 101 US

April 1981 Heavy Love Affair/Far Cry
October 1982 Sexual Healing (vocal)/Sexual Healing (instumental)/
Turn On Some Music/Star Spangled Banner
3 US/4 UK
December 1982 My Love Is Waiting/Rockin' After Midnight (UK only)
February 1983 'Til Tomorrow/Rockin' After Midnight
May 1983 Joy/Turn On Some Music
March 1985 Sanctified Lady (vocal)/Sanctified Lady (instrumental)
101 US/51 UK
May 1985 It's Madness/Ain't It Funny (How Things Turn Around)
November 1985 Just Like/More
May 1986 The World Is Rated X/No Greater Love
May 1986 I Heard It Through The Grapevine/Can I Get A Witness
(UK only) 8 UK
November 1990 My Last Chance/Once Upon A Time (with Mary Wells)

ALBUMS

This list does not include bootlegs or every posthumous compilation.

June 1961 *The Soulful Moods of Marvin Gaye*
January 1963 *That Stubborn Kinda Fellow*
September 1963 *Live On Stage*
April 1964 *Together* (with Mary Wells) 42 US
April 1964 *Greatest Hits* 72 US
June 1964 *When I'm Alone I Cry*
November 1964 *Hello Broadway*
January 1965 *How Sweet It Is To Be Loved By You* 128 US
November 1965 *A Tribute To The Great Nat King Cole*
May 1966 *The Moods Of Marvin Gaye* 118 US
August 1966 *Take Two* (with Kim Weston) 14 US/16 UK
June 1967 *Greatest Hits Volume* 2178 US/16 UK
August 1967 *United* (with Tammi Terrell) 69 US
August 1968 *You're All I Need* (with Tammi Terrell) 60 US
August 1968 *In The Groove* 63 US
May 1969 *M.P.G.* 33 US
May 1969 *Marvin Gaye And His Girls* 10 US
September 1969 *Easy* (with Tammi Terrell) 184 US
January 1970 *That's The Way Love Is* 189 US
May 1970 *Greatest Hits* (with Tammi Terrell) 171 US/60 UK
September 1970 *Super Hits* 117 US
May 1971 *What's Going On* 6 US
December 1972 *Trouble Man* 14 US
August 1973 *Let's Get It On* 2 US/39 UK
October 1973 *Diana & Marvin* 26 US

April 1974	*Anthology*	61 US
June 1974	*Marvin Gaye Live*	8 US
March 1976	*I Want You*	4 US/22 UK
September 1976	*Greatest Hits*	44 US/56 UK (as *The Best Of Marvin Gaye*)
March 1977	*Live At The London Palladium*	3 US
December 1978	*Here, My Dear*	26 US
January 1981	*In Our Lifetime*	32 US/38 UK
November 1982	*Midnight Love*	7 US/10 UK
September 1983	*Every Great Motown Hit Of Marvin Gaye* (*Greatest Hits* in UK)	80 US/13 UK
February 1984	*Compact Command Performances*	
May 1985	*Dream Of A Lifetime*	1 US/46 UK
November 1985	*Romantically Yours*	
March 1986	*Motown Remembers Marvin Gaye*	
September 1986	*Compact Command Performances: Volume Two*	
September 1988	*A Musical Testament 1964–1984*	
October 1990	*The Marvin Gaye Collection*	
May 1997	*Vulnerable*	

Major Tours

This is an incomplete list due to the lack of existing records, but I thought it would be worth including the tour schedules which came to light during my research. Hopefully these can be added to in future editions.

1962

As part of Motortown Revue, with Mary Wells, Mary Johnson, Contours, Supremes, Sammy Ward, Miracles, Marvelettes, Vandellas, Bill Murry, and Choker Campbell and his Show of Stars Band.

26 October–

1 November	Howard Theater	Washington, DC
2 November	Franklin Theater	Boston, MA
3 November	New Haven Arena	New Haven, CT
4 November	Memorial Auditorium	Buffalo, NY
5 November	City Auditorium	Raleigh, NC
6 November	County Hall	Charleston, SC
7 November	Country Club	Augusta, GA
8 November	Bamboo Ranch Club	Savannah, GA
9 November	City Auditorium	Birmingham, AL
10 November	City Auditorium	Columbus, GA

11 November	Magnolia Ballroom	Atlanta, GA
12 November	Fort Whiting Auditorium	Mobile, AL
13 November	—	New Orleans, LA
14 November	College Park Auditorium	Jackson, MS
15 November	Memorial Auditorium	Spartanburg, SC
16 November	City Armory	Durham, NC
17 November	Township Auditorium	Columbia, SC
18 November	Capitol Arena	Washington, DC
20 November	Civic Auditorium	Greensville, SC
21 November	Palladium	Tampa, FL
21 November	Palms	Bradenton, FL
22 November	Armory	Jacksonville, FL
23 November	Auditorium	Macon, GA
24 November	National Guard Armory	Daytona Beach, FL
25 November	Harlem Square	Miami, FL
26 November	Skating Rink	Orlando, FL
27 November	Field House	Tallahassee, FL
28 November	Long H. S. Gymnatorium	Cheraw, SC
29 November	New Park Center	Charlotte, NC
30 November	Memorial Auditorium	Louisville, KY
1 December	City Auditorium	Memphis, TN
2 December	Fairground Coliseum	Nashville, TN
3 December	Civic Auditorium	Pensacola, FL
5 December	Mosque Auditorium	Richmond, VA
7 December– 16 December	Apollo Theatre	New York, NY
17 December	—	Pittsburgh, PA

1964

13 September	Fox Theatre	New York, NY
28–29 October	Civic Auditorium	Santa Monica, CA

1966

26 May–8 June	Whiskey A Go Go	Los Angeles, CA
5 August	Copacabana	New York, NY
December	—	San Francisco, CA (supporting Otis Redding)
December	Sports Arena	Los Angeles, CA

1967

12 March– 1 April	Coconut Grove	Los Angeles, CA (with Tammi Terrell)

14 October	Hampton Sydney College	Farmville, VA (with Tammi Terrell)

1968

29 December	Miami Pop Festival	Hallendale, FA

1969

17–25 January	Mr D's	San Francisco, CA
26 January	San Diego State University	San Diego, CA
2 April	San Diego State University	San Diego, CA

1972

1 May	Kennedy Centre	Washington, DC
September	—	Chicago, IL (benefit for Operation Push)

1974

4 January	Coliseum	Oakland, CA
May	Carib Theatre	Kingston, Jamaica (benefit for Trench Town Sports Complex)
May	National Stadium	Kingston, Jamaica (benefit for Trench Town Sports Complex)
August	(20-date US tour with 20-piece orchestra and Ladies Choice vocal group)	

1975

—	Maple Leaf Gardens	Toronto, Canada (benefit for football players)
November	Cow Palace	San Francisco (benefit for Glide Memorial Church)

1976

Supporting acts included the Temptations, Staple Singers, Stylistics, Black-birds, Smokey Robinson, and Harold Melvin and the Bluenotes.

15 May	—	Denver, CA
11–12 June	—	Oakland, CA

18 June	San Diego Stadium	San Diego, CA
25 June	Atlanta Stadium	Atlanta, GA
27 June	Hampton Coliseum	Hampton, VA
3 July	—	Houston, TX
4 July	Convention Hall	Atlantic City, NJ
9 July	Royal Stadium	Kansas City, KS
10 July	Shea Stadium	New York, NY
17 July	Milwaukee County Stadium	Milwaukee WI
23 July	Riverfront Stadium	Cincinnati, OH
31 July	JFK Stadium	Washington, DC
7 August	Pontiac Stadium	Detroit, MI
		Support act Rose Banks
27 September	Albert Hall	London
28 September	Apollo	Glasgow
30 September	Empire	Liverpool
1 October	ABC	Manchester
2 October	Bingley Hall	Birmingham
3 October	Palladium	London
5 October	Winter Gardens	Bournemouth
10 October	—	Amsterdam
12 October	—	Paris

1977

(autumn tour of US with Luther Vandross)

1979

(tour of US by bus)

August	Circle Star	San Carlos, CA
September	—	Gary, IN
9 November	—	Hawaii
		(then Japan)

1980

Support act Edwin Starr

13 June	Albert Hall	London
14 June	Odeon	Birmingham
15 June	Rainbow	London
18 June	Fulcrum Centre	Slough
19 June	The Centre	Brighton
20 June	Apollo	Manchester
21 June	Usher Hall	Edinburgh
22 June	Southport Theatre	Southport
4 July	The Venue	London

1981

13 June	Hippodrome	Bristol
16–18 June	Victoria Apollo	London
20 June	Victoria Apollo	London
24 June	Gaumont	Ipswich
25 June	Apollo	Manchester
26 June	St George's Hall	Bradford
27 June	Odeon	Manchester
28 June	Southport Theatre	Southport
30 June	Hammersmith Odeon	London
1 July	Gaumont	Southampton
4 July	Casino Kursaal	Oostende (Belgium)

1983

13 February	Forum	Los Angeles, CA (NBA All Star game)
23 February	Shrine Auditorium	Los Angeles, CA (Grammy Awards)
25 March	Civil Auditorium	Pasadena, CA (Motown 25)

Midnight Love Tour

15–16 April	Golden Hall	San Diego, CA
21–25 April	Circle Star Theater	San Carlos, CA
28 April	Assembly Center	Baton Rouge, LA
29 April	The Summit	Houston, TX
30 April	Municipal Auditorium	Mobile, AL
1 May	Fox Theater	Atlanta, GA
5 May	Saenger Theater	New Orleans, LA
7 May	The Reunion	Dallas, TX
8 May	Hirsch Memorial Coliseum	Shreveport, LA
17–22 May	Radio City Music Hall	New York, NY
26 May	Sun Dome	Tampa, FL
27–29 May	Sunrise Theater	Sunrise, FL
30 May	—	Tallahassee, FL (cancelled)
1 June	—	Memphis, TN (cancelled)
3 June	Hampton Coliseum	Hampton, VA
4 June	Richmond Coliseum	Richmond, VA
5 June	Capital Center	Largo, MD
16–19 June	Holiday Star Theater	Merrillville, IN
23 June	Rockford Civic Center	Rockford, IL
24 June	Checkerdome	St. Louis, MO

25 June	Myriad Arena	Oklahoma City, OK
26 June	Kemper Arena	Kansas City, KS
28 June	Municipal Auditorium	Omaha, NE
1–4 July	Front Row Theater	Cleveland, OH
8 July	Civic Arena	Pittsburgh, PA
9 July	Spectrum Arena	Philadelphia, PA
11 July	Canadian National Expo	Toronto, Canada
12 July	Boston Common	Boston, MA
14 July	New Haven Coliseum	New Haven, CT
15 July	Meadowlands Arena	East Rutherford, NJ
16 July	War Memorial	Rochester, NY
17 July	Laurel Race Track	Laurel, MD
21 July	Augusta Civic Center	Augusta, GA
22 July	Charlotte Coliseum	Charlotte, NC
23 July	Greensboro Coliseum	Greensboro, NC
24 July	Leon County Civic Center	Tallahassee, FL
27 July	Billy Bob's	Fort Worth, TX
29 July	Nashville Civic Center	Nashville, TN
30 July	Civic Center	Lake Charles, LA
3–7 August	Greek Theater	Los Angeles, CA
12 August	Celebrity Theater	Phoenix, AZ
13 August	Santa Barbara County Bowl	Santa Barbara, CA
14 August	Pacific Amphitheater	Costa Mesa, CA

Index